The DIVINE TRILOGY

The Story of Union through the Teachings of the Masters

all Love & Light to you. Embrace the Divine Perfection you are. always — Joni

VICKIE MARY FAIRCHILD HOLT

Vickie Mary Magdalene

BALBOA
PRESS

A DIVISION OF HAY HOUSE

Art Credit: Alixandra Mullins

Balboa Press books may be ordered through booksellers or by contacting:

Balboa Press
A Division of Hay House
1663 Liberty Drive
Bloomington, IN 47403
www.balboapress.com
1 (877) 407-4847

Print information available on the last page.

ISBN: 978-1-5043-2729-9 (sc)
ISBN: 978-1-5043-2731-2 (hc)
ISBN: 978-1-5043-2730-5 (e)

Library of Congress Control Number: 2015901440

Balboa Press rev. date: 12/31/2015

Book 1

THE GREATEST LOVE I
HAVE EVER KNOWN

By Mary Magdalene

CONTENTS

ACKNOWLEDGMENTS

Special thanks and deep gratitude go to all my friends—you know who you are—for your love and support, without which I could not survive, much less enjoy, this amazing journey. I love you all. I would like to name those who have directly contributed to the editing, transcribing, and publishing of this book first and then to the others in my life who have contributed to my heart.

To Judy Evans, who graciously transcribed my dictation of *The Greatest Love I Have Ever Known*, and deciphered my sometimes, difficult writing, and who patiently typed edit after edit.

To Ray Ash, my dear friend and companion on the journey, whose computer skills helped me edit and bring this book to fruition, you are my spiritual soul-friend who lives and breathes Spirit and who delightfully walks the walk of a true spiritual seeker. Your positive, uplifting support has carried me through many of my dark nights. Thanks for your love and support and believing in the Truth of these teachings.

To Marilyn Green, my spiritual guru, long-time friend, and sister, whose direct knowing of spiritual Truth never ceases to amaze me. Marilyn was the first to read the entire book. When I received her message, "Congratulations, Vic, this is the real thing. This is the Truth. You can trust the Source is who you think it is," I cried and knew from my heart that it was true. Thank you for always being with me when I needed you most.

To Pam Tate, my dear soul sister and sister on the path, you share my ongoing longing for connection to the love of God; our hearts are one. Thank you for listening to all of my writings, and I encourage you to continue yours. Without your love and editing and formatting, these books could not be brought to the world. Your heart is one of the purest I have ever known and you embody the Mother energy so divinely. I bow to you in humble gratitude.

To Lorna Symthe, who holds within her such a personal and deep connection and devotion to God, you are an inspiration to me. Thank you so much for typing *The Book of Sarah* and always reappearing in my life, just when I need you the most.

To Cheryl Ames, thank you for your sincere help and for volunteering your precious time to type *The Book of Sarah*. I loved being with you and so enjoy your presence.

To Laurie Adkins, you are my dear, reliable and loyal friend on this amazing adventure. We are on an incredible journey in life and are aligned in true cooperation in creating Love Yoga. Thank you for all of your time and assistance in reading and editing this book with me. You are extraordinary and essential to this mission.

To Denise Bosma, thank you for finding Nancy to help edit the first book and your generous financial contribution to pay for it.

And special appreciation:

To Lawrence Holt, you say you are not a seeker, and yet, as all seekers do, you were looking for Love and through the union of our hearts, the search was over. You have been my most challenging and revealing teacher, for during those years without you, I was challenged to find God, and through that dark night, I was enlivened with Truth. You are truly an instant mirror of my ego's shortcomings. Being in love with you has taught me volumes about what Love really can be with a marriage partner. Thank you for loving me.

To Sue Telintelo, for continually asking, "How's it going with the book? I want to read it. When are you going to get it out there?" Well, Sue, here it is!

To Paula Davis, we have laughed and cried and searched together for the keys to the kingdom and the prosperity of knowing Spirit, in order to live a life of abundance in all areas of our lives. Jesus was right, of course, when he said, "For where your treasure is, there your heart will be also."

To Jim Strittholt, my long-time friend, who was first to witness my writings, you were right. And now we have our answers. All of your questions, my brother, can be answered from within you. Thank you for your friendship, and for all your efforts, hard work, and tireless devotion to save our great Mother Earth.

Joyce Supriano, you embody the core of Divine Mother. Thank you for your loving spirit and believing in the teachings of Christ, and for sharing the statue and books of Mary Magdalene. You are my family.

Especially to my parents, Jack and Billie Fairchild, who taught me that I can do anything I put my heart and mind into, and to believe in God, however, I know that to be. For my life, for your love, for your support, and all that I learned with you, I am eternally grateful. I love you. Thanks for believing in me.

To my patients and clients, you have taught me the true nature of healing and the divine miracle.

To all my yoga students, you are my teachers and spiritual community.

Thanks to Dana Pilolli, my partner of 20 years. Dear friend, you are my soul family. You embody integrity and honor and the truth of the spiritual warrior. I will be forever grateful to you for encouraging me to write, to listen to my inner voice, to trust myself, to study, to teach, and to heal. You believed in me when the clouds of doubt and despair overtook me. You listened openly and offered your deep profound wisdom so freely and effortlessly. What a joy and honor it is to know you. The conversations we have had are the most deeply profound and meaningful I will ever know. In humble gratitude and loving devotion to your heart and soul's journey, I bow to you.

To all my teachers, your wisdom is inside me now.

To my Inner Guru, Namaste.

To God, thank you for the teachings and this book, and the gift of the breath of the heart and the journey of this life.

And to Mary Magdalene, Sarah and to Jesus Christ my Beloved, words cannot express. You know my heart and now, I know yours. We are one. OM.

PREFACE

Will you write the book for me? Will you write the book for me? The words repeated over and over in my mind like my inner voice, but different.

It depends on who you are, I replied.

"You know who I am," the voice said. And I did.

So the journey of writing this book began in 1996. It came as a stream of consciousness. I would sit down with a pen and write, not knowing what was coming next. I would feel an amazing presence of love and wisdom and truth and direct knowing coming from what felt like was my very own soul. Sometimes, the feelings and emotions were so overwhelming I would have to stop to cry as I was so overtaken by my own deepest yearning to feel and meld with the heart of God. Sometimes, the presence of Love through Jesus Christ Himself was so utterly overwhelming I would just bow and cry out for the Light to take me Home. Sometimes, I would fall asleep writing in the middle of a sentence and I would wake up and finish it, without knowing what was written before. It was the easiest and most effortless thing I have ever done.

My own personal journey delayed the process along the way: things like divorce; a back injury followed by excruciating pain and eventual back surgery; two car accidents; reorganization of my business; a major house move; two business moves, and, well, you know—life stress. And yet, I would come back to the book and the words always brought me comfort. The Presence and the Truth in the words always brought me back home to my true Self. I felt love and inner peace.

I asked questions of Christ and received answers, some of which I have shared here. I felt somehow like I was myself Mary Magdalene. I knew about divine tantric union, but I wasn't sure why or how I knew.

I now believe we all know about this. Having had my own deeply spiritual and mystical experiences, I also know about the most amazingly desperate times of the dark night of the soul. I have experienced the blaze of light that accompanies the glory of grace piercing through the illusion of fear. And through reunion, I have been delivered back to the brilliance of God's love and light.

It is so easy to forget and to get lost in the illusion of separateness, this much I know. If these writings can help even one soul remember, then this book will have served its purpose.

Is the story true, you ask? This you must feel and decide for yourself. I know other books have been written about Mary Magdalene and her gospels, but to date I purposely have not read any of them to keep my own channel and mind clear. My friends have told me that some of the teachings in this book, as well as other, earlier inspired writings I have done for them, are consistent with the teachings of Jesus as found in the Gospels. I always reply, "I didn't know that," as I have never read or studied the Bible.

When my first awakening occurred, over twenty years ago, and my inspired writing (I never know what to call it) began to emerge, my dear friend Jim said, "You will write three books," and he was right. During the writing of this book, I was indeed told there would be three books. The writings always ended with, "Your Beloved, Jesus" and I responded saying, "Now I am having illusions of grandeur!" However, I now know that His Presence through Christ is real—more real than the illusion of any of my ego's false, fear-based thoughts. And so for me, yes, this story is true.

Know this—the Divine calls to you to awaken. The Divine waits with loving patience and great compassion. "All souls will return Home to Love, and all souls will awaken, my dearest Vickie Mary," Jesus would say to me. "Fear not, *everyone* returns Home."

I pray that you are blessed with the awakening and remembrance that Christ promises and that you enjoy these teachings. May you feel your own inner truth, and may the Truth embedded in these words come alive inside your own heart. For as Jesus said, "...the Truth shall set you free!"

It has been my greatest blessing and gift to be a part of this amazing process. I am extremely grateful and bow in humble gratitude to Mary Magdalene and Jesus Christ for their amazing souls, their love and their great sacrifice. I am eternally grateful, also, to those in Spirit World, who support me and use me as a medium for these truths.

To Amma (*Mata Amritanandamayi*), my Satguru and Blessed Mother who serves me from the deepest love of divine grace and who has saved me from the dark night of the soul so many times I have lost count, I bow to you.

To God, the Almighty Spirit, words cannot express my deepest love and devotion, for you are *The Greatest Love I Have Ever Known*. With you, I continue this most amazing journey of my life and to you, I shall return Home.

To all beings: Namaste. We are one. OM Namo; Jesus Christ, my Beloved.

Note to Reader:

I have to the best of my abilities used appropriate formatting to accomplish a flow in the writing as it was given to me. At times, I was challenged by the "rules" of capitalization. I chose to capitalize words that could be another name for God like Truth, Supreme Being, Almighty Presence, the One, Love and so on and at other times when it intuitively came to me to do so. Please overlook any perceived discrepancies and focus on the content, which I feel is profound in its timely message to humanity. There are great beings of light helping us in the unseen realms, for which I am eternally grateful and I bow humbly to their knowledge, love and devotion to our journey and to their most Holy Presence. Thank you for reading <u>The Divine Trilogy, The Story of Union Through the Teachings of the Masters.</u>

Vickie Mary Fairchild Holt

CHAPTER 1

The Deepest Love I Will Ever Know

When all else fails to satisfy human hunger the wise soul always turns to love through prayer, through thought, through words, through deep yearning and longing. Love is both the grounding and the uplifting force that creates all balance and harmony in the world. It is this satisfying experience that we all crave. To that end I would like to tell my story in an effort to encourage and console others. Even to the one who writes these words I offer some advice and a story that encourages you to never give up hope of finding the true source of love. There may be many manifestations, but there is only one source. So why not go to the source and remove the obstacles that prevent the seeing, the knowing, and the direct experience of love?

When I was only five years old, I had already given up hope of unconditional love. My mother had long since forgotten her own true nature and struggled in a world of ignorance, intolerance, and abuse. Seeing the Divine Feminine treated in this way at such an early age led me to feel disrespect and downright disgust at our womanly bodies, which seemed to dictate and entice the masculine attention. *So why not be in control?* I said to myself. I will use this feminine form and its seeming power to seduce the masculine to succumb to my infinite power of beauty and release this feeling of self -condemnation. For it was, of course, false power and false identity that was acting out and behaving in such an ill-suited manner. Enticing the masculine has not changed so much over the millennia. Lower-consciousness men have always acted from their lower nature, so they are very easy to read, seduce, and predict.

So what was I to think when I met a man who could not be tempted by my acts of seduction? *I am only interested in your soul,* he said. *That was put to rest long ago,* I said. It has failed to serve any needs I might have here in this small miserable world. There are so many men, but so few who truly care about the needs of the feminine. For the masculine ruling the earth seem to care little about love, relationship, compassion, kindness, or gentleness. Rare it is to find one who can remain truly present with a woman who is fully in her power. Rare it is to find a woman who has the courage to remain fully present in her gentleness. She succumbs to the aggressive power of the masculine and becomes narrowly directed and one-point focused, missing the bigger picture and neglecting her own needs, and thus, is unable to provide for those around her.

I did not know I was searching for the balance of the feminine and the masculine until I met the Master. He came to me first in a dream and said he would be coming for me. He said I should go to the town square and join the group gathered there around a man who talked about spiritual truths. I awoke in a panic, in a sweat; this dream was so real and so unlike any other. It was as if there was someone inside me and I awoke with a start, gasping for my own breath and searching the simple exterior of the room for the presence I had felt. And yet, no one was there. There remained only this feeling of desperate longing for the morning to come quickly and for this extremely dark night to end.

When I got to the village square in the morning, there were the usual faces and activities, sales and exchanges and typical community gatherings. So I did not see anything or anyone out of the ordinary. I continued walking, hoping to find this man from the dream, so peaceful and loving was his presence. I could *feel* him inside, but what did he look like? Would I recognize his face? I sat down to have some food and drink and to await this man of the dream, but alas, he did not come. *Well, so much for dreaming,* I thought. I must have been delusional to think someone like him could really exist in this world.

Love will set you free, I heard a voice inside say.

"Love?" I said in response. "What the hell is love? Only a child's tale."

Look to the east and walk to the end of the street and you will know.

I felt myself arise and start to walk. Now everything around me disappeared in a blur and I came upon a small gathering of people, five men and three women. They were clustered in a group and talking intensely among themselves. I ventured over to them to ask if they had seen a man today who talked of highly prophetic things. As I approached I saw a simply dressed and humble looking man sitting on a rock in the center of them. He looked up and our eyes met suddenly. I gasped and felt that same gripping feeling in my heart that I had had in the dream.

Come to me, he said. Not with his words—but with his eyes and heart. *Sit with me. I have been waiting for you.* No one else seemed to hear anything. They kept talking, not even noticing me. I wanted to turn and run away out of fear of this strange phenomenon and out of a premonition that if I remained nothing in my world would remain the same. My life would be forever changed.

"Come sit with me," he said. This time I heard the words out loud. "We are talking about deep matters of the heart, unlike what you might hear in the temples. Will you join us?" And in that moment I knew I would be joining them now and I would be joining him forever.

I felt myself sit down beside him and I could not stop looking at him, peering deeply into his eyes and sensing deeply into his heart. I felt our souls reunited in a sea of bliss and a sacred matrimony that was at once familiar and forever ecstatic. Could *this* be love?

I have experienced pleasure, love, emptiness, nothingness, anger, frustration and even fear and resentment, but never *true* Love. I have felt fleeting moments of happiness and long periods of sadness, sometimes so deep I felt I had fallen to the bottom of the well drowning in my own misery, forsaken by Love. And who could change that? A man? No. Never. A mere mortal man has too many self-serving traits to be worthy of the grace of a woman's true love, and yet here was someone who looked like a man, but like no other. He could see me, the part of me that I had forgotten way before my birth and series of incarnations. I felt as though I was looking in a mirror and the only thing that was real in this mirror was Love—the pure ground of all reality. And yet, there was a man with gentle, caring eyes and a soft yet bold face and a smile that could melt the biggest glacier. No one before and no one again, I thought, no, not ever. If today were to continue on and never end, I would feel the greatest joy. And if the day should end and my life with it, I would feel forever content and satisfied, to my very soul. Yes, most certainly, this must be Love.

"The soul is manifesting this reality right now. You are the center of the universe, for within you lies the kingdom, and you, the Divine Creator, rule. It is not the small self I refer to, it is the one who witnesses the All being made manifest in the present moment. To experience your greatness, you need only to witness all your thoughts and notice how repetitive they really are, and truly, not of much substance. But what if you could consciously begin to imagine a new way, a new being, a new creation of what you desire? If your thoughts are pure, then all your desires will come to you. If you choose to stay hidden in the dark of night, then that is all you will perceive, the darkness. But, if you choose to see the light and to live in that light of day, you will experience your own brightness, which has been illuminated. The soul longs for the light and is always watching for the glimmer that gives hope for a new beginning, every moment fresh and new, the soul energy constantly renewed. It is to this end that every soul strives to remember and embrace the truth of their essence."

And so I was left to ponder these words and to self-reflect about what I wanted to choose to believe, lies and illusions based on former experience, or truth and wisdom based on the essence of the light and true reality being embodied by this one soul who spoke from the heart of God.

He said, "Love is kind, thoughtful, caring, and given from a genuine open heart through acts of gentleness and tenderness and out of compassion through grace."

Grace? Now what was I to think of grace? That it is bestowed upon the favored few? Those who do not have to worry about money, shelter or where their next meal is coming from? Well, that has been my experience, and yet this man was simple, not self-righteous, selfish or self-serving. Or at least, if first impressions were right, for this man was different from any other I have ever known.

"Grace is a gift from God," he said.

Ah, and who was this God about whom he spoke? Certainly, no one had ever seen him in the streets, at least not here in Jerusalem, or even in Nazareth to my knowledge. And certainly by the looks of things, he hadn't walked in any of the many other places either.

"You cannot find God outside," said Jesus. "You must first look inside, and then you will find the divine is everywhere. There are times when the human heart just opens up and falls into love, and if there is an object of that love, then clinging and attachment come. Then love disappears. But it only disappears from the experience; it never really disappears. For love is the very matrix upon which and through which all creation is enlivened and manifested. So to love is the greatest gift you can give to another, but especially to yourself, for then you master the art of being human. Humanity was created to manifest love and joy in the world, to celebrate the infinite possibilities and varieties of creation. You truly must awaken to your divinity, and then you will know the heart of God, sitting right here every moment of every day."

Jesus touched the center of my chest where I felt a magnificent rush of energy pulse through me like a wave. It swept away my fear and released the dusty cloud of doubt and ceaseless thoughts that were running through my mind. There was no turning back now, for there was nothing back there that I needed. I knew I had to know this love of which he spoke. I needed to understand these teachings, not through my head, but directly through my heart. *So I have found my teacher,* I thought, *and the deepest love that I will ever know.* For in that moment I knew that we would be the greatest of friends, the most beautifully tender lovers I had ever known, and I knew I would have a child with his face, and we would carry this lineage through, until time did end, and we would walk through the garden of grace, hand in hand, loving each other into eternity.

There is that child's tale again. The *happily ever after* ending I sought. *Now Mary,* I thought, *don't get too dramatic, you know how you are. Settle down and feel your feet and get grounded here and now.* I am going to have to do something about these thoughts for they were spoiling the entire experience.

"You can't feel love and fear at the same time," Jesus said. "Focus on the heart. Train your mind and surrender to your heart and then love will have a chance to shine. Put aside the ego's thoughts and sit with the purity of love. Focus on it night and day and then the seeking for meaning will end."

Such a philosopher, I thought, and yet the experience of my heart was telling me something different. There was a profound ring of truth to those words. I am going to listen to the new voice. This new voice makes me feel good inside. I feel happy and it makes me feel like singing. That must be what the birds are talking about. They know all about grace for it illuminates their voices.

CHAPTER 2

Love

Love is what I focused on, just like he said. Whenever the negative thoughts came back, I would catch them and focus on love and the feelings I had in his presence. I repeated love over and over again, sometimes singularly, sometimes in the form of a sentence. *I love. I am loved. I feel love. I live love. I know love. I am experiencing love. Love is....*

I could never fill the blank in after *Love is* because I really did not know what love was. Was it God? Was it an experience of the truth? Words are so useless sometimes, and yet, this word love seemed to be exactly what I needed. And if repeating this over and over again could make a difference in my life then why not try it. So I did.

Jesus said, "Love is like a letter that is never written and yet, everyone knows what is said, for it is written in the soul. For to love and be loved is all that really matters. Everything else flows from this one basic truth. If you learn nothing else from these teachings, know this: to your own soul be true, for Love will make your heart sing and your spirit fly. Ultimately, no one can thrive without it and, in the end, no one really lives without it, they just do not *feel* it. If you are inside love that is all you feel, so the ecstasy of falling in love is like reunion with your lover over and over again. The ultimate love is the Inner Beloved loving you, endlessly. Most people will never share this kind of ecstasy. Ecstatic reunion can only come from a fully surrendered heart, which has been opened through grace. Devotion and spiritual practice lead you to the gateway of the soul, but it is grace that has the key to open it. So, the purpose of loving devotion is to find the key to the heart for it is the direct pathway to God."

"Wait a minute," I said. "I have trouble with this God of which you speak. Is He a person like you and me? Where does He live, inside of us? I really do not believe that I, acting from the heart of love and God ultimately, know everything, create everything and permeate everything as you teach. That feels too overwhelming. What do you mean by God, Jesus?"

He said, "Well, if I could explain this truth to you, I would need to speak in parable and story, for the little limited mind does not have access to the entire truth, only the Great Mind could possibly know the nature of the universe. This is what you are really asking. What is the nature of the universe and who am I? For when you ask who, or what, is God, you speak of all things and the potential to create an infinite number of realities. In the end, everyone will have her own individualized experience of God because each of us holds the key to the doorway of heaven."

"To speak of God as any one gender is quite ludicrous," I laughed, "for then what would the other gender be, an un-God? If God is all there is, how could we not find this truth in everyone and everywhere we look?"

"If you need to know God as human, you need only to feel inside a human heart," he said. "But so hard that is to feel into a human's heart. So many doors bar the entrance, doors of fear, anger, anguish, sadness, and grief. Eons of suffering and ignorance are the locks on these doors that have held the human heart imprisoned for so long. They are held hostage by their very own feelings and emotions, fraught with ongoing thoughts and beliefs that defeat its greatest desire for lasting union with Love. If you ever experience in this life even one moment of this blissful reunion, you will spend the rest of your life seeking it, so profound is that love you seek."

"Well, then," I said, "why is it so hard to experience this profound union, especially if it is our true nature? Why does existential love have to be so hard? Why this human tragedy of forgetfulness and illusion? Why not Eden here on earth? Why not love versus hate, peace versus war, acceptance over fear? Why do we flee from our intimacy with love? Why not just relax and surrender completely?"

Jesus replied, "That *is* the path to Love—surrendering all obstacles and fear, all the forms fear manifests. The ego, however, fights to survive, so it takes an enlightened soul to awaken, or a desperate human. Both draw grace like a magnet. Grace is always drawn to devotion. Grace is preordained destiny for all those who focus on the kingdom of God, known by many names and experienced as love."

"Why, Jesus?" I asked. "Why so much suffering in the name of God? Why in the name of the One, the true source of love, does so much conflict arise?"

He said, "It is because the very nature of God can subtly or dramatically vary depending on the nature of the soul having the experience. It is why so much is written about the mystical experience, and yet, the roadmap to the territory is so varied. There is no one way to know God, and no one religion has the one answer, the rules, or the dogma to get you there. The true seeker needs a pure intention to know God, and this intention will bring the experience of the Infinite close. Then it is necessary to let go and let God, for God's love is the key that opens all doors and removes the roadblocks to the mystical experience. Once there is true surrender, a melting into oneness occurs and at the meeting there is love. Once you surrender to the true source of love, there is only the experience of the Source. Love has been known by many names and called by false diction, and yet, the union of which the mystics of the East speak is truly beyond any human experience of ego love."

"What is this mystic experience that you speak?" I asked. "And who are these masters of the East? Who do *they* worship?"

"They are seekers," he said, "Who have found what they have been searching for. They were able to touch the Heavenly Father of which the prophets speak, and when they melded with their God, they discovered the nature of the entire universe. It seems that this God is not made of gold or something outside the physical form. It is, indeed, inside each and every one of us. And you too can know God, for you too are the messenger for grace to flow through. It is to this stream of grace that all souls return. There really is no place called heaven. The experience of heaven is known in the East as ananda, or bliss. When the seeker finally merges with the One, there is an experience of reunion and this produces a feeling of ecstasy and physical exultation. It is the most familiar feeling one can ever know. Like seeing a child to whom you have just given birth, there is something very familiar and very sacred, like you have done this before. It is because you have been with God this whole time. If you are still, you will feel the presence of God. It is unmistakable. There is an innate feeling of peace and calm, a stillness that carries infinite potential. In fact, some seekers call God the Infinite because there are so many possibilities that can emerge or that can be produced, if only one allows the merging to occur."

Jesus went on. "I am with you always. Forever, I shall love you. Humans want a God with skin, muscle, and bone, a human form like their own, so they worship a God with a face, and yet God has no face. God is the expression of pure light, a joy so great that all faces are born in a blaze of such beauty and glory that the personification of God is born just so love can experience itself. Love is so close, and yet being human allows for an illusion of separation. The truth is quite simple. All one must do is to choose love. Keep the desire to know and experience pure love in your mind's eye and feel the existence of whatever form of love you choose, for love is everywhere."

"Wait!" I cried. "You must stop this fantasy. This oneness that you speak of is hardly accessible to the normal person. Excuse me kindly, but I do want love in human form. What is the use of this existential love if it has no expression and no form? What if all I ever wanted was to look into the face of a man who could really see me and love me heart to heart, hold my hand and touch my face and express the Infinite here and now, to speak kind words while caressing me softly? Why is this so hard? Is it a sin? Why can't men be loving and expressive? Why do I yearn so deeply for this kind of expression? I understand other sources of love. I feel it in the temple, looking at the sky, smelling a flower. I even feel it in the face of a child, and yet this is not my deepest yearning, nor do I feel fulfilled. There is emptiness, a hole that wants to be filled. Tell me Jesus, is there no love for me like this? Is there no man that is capable and willing to love and meld to the point of this ecstatic union?"

"The mystical truth of our being is always touching the Infinite," said Jesus. "The human expression of Spirit has certain physical needs and there is a built in reflex and desire that helps to create experiences to get these needs met. You can have both, the physical and the metaphysical love. Both are yours by birth. Now you need only to choose."

And so I sat contemplating these words of wisdom. What is it that I am to choose, love solely for itself? Can I choose love in any form I desire? Can I manifest my heart's desire as the ultimate lover? Can I find a man to reflect his greatness and share his magnificence in such an utterly astonishing form as a human being? Is it *human being* versus *human doing,* or is it Spirit being versus Spirit doing? Interesting concept. But how is it I get so lost in these thoughts that once again I have chosen to follow this train of thought versus my heart's desire that always leads me back to the One?

It is truly a humbling act—to surrender our thoughts that are, alas, not as profound as we would like to perceive. If we could turn our intention and focus onto the heart, we would know. Know what? What do I *feel* when I focus on my heart? A soft voice inside me said:

Sit with your heart for as long as it
takes until the answer appears.

The answer came as this: It depends on the day. Today I sense layers of fear, past hurts and disappointments, struggles from the past, pain, grief, sadness and a sensation of pulling in, hollowness, emptiness, nothingness, deep sorrow, yearning, hope, longing, releasing, so many layers of suffering, eons of experiences, lifetimes of learning, all deep within the confines of this beautiful energy center known as the human heart, pumping to dissolve the doubt and release the fear so the flow of arterial blood can carry the truth back from soul to body. It travels through awareness straight to the brain, and with mindfulness and devotion it flows back to the heart, the source of all truth.

CHAPTER 3

Conversations about God

Jesus said, "Great and small, near and far, they will come to the center of their own heart and humanity will be healed, people cleansed of all their perceived trespasses and sins, all of which do not exist, except in the consciousness, limited by the small mind, and limited by their small knowledge of reality."

And so we continued these conversations with me ranting and raving about a God that may or may not exist, expressing fear of, just about everything. I expressed my disappointment in myself, my life, and complained about everything else. He sat listening with a seemingly unending patience, offering me advice and a new way of looking at reality, my world and myself. And yet, what I was aware of more than anything else was the feeling I had when I peered into his eyes, and the way he looked back at me, as if he knew more about me than I or anyone else ever did or could know. For the light that shined through those eyes could light up the galaxy and heal the most tattered soul. And in this moment, that soul would be me. What an honor to share time and space with such a brilliant man who seemed to possess the knowledge of the Universe and the humility of a lowly servant.

He would say, "My master is the one who created the All, the One who manifests as the many. I bow humbly to the Source of the One who has given me life and a chance to save humanity from itself. For through God-Realization we can *all* be saved from the suffering that comes with incarnation. By tapping into the infinite power of the Creator, you can redeem your life and awaken to the Truth. That is why humility leads to greatness. To bow before the Almighty is to bow at the lotus feet of the *Satguru,* the Master Creator of this entire universe. That kind of power is completely beyond the human mind's conceptual capacity. It is truly a great undertaking to play God, and yet once you tap into the great river, you are intoxicated with grace and she will show you the gateway to the heavens."

"Jesus," I asked, "is it possible to view this Creator of whom you speak? Why is it that I have never felt this love or experienced God? How can *I* find what it is that you have found? Why are we so incapable of perceiving this love that you speak of so highly?"

He said, "It is interesting that so many seek the kingdom of heaven somewhere *out there,* and yet the true kingdom is right here." He touched his heart, smiled, and continued. "It is not possible to see or to know God without opening your heart to the divine miracle. You must sit and contemplate what it is you really want. Do you want to truly know love and the riches of the kingdom? Then you must be willing to do what is necessary and be willing to throw away preconceived ideas and previous beliefs that no longer serve you. Your thoughts and your feelings must always be surrendering to the yearning in your heart that seeks to know true Love—love that cannot be created or destroyed, but that is always constant—the ground of existence and the essence of your being. If you focus inward with the one-point focus you will find that which you seek."

"How long does it take?" I asked.

"For most people, it takes lifetimes," he replied. "Less time is needed for the true seeker and those with a pure heart. Whatever time you spend in meditation and focusing inward is like a treasure chest of gold. What is your name, dear seeker?"

"Mary. Mary Magdalene," I told him. "I fear you shall never come here again, for there are so many who doubt and have no interest in these things, but I request time and counsel with you, if you should be so kind. I would like to study with you if you are a teacher."

"I *am* a teacher," Jesus said, "but not with messages from some ancient text. What I speak to you is what I know, for it is my direct experience. Years have I spent traveling, searching for my own answers and then one day I was with a master teacher and he asked me to open to my true self, and told me I was ready to begin my ministries and to teach what I knew. The master teacher touched my head here," Jesus said, touching the middle of his forehead, "and told me to see the One I sought. What happened next was so astonishing that words fail to describe the ecstasy of the awakening."

"It was like coming home to the garden of pure love. God was everything, and the entire universe did I see, the creation of heaven and earth and the pristine Presence of pure illumination. This world as we know it disappeared, and the man who searched plummeted head first through this tunnel of light and emerged in a new galaxy bursting with radiance. My body disappeared and a new body appeared. The vibration of this new body was very high and very finely tuned to play the music of the angelic realm. So intoxicating was this experience that who I thought I was completely dissolved, and my soul was drunk on *amrita*. The nectar was so sweet, my old body could no longer tolerate it and it exploded into ecstasy. This new body of light surrounded me. My soul was uplifted and I felt the wings of the angels arouse the DNA of the new me, and I was born again and again and again. Each new version was higher in vibration from the last, and each time I felt myself die thousands of deaths, lifetimes they could have been, but all in rushes of experiences, and I watched and I became at the same time. It was as though my soul was rescued from incarnations to be here right now in this moment just to be with you."

And then, I knew before me was the embodiment of Love. Pure, exalted Presence. And I fell in love as his hand touched mine.

"I can teach you and share with you the majesty of creation," Jesus said, "but I must warn you, there will be great sacrifice involved. To enter the ocean of bliss, you must surrender who you think you are, and trust that the you that emerges is the authentic one, the self that you are meant to become. There are layers of enlightenment, and I have traveled through many experiences in this one lifetime equivalent to a multitude of times on this earth. It is not realistic to expect others to do the same, although it is always possible for the true seeker to find the sacred heart. If you set your sights on the highest goal possible, then your soul will design a program just for you. The right place and experiences will be designed just for you. Layers of understanding can be generated in just one lifetime, although many are usually necessary."

Jesus paused, and then he said, "This feels like enough for one day; why don't we just walk together for a while?"

So we left the town square and began to stroll through the streets, side by side. I wanted to take his hand, but I thought that might be too presumptuous, so I moved closer, just so I could see him better. Standing next to him I could feel a pulsation emanating from his body like a wave of energy passing through me. There was this uncontrollable urge to meld with him and lose myself and get lost in this world in which he lived. For what would I leave behind, really? What could possibly come close to the magnitude of sensation that I felt whenever I came near him?

"Tomorrow," he said, "perhaps we can meet again. If you are interested, there is a group of us meeting over there on that hill. I hope you can join us."

I said, "Thank you, yes. What time?"

"Noon," he replied. "I shall wait for you. For now, I must go. It was lovely, dear Mary. Your presence is quite refreshing and delightful." He bowed his head to me and walked away.

Love is never something you expect to happen, it just happens. No forcing it or coaxing it or encouraging it to appear can make it happen. Love just appears and one wonders why you would choose anything else. Love seems to choose you.

CHAPTER 4

Studying with the Master

The next morning I arose early to study what he said and to prepare myself to take in more information. I was not quite sure what this would entail until I found myself sitting cross-legged on the floor praying. *Please, God, make me worthy of this teacher and his teachings. Help me to be open and to be humble as I find myself surrendering to his light.*

I could not help but wonder why I had met him or how things would unfold, but the soft unassuming demeanor and the light in his eyes made for a magnetic combination. So many other men are of lower caliber— arrogant, self-righteous intellectuals without any intelligence at all. I am ready to engage with a man who actually knows of the kingdom; someone, who feels he can help others to know love and to live a good life. He has such compassion. He is extremely magnetic, and I am so drawn to him.

I was anxious to get to the meadow to meet with him, so I hurried through a simple breakfast and made my way through town out to the countryside to wait for him. He was already there, sitting on a rock with his eyes closed, sun pouring onto his sweet face. I sat in front of him and waited silently for what seemed to be three to five minutes before he spoke.

"Good morning, Mary. How did you sleep?" He said. His eyes were still closed but I could feel him looking at me. I felt as though I was being seen for the very first time, and a great wave of peace came over me. *Everything is OK now; there is no trouble and no strife, only this moment of great peace.* These words were not spoken, and yet I could hear them very clearly, as if he had spoken them aloud. I felt as though I was floating and yet very grounded at the same time. I did not know this feeling could exist, for I had never known such a feeling before. So I relaxed fully into the moment and fell into what I later learned was a state of expanded consciousness known as meditation.

Things like this happened all the time with him. I would be with him and the entire universe would open up. Love has an incredible way of producing magic, and this moment was pure luxury. Nothing else mattered. It was just he and I. I could have died there and then, and I would have been happy to do so, I felt so fulfilled. Nothing could possibly match this sense of peace where everything in the universe stops in ultimate perfection. What divine bliss.

"*Om Namah Shivaya*. I am love," said Jesus. "Chant this phrase whenever you need this state of consciousness to return. It opens up the gates of the mystical waters."

I had never heard these words before. He said they were used in India and were part of an ancient language (Sanskrit) that has the divine inside each individual syllable.

"The vibratory state represents different aspects of the universe. They are embodied inside our physical form," Jesus explained. "There are light centers at the center of the spine, connected to the spinal cord, that are energy vortices that spin with a certain vibratory light that keeps us embodied here in the Now, and keep us connected to the Creator. They are messenger centers that have been coded with information that when awakened to their fullest potential, take you back home and purify you so you vibrate at your highest level. When all these *chakras*, as they are called, are open, there is an ecstasy that is purely indescribable bliss and the vibration of the soul emerges as pure, radiant light."

I asked him, "Jesus, how do you know of these things?"

"I have been instructed by the mystics and the ancients and visited by masters who have gone before," Jesus replied. "I have been told that I am one who will carry on these teachings and enliven love to return to this land. For, as it was in Eden, so it can be here on this earth again. I am the messenger of the heavens who reign upon this earth, and I shall not tarry far from this path, for my mission is to awaken twelve of the most interested here. We shall pass these teachings down through the ages until all will be Eden again."

I asked, "But Jesus, how will you know who these people are?"

He said, "I will know by their soul resonance and the look in their eyes. They will also awaken and it will be known to them. Together we will bring down the temples of hate and prejudice and in their place erect a monument of the heart, so everyone will know the true temple of God is right here."

He touched his heart, and I smiled for I knew well, because somehow, I knew of this temple of which he spoke. I have felt the pain of a broken heart and the joy of an open heart. This was truly the center for feeling and expressing love, and I knew I wanted to know everything I could about the temple of God. For my life, as I had known it so far, was dismal, dark, and depressing, with only glimpses of light. The eyes of all those around me were cold, calculating, or empty and devoid of any real compassion or love. Why not choose love over hate, abolish the God of war and replace it with my attention and focus on this God who wants only good to come to the earth?

"Teach me Jesus," I blurted out. "Teach me all that you know. I want to be your finest pupil."

He replied, "Ah Mary, you will be, for you have already been chosen as one of my disciples. Indeed, you are the first." Love gleamed from his eyes and he smiled. That smile could light up the heavens, and I knew the words he spoke were true, I was meant to be here and I was meant to learn these truths and pass them on.

"Jesus," I said, "I am an open book for you to write. Inscribe me with the words of truth and emblazon love in my heart, and I will serve you until my death. And if there is a beyond, then I pledge to you my loyalty for eternity."

He looked right through to my soul and with words unspoken, held my heart in his loving hands and I fell asleep to the outer world and entered the kingdom of which he spoke. Everything else disappeared, and all there was, was he and I.

"Mary," he said, "it is time to go now. There are others we must contact today. So easy it would be to remain here with you, but let us travel together and find the others who are to join us. We will not have to travel too far." He whispered the words so as not to disturb the magnificent peace that had entered my heart.

Together, hand-in-hand, we arose and walked through the meadow down to the ocean. There were men gathered around their boats, ready to go to sea. Two stood among them whom Jesus seemed to know and he called them by name, Peter and Andrew. Young and strong, quite handsome, I thought. They talked together for a while and I stood looking out to the ocean. So beautiful, I thought. How far does it go? I had never been on a boat, nor did I care to do so, but I really enjoyed standing nearby, smelling the air and drenching my eyes with the beauty of the blue sky and the colors of the horizon.

"Mary," Jesus interrupted my thoughts, "I would like you to meet your brothers, Andrew and Peter. They are among us with their hearts and want to explore the meaning of life. I told them we could meet for a while. Is that good for you?"

I said, "Of course," and we arranged it for after the evening meal. They seemed nice enough, but they looked at me quite oddly. A woman was not allowed in the temples, and they wondered about my ability to comprehend such life-enhancing talk, and yet I knew the yearning in my heart and the questions of my mind. *I will be his finest student,* I thought, *you will see.* The days to come were filled with ecstasy as he spoke of love and the power of it to transform the world and the heart of humankind. He said he was sent on a mission to reintroduce God as love to the world and to bring peace back to the kingdom of heaven and earth. I said, "What an enormous task!" How could one man, or even twelve, ever accomplish such a mission? He said it would, indeed, start a new way, and that the mission would continue for many generations and that our heirs and the ones that come after will continue the teachings. In this way new generations would emerge that would prosper from our initial efforts.

So hard it is to imagine a notion of peace and a people of loving, kindness.

"Mary," Jesus said to me, "there *will* be a time when women will be seen as equals to men and they will no longer need to sell themselves to eat, or to survive. There will come a time when the Divine Masculine, in his clarity and strength, will protect and serve the heart of God. And women will blossom into beautiful flowers and display their true colors as the Divine Feminine, powerful in their compassion and a true gift to this earth. Fear not, for the mission will succeed. It will continue long after we are all gone. We will commit to this mission, and together we will remain incarnate until this mission is fully embraced by many. All *will* be Eden again, for we will see to it. Every soul will awaken. It is the vow of the bodhisattva to ensure it and support and incarnate as long as it takes for every soul to awaken and remember and it should not be taken lightly."

I knew I must contemplate this vow to serve humanity until every soul awakens. That truly would take a long time, if not eternity. But if I could serve side-by-side with Jesus for eternity, then I was definitely interested in this job, and indeed, I was interested in the mission, for to bring love could bring the end of suffering. No longer will women need to choose between their dignity and their ability to survive, between stealing and eating, or starving themselves or their children. Yes, indeed, the suffering must end. In the name of Love, from the heart of compassion, truly this suffering must end.

"Remember, Mary," said Jesus, "everyone has his own mission and lessons to learn. It is not our job to interfere with the journey of even one soul. But we must educate them about their choices so their free will is used with great care and mindfulness. We must all learn to help one another and to serve the greater good, even if that means some inconvenience and mild discomfort to ourselves. Self-sacrifice can be self-serving, for it serves one's higher source. Serving the highest good is always the best choice, but we must educate the people and turn their hearts to love. This is the only way."

Well, I thought, what a mighty and noble goal that is, but what can one person accomplish? There are so many people; it really *will* take forever.

"Not forever, Mary," I heard Jesus say. Can he hear my thoughts? "We must start now. One person can do a great deal, and together we can do even more. Most people are sleeping, going day-to-day, without even dreaming of a better tomorrow. They are followers of whatever the set norm is of the day. They have no original ideas and no way to think through their own problems, let alone for an entire community. This is because they think with their small minds and have lost the ability to listen to their Great Mind. The thoughts that come from the Great Mind are inspired and are imbued inside the source of their being. This voice is the voice of God, and it takes only one person to speak it and to lead others to their own inner voice. Then, coming together, we can make a difference."

"Master," I said, "I pray this is true, and I vow to help you complete your mission and make it my own. I am not knowledgeable about such things, but I will learn from you and follow your example. Never before have I known the course of my life. Now there is a clear purpose, a clear path to my life. It feels really good to have one now."

What had I just said? The words just came through without a prior thought and before I could even contemplate. It was like something else inside me knew this was true and my path was to become a devoted follower of this man known as Jesus and to serve and inspire humanity to awaken to their true nature, inspired to knowing the Great Mind.

"Actions taken from this higher knowing always serve love," he said, "always serve the highest good. When one acts from the source of love, there are no regrets. There becomes a sense of completion, contentment, and peace. Love is meant to reign over this earth and heal the masses of their self-perceived importance and end the trite bickering. Murder, war, and rape will become a part of the hideous past of humanity, and generations will learn from the lessons of the past. The more people awaken, the more people will be drawn to them like a magnet. They may not even know why, but they will come and surround them and unconsciously want what they have. They will want what the enlightened being knows. Love is the true nature of each soul, and the more light that shines, the more a magnet for greatness they will become.

"A leader of the way of love must remember this and be crystal clear in their intentions and way in the world. For with this light comes great power, and if this power is not understood, and not under inspired control, it can be dangerous and even devastate lives. The ego cannot withstand the kind of power that the Great Mind wields. Only the Higher Self, which is the seed of God, can sprout and blossom beauty into the world. The ego was indeed created to serve God, create beauty, and to bring love to the world. The enlightened soul merges with this higher power and serves through oneness versus separateness and ignorance. For when one is separated from her higher knowing, she acts out of fear, and fear brings suffering. Fear is the opposite of love. You cannot be in fear and love at the same time. Every moment each individual has the free will to choose between love and fear. And each time the master teacher inside asks *which will it be?* Humans must work with their thoughts and choose love, if they are to experience happiness. For inside love is much joy, and inside joy everything else disappears.

"The Master can perceive the suffering of humanity but knows the greater truth. The Master can serve with great love and compassion and help heal the pain of humanity, but only by choosing love can each individual ease his suffering, and only by choosing a God of love, almighty in His power, can a person end his suffering. Love is the only way."

And so our conversation ended. I was left wondering, *how does one become a master?* Do we master our thoughts, our beliefs, and our desires? Do we study with a teacher who can grant us immunity from the journey – the pain and suffering that accompanies it, or do we work as slaves to the outer ego run by desire? The master truly must have special skills and talents along with his teaching and the gifts that he has brought to this life. For how could a simple human being born in ignorance and poverty ever become a master?

Later, I was to hear the answer. Self-mastery was truly the mission of this life. To have control over our thoughts and beliefs, feelings and emotions, we must not succumb to our weaknesses. We must be willing to lay down our swords of self-delusions and ignorance and fully surrender to our higher source, which is the seed of God, and then sprout into our true mission. Once our mission is truly acknowledged, we can serve the seed of God and can bloom fully into the beautiful flowers our souls were created to be. Love will find a way to remove the obstacles, especially if we ask for help. Over and over again, we must ask for help and surrender to the one true voice of Truth—the voice of God. That would be music to my ears. It is no simple task to hear the voice of God. How is this even possible? I have found all these questions coming forth. I would need to save them until the next meeting.

CHAPTER 5

The Nature of God and the Great Mind

This time there was just a small group of people gathered, and I sat in the back and listened for quite awhile before I spoke out my first question.

"Jesus," I asked, "how do you listen to the voice of God? How do you know which voice to listen to inside? There are so many voices in my head. I find it very confusing. Are these all *my* thoughts?"

Jesus replied, "That is a very good question, dear Mary, for I often wonder myself, what voice shall I listen to? Is there one right way to hear the voice of truth? My experience is that you must first quiet the thoughts of ignorance and repetition. Eliminating the thoughts that continually repeat throughout your day is the first layer of release. You must first recognize these truths for what they are and then let them go without attaching or clinging, and without effort. Other thoughts will then come. These are the thoughts of the judging mind. These thoughts all have opinions and experiences upon which to base them. These thoughts are often repetitions and replays from the voices you often heard in childhood that come back to haunt you in different forms and in different situations. When these thoughts disappear, the mind will feel clear of the chatter or chit, as some masters describe it.

"In the next layer are deeper beliefs and feelings that have been buried there. This layer is unconscious, but very powerful. They often dictate our actions, responses, and reactions to our world. This is the layer of consciousness that most of us need to recognize, in order to change ourselves consciously.

"There is another layer that, when permeated, can give you great insight and vision. This is the intuitive mind. This aspect of self is directly connected to the Great Mind of God, and can provide you with the wisdom you seek. This is an aspect of self that will link you directly to Spirit, and will help you feel and live out your responses based on inspiration. If we all lived more from this part, we could get along much easier and with more friendliness and kindness.

"Once this veil is penetrated, you enter the realm of no thought. There is a field in which you enter where there is pure vibration, pure presence. In this state of awareness, there is a deep stillness and quiet that feels thick and often even dense. If you completely surrender to this presence, then you will be pulled into love, and your outer body will dissipate in your awareness and you will know ecstasy beyond your wildest imaginings. Inside Love you will feel at home, enormous peace and Presence. There is a feeling of deep trust that everything is perfect as it is. There really is nothing to do except to help others to get back to this knowing, for this knowing is God. God the Father, God the Mother, the Lover, the Friend, your constant companion, the Supreme Almighty Being that is pure, exalted consciousness, the one you feel, the one who is seeking you, the finest creation known, for this is your Creator, your Personal God."

After a bit, I asked, "Jesus, is there one God or many? How does that work that God can be masculine and feminine?"

He replied, "God is hard to conceive by the little mind that sees only the two-dimensional world. Reality is much greater than the eye can see. Reality is actually pure consciousness, a field of vibration that can manifest anything at any given moment. Your thoughts actually create, so what you need and desire is manifested in your reality. If, you need a father, here I am. If you need a mother, there you are. And if you need a friend, here I am, and so forth. The spark of creation is inside every living being and is in all things manifest here. Your free will can co-create with God, so beware of your desires. If you truly want to know your God, you must persist through the veils of illusion, thoughts, beliefs, and feelings until you get back home to love. Then, and only then, will you know, about that which I speak. Love is the direct experience of union with God. There is no other."

"Jesus," I asked him, *"are you God?"* When I am with you I feel so much love and inner peace that I never want to leave you. I walk away with a sense of deep contentment and love, only to find myself the next day yearning to be in your presence. I am sometimes overwhelmed with the words that you speak, but when I let go of the thoughts, I am left with a deep opening of my heart that brings a smile to my face and tears from my heart, for it has been a lifetime of yearning and seeking. I seem to have an insatiable desire to feel love and now that it is here, I feel many parts of me wanting your attention. It is as though when I am with you I am with God.

"Like a friend I can share my deepest yearnings, and like a father, although I don't remember much about my life father, I feel safe, comforted, and protected. And yet, the woman in me, well, she has been far in the background for a long time now, and maybe I should keep her there, for her needs are many and very complex. The child in me knows all you need is love, and yet, the woman in me does not seem to know the first thing about love and doubts the existence of this God that the temple priests talk about. Their God, I know not, but this God-like man who stands before me is the closest to God *this* woman has ever known." I paused, and asked again, "Jesus, *are* you God?"

"I am at the deepest, most basic level, God as man," he explained, "and when I shed this body of man, I will return to the heavens from which I came. For my soul mission is to open up the heart of humanity, and bring love back into religion. I have come to encourage the dissolving of all self-limiting beliefs and to teach people how to free themselves of self-defeating thoughts and actions that do not serve their highest good. I was given a task, a great mission to accomplish and every day the path is made clearer. I have known that the Infinite Presence, known to some as God, is inside of me and that the ego that calls itself Jesus is a servant to the master of love. Love is my only master, my only truth. Everything else pales in comparison. There is no other lover that can match the ecstasy of my God. When I am inside this love and everything else disappears, then, I am God. I am that. You are that. We are *all* that, and yet some would lead us to believe that we cannot touch God let alone *become* God. For God as love, does not exist in Judaism or any other religion that exists on this planet today. There is no greater truth than knowing about the feeling of love and truth inside you. And yet, unnourished and unacknowledged, it dwindles to a minute aspect of your awareness and appears and disappears quickly. In reality, it only disappears from your awareness. When you fall back into love, God reappears in your awareness and you never want to leave. There comes a time that the devoted soul remains in love and the ego masters servitude and steps aside for the inner master to dominate. In this way, each soul has divine sovereignty over its own destiny, for choice dictates freedom. The freedom to choose is action in its purest form, which is destined to love. Love is, after all, the prime directive. It is all you are required to do. If you choose not to love, then suffering will overtake you, and you will not know freedom. You will know only slavery, and the pain of separation. Why choose pain when you can choose love?"

"So I am God?" I asked.

He replied, "Only when you know God can you be one with God, and only by being one with God can you know God. Only by being completely dissolved into the oneness can you be one with God. But no one is all of God, for the presence of God is ever present as a field of energy constantly manifesting all things. In the ultimate reality there is nothing unless you are there to perceive it. If you cannot perceive God, then God does not exist for you. There is a cloaking that happens, and God disappears back into the presence until you are able to perceive love. Love is always present. It is only your level of mastery over your own universe that conquers the demon of illusion. Self-delusion avoids self-mastery, so you are not in God-Realization. And that is more the nature of your question. What is God-Realization? I am God-Realized, for I am able to realize the truth of the Universe, but only after lifetimes of searching do most students know this truth. I have been sent on a very special and specific mission.

"Everyone has the potential to be Self-Realized. It is up to you to choose God and to choose to become one with God. Once you choose that you must focus all intention in this manner and deviate not to the tasks of the outer world. Do what you must each day and keep all thoughts on wanting to unite with God. In this way your mind will clear and you will then be able to perceive God."

"Jesus," I asked him, "what is *my* mission?

"To become one with God and a master of love," Jesus said. "And if you choose, to join me in my mission to save this world from self-imposed misery, thereby easing the suffering caused by separating ego self from God-Self. I love you Mary, as I love my God, for inside you is my Master. That is what is meant by love thy neighbor as thy self. God is inside each person, looking out. When the veil of illusion is removed, then it is very evident. Try it with me now. Look into my eyes and dissolve all else from your awareness. What do you see?"

I moved close and blurred my vision to exclude everything except Jesus. What I saw was indescribable. Everything fell away and I fell into Love. Nothing existed but that moment. Time stopped, my heart stopped beating, and we were suspended in a timeless state. I felt the presence of love and a voice inside me spoke.

The voice said to me, "I am always here, loving you. Nowhere can you go that I am not there. Nothing you say or do can stop me from loving you. Nothing you feel will ever match the love I feel when I look into your eyes. I am you and you are love manifesting. Nothing can match the beauty I see when I look through your eyes. I am all there is. I am Love."

And then the entire universe opened, and I was swallowed up in its vastness. I could sense oceans, mountains, deserts, flowers, tundra, sky, and clouds all made of this same stuff, this energy, all vibrating at a certain frequency, but all manifesting as love—powerful but gentle, expanded and peaceful. Layers and layers of knowing came to me. The nature of the universe revealed a holographic projection of my own mind, vast and exhilarating with infinite possibility. This went on for what felt like forever with many layers of reality being revealed. When I came back to Jesus, he was sitting, smiling. Everyone else had left and there was only he and I, gazing into one another, reflecting divinity back and forth into forever.

"Jesus you are my male counterpart; you are the male aspect of me."

"And you Mary, are the feminine aspect of me. We are twin souls joined at the heart."

Jesus spoke to me. "Only free will can break this bond, Mary. I promise to always acknowledge our union. I am forever wed to you and I am forever joined with you. This union is sanctified by the highest power in me and the highest power in you and can only be broken if you choose to leave me."

"But why on earth would I ever want to leave you?" I told him. "I am forever yours, Jesus."

"Mary," he replied, "Know that this vow is forever, and the love we experience will be like no other man or woman. Know this and love will set you free eternally."

And he said to me, "I, Jesus, take you Mary as my twin soul, married in mystical union now and forever, together again, as one."

I replied to him, "And I, Mary, take you Jesus as my one and only now and forever. Never will I betray your love, for inside God, one with you I will remain forever more."

"Mary," Jesus said, "Always remember this moment. No matter what lies ahead, always remember now and the veil will never reappear. Know this truth for it will keep you free."

I fell so deeply into love that nothing else mattered. I closed my eyes, but I could still see his face, glowing, magnifying the radiance of love, self-illuminating self, love magnified into two, the reality of illumination finally revealed. And then there was only love, and there were no words that needed to be said. Without touching, I felt him. Without seeing, I saw him. Without light, I was ablaze. Ecstasy moved through me in waves—wave upon wave of never-ending ecstasy like no other moment again. Never again in my life, such passion would I feel. This moment was forever blazoned in my soul. The Mary that I knew died that day, and the Mary Magdalene that was—wounded, bitter, confused, angry, sad, and fearful—dissolved. I was held in such love, that the Mary of the past was replaced by light, and I was bathed in renewed faith and hopefulness. Then an *Is-ness* that turned into a sense of *Being-ness* came upon me and I was reborn. I looked up and night had set upon us, the stars beginning to form in the sky. He sat still, eyes closed, smiling. I moved toward him and he opened his arms, and I nestled close to his heart. We lay down together and fell deeply asleep.

CHAPTER 6

Union: When the Two Shall Become One

I awoke with a start to see a lamb pressing its nose into my face. I cannot believe I slept overnight in a field. What in the world will people think? *Remember this moment, Mary, and no matter what lies ahead, always remember now and the veil will never reappear.* Then I did remember and an utter calm came over me. There he was standing overlooking the mountains in the distance. I got up and walked towards him and he touched my face and I felt again that powerful radiance. Love overcame me again, and I began to giggle with a young girl's innocence and only the experience of unconditional love was in the air.

"We really must go and make preparations for a real bed, Mary," Jesus said to me. "What will the people say if I do not have the proper house for us?"

"Jesus," I said, "what do we do now? Do we get to live happily ever after?"

"No, Mary," he said. "Life is not simple here, but we shall let our families know of our love and make preparations for a proper ceremony, so you will not be looked down upon. I could not stand for that. We will make the ceremony simple, and ask only those people who mean the most to us to come to bless our union. You know I am but a poor carpenter by trade, but you will never want for anything for I will truly manifest it for you. Love will see to it that we have all we need."

We walked down the mountain into our small town, and I returned to my home to tell my mother of this glorious news.

"How can you prepare to spend the rest of your life with a man you know nothing about?" Mother said to me. "Why have I not heard about him before?"

"He has just come to us, Mother, and I have known him like no other," I told her. "The feeling I have inside is enough for me. You will have to trust me. This is the only man I will ever love, and I will marry him."

"So be it then, Mary," she said. "Let us prepare."

Jesus came to dinner that night, and my mother immediately understood our connection and could feel our love. She said she was honored to have him as a part of our family. My brother came by later and he also felt Jesus's charm and he was pleased for both of us. My sister was initially jealous, but then she too was charmed by the magnitude of his presence and I knew love would see us through.

He worked hard in the next two weeks completing his projects and teaching at the end of his day, and I took to preparing his food and keeping him warm at night. I wanted everything perfect, so I made all the arrangements in great detail, leaving no stone unturned.

It was three weeks later when the guests arrived at the temple and the ceremony began. His mother came into town for the ceremony and she and his father were very pleased, open and warm. His mother was also named Mary and said she too was a part of his mission and counseled me on the nature of his ministries and told of the divine experiences she had had since before his birth. She and I talked for hours about his life and her role to help him complete his mission here. I know she wanted me to be happy, but warned me of the trouble his ministry was causing and the conflict it created in the temples. She said he talked of a loving God and the presence that could be found in all beings. The king was very angered by this and the priests were extremely sensitive to any threat to their power over the people. Interesting, how power corrupts, even among so-called men of the cloth. The holy ones were not always so holy, and definitely not too open to new ideas.

Some of Jesus's teachings were based in Eastern philosophy, and he had amazing master teachers whom his mother Mary had met. Her first *opening experience,* as she called it, was when she was visited by a messenger from God who told her of this soul, soon to be known as

Jesus and the profound effect his life would have on so many people, now and for generations to come.

The messenger told her it would be her responsibility to provide shelter and food to eat, as well as food for thought into the mysteries of the universe. There were three teachers that came to her and offered to teach Jesus so he could remember from his earliest memories who he was and his mission. Layers of knowing would be opened to him, based on Mary's love and her first meeting with Angel Gabriel, as she called him. Mary and I became very close friends and ended up spending much time together. Jesus's father, Joseph, was more distant, but still very kind. He was more traditional, as he liked to call himself, and honored the teachings of his church and was considered an elder in his temple. He felt, in this position, he could temper the emotions that others had about Jesus's beliefs and teachings and in this way could keep him safe. Joseph was a simple man who took over the care of the other children when Mary and Jesus traveled. I had no idea such a thing was possible, but Mary made sure Jesus was able to study and become the master he came to be.

"The knowledge he has is really beyond the books," she said. "I wanted him exposed to the teachings of the *true* Holy Ones, not the power hungry men in this town. They are not good enough to carry his shoes," she said. "They may never know his kind of wisdom."

And so it was that our conversations in those early days were talk about Jesus and his mission and the truths that were revealed to Mary.

The ceremony was quite lovely, and very powerful, for the force of this union was so strong. We moved directly into the small house he had built for us as soon as it was completed, and we consummated our union in the beautiful field where we first fell in love under the stars of God's creation of the heavens and earth.

That union was beyond any other physical experience I had ever had. He was gentle, slow and soft in his touch, spending hours touching me and talking to me rocking me, and holding me. I was wondering if we even needed to experience anything like intercourse for I was already in such ecstasy that I did not know if my body would explode if he penetrated me. But the waves of ecstasy carried him right into me, and it was as if we had been created out of one mold. We fit together perfectly and he was electrified by the penetration. He fell back and I moved on top and then I would glide with him as I moved with waves of ecstasy that came in a rhythm. I just surrendered moment to moment, and let my body experience the deepest pleasure I had ever known. I was making love with God, and there was no doubt that a child would be born of this union and she would become a teacher pure as he, for the angels were singing her name as we moved the dance of love—*Sarah, Sarah, Sarah.*

CHAPTER 7

Life with Jesus

The days to come were a mix of simple daily tasks, working and sleeping and eating and loving, all the while learning and growing in his presence. I would experience such peace and exultation. I never knew what to expect. I just knew how much I loved him and that I would do anything for him.

This lasted several years, and the birth of Sarah was a great moment for both of us. She truly was angelic and became the apple of our eyes, and I looked forward to every moment we were all together. Mother Mary and I would take her with us everywhere we went, and she became a favorite topic of conversation at the end of our day as we described to Jesus all the little nuances of her development. We had just five years of bliss before the trouble began.

"Mary," Jesus said to me one day, "we need to prepare for what is to come. There are rumblings about a new ruler and his laws, affecting everyone. We can no longer stand by and allow people to suffer because of his ignorance. You know I have spoken about only love and self-mastery, and yet he interprets it as blasphemy and a threat to his power. I am afraid for you and Sarah, and I must make sure you are safe. I want you and Mother to take the family and go away for a while whilst I work things out here."

"No," I replied. "If we go you come with us. You cannot change people who do not want to change, or are unwilling to open their eyes and hearts to another way of being. We must stay together no matter what. Let them do what they must, but I will never be without you, and I will not let anyone hurt Sarah. I feel we are protected, don't you?"

"In the greatness of the universe no harm can come to anyone," he said to me, "but in this three-dimensional, physical reality there is trouble at hand. Peter and Andrew are writing everything down and are coming up with a new testament to our teachings, and this is creating quite a stir. I must sit with this and commune with God about what is to come. Please come with me and let us sit together."

He sat for hours in silence and what came was too impossible to even imagine. I could sense great fear and anger from many around us even as the angels of mercy were overseeing great turmoil in our land. We would be asked to endure great suffering for the good of all. Jesus was given details into the unfolding story that was upon us. He began to prepare me by giving me insights into his vision and preparing me to carry on the teachings if something were to happen to him.

Jesus said I would need to leave with his mother, Mary and Sarah and the few others in our merry band of devoted followers, and we must not lose sight of the glory of God and the divine perfection with which all things are created. "Remember, Mary," he told me, "the illusion is that this is the only reality, but we know of the greater magnitude of our teachings and the implications. We are planting seeds for generations to come. The people here now are mostly not ready for what we have to offer, however, in the perfection of God's plan, everything will unfold as it is meant to be. I cannot remain here long enough to see Sarah to maturity. My time here is short. I am needed in the nether world where my power will be stronger out of the body than it is in this one. This body, no matter how high a vibration is generated, is still limited by form. I must eventually leave this body to better combat the forces of evil that are moving upon us. I will merge with my Father and together we can influence and help more people."

He continued, saying, "I will need you to be strong and to always, *always* remember our union. I have planted my seed inside the womb of the Goddess, and God has planted the seed of love in your heart. Let the two come together and disperse the wisdom to the masses. I will come for you and take you home when your time to leave your body comes. And, as long as you are alive here, I will remain with you. Even though you may not see me as you do now, you will always know by the feeling you have here."

As he touched my heart I began to cry great tears of grief as I realized I would outlive him. I knew of the future he spoke of and I understood the wisdom and vision he had, but all of a sudden I felt a sword cut through my heart and a feeling of desperation overtook me as I begged him to leave now.

"But Jesus," I pleaded, "we have choices, remember we can choose; we can co-create; we can manifest anything. You are God—why would you choose such a fate as this? Why not choose life; live until old age takes you? Stay with Sarah and me. Do not leave, not like that. How can you be so sure that this is the only path? Jesus, don't leave me. I cannot live without you, and I do not wish to go on without you."

I felt my weakness as human and as ego. I could not bear such things as I had seen, and yet, I knew humanity had born much suffering and I too must confront our destiny, and together, do what we could to make a difference.

I prayed for hours. I begged God, pleaded and bargained and prayed some more until my eyes were swollen shut and I could cry no more. I curled up into his arms and fell asleep as I had that first night and prayed I would awaken with him in the promised land of heaven with all the past behind us and only love in our future.

"Fear not, my dearest Mary, I will not die. I shall rise and come to you three times before we say goodbye. Remember, even in death there is birth. Remember how the Mary in you died and you were reborn and how I described my own rebirth? When I leave this body, I will again be reborn into a new plane of existence. Do not let the illusion of this physical world create suffering for you. I will come for you.

"This love we have is so deep, so transcendent, that it eludes time and space. It expands and creates new galaxies it is so potent. You, dear Mary, are extremely thoughtful and if you choose to remain inside love you will avoid the dark night. The dark night of the soul has consumed many, but it need not consume you. Stay in love, my dearest, and you will remain free. The pain of the physical body is unavoidable, but the suffering of the soul can be avoided if you keep your inner eye on the light and the mission we are on. The Almighty Father has a plan of which we are all a part. Keep your eyes and ears open to this and this alone, and you will remain free. You and Sarah will be cared for and the ministries will continue through many incarnations. Awaken to the One and only and keep your focus on our love so you are not blinded by the illusion of separation. Pray with me, dear Mary, and feel your connection to the One, our connection with each other, and the divine trinity that is created between us."

And so that night we prayed, for our bodies, our minds, our souls, our hearts. We prayed for all of humanity to awaken to the truth and to use this story to awaken the love that resides inside each heart. I needed to lay aside my own feelings and emotions and remember what I agreed to do and my vows as the bodhisattva, the Goddess of compassion, to remain embodied until each soul remembered. This exit of Jesus's body would be remembered for eternity, for how could anyone deny such a soul as his as not being enlightened. How could anyone deny his majesty or the magnitude of his connection with Love? How could anyone sacrifice his life so that generations later, others would look to him for compassion, love, and hope? He said the most important part of the story was not the suffering, nor even the pain of betrayal. He said the most important part to remember was our love and how it would transcend death and even in the darkest hour, our love would shine and illuminate the world, that this ground would become sacred as others would look to us as the saviors of hope, of faith and, the greatest of all, love. He said I would continue with the teachings and that he would remain with me in his spirit body until I too left my body. He said he would be not only with me but, with all of us, for in death he would be reborn back into the divine realm that permeates all. He said not to fear ego death. By totally surrendering the story of our lives, we could accomplish great things—things the ego cannot even dream about. So I prayed that I too could know these things and trust the divine plan that was laid out before our incarnation here.

But I could not help but wonder, *what was I thinking to agree to this?* To fall in love with a savior, the most perfect man ever. How could I think I could carry on without him? How could I ever be happy again? And then I remembered the child I had carried and the overwhelming feeling of love in my heart, and I knew indeed he would never die, that our love could never perish, and all I needed to do to rekindle that spark was to remember.

"Your gift and lesson in all this, Mary, will be your great strength and courage that you will develop, and you will carry on the wisdom, and reveal to many the knowledge of truth," Jesus told me. "Your lesson will be to trust. For in order to avoid the pain, you will be forced to remember the truth, which is, we do not die. As souls, we continue to grow and evolve and live on lifetime after lifetime as we choose to do so, for free will reigns. Even in death and transition we are connected to our source and if we surrender <u>our</u> will and align with the divine, we fall back into love. And inside love is this great joy. No fear can harm you here. Only grace resides and the river of grace is ever flowing and ever knowing. Choose not fear, dear Mary. Always choose love.

"Let us now lie down together and embrace each other and allow our physical bodies to relax and feel safe. For now we are together and we must imprint this knowing in our deepest physical memories so we can never forget."

As we connected to one another I felt the union of our spirits, and the oneness was so comforting that my body deeply and completely relaxed, and I fell fast asleep. When I awoke, I felt refreshed and greatly enlivened with faith and great hope for our shared mission.

CHAPTER 8

A Mission of Love

"Jesus," I said one day, "it is truly the mission that allows me to carry on, for if I stop and allow my body to feel the underlying fear, I would be completely immobilized and depressed."

"Fear not, my dearest Mary," he told me. "The truth will always set you free and fear retreats into the darkness from whence it came. The light of your being is too great to allow fear to get too strong a hold on you. You are the bodhisattva. Compassion is your mission. My mission is different. I came to enlighten and enliven the masses to their truth and to deepen their connection to the divine. There has been too much stress placed on the written word, and not enough on one's own experience of God. We must teach them more about love."

I pressed him, "Why is love so hard for people to feel? Should not love be the most natural experience of all?"

"Yes, Mary, this is very true, but fear is the enemy of love and most people succumb to fear in their ignorance of the unseen world. For those people who choose love, grace enfolds them and delivers whatever their heart's desire might be."

"So, if I choose love, you will be free of this great burden? For it is my deepest desire to be with you for eternity; to live out our lives and to accomplish our mission *together*. Why can't we have it all?"

"For love will answer your deepest desire," he told me, "not accommodate the fear of your ego. Your deepest heart's desire is to meld with love and never to return to fear. If your desire is to spend eternity with me, then it is forever granted, for I too wish to be with you. That is why the physical body must eventually disappear, for only when I am one with my Father/Mother can I be with you forever."

"But, Jesus," I protested, "can't we extend our time together here?"

"Trust, Mary. Trust this love," he said. "Focus on what you know. Stay present in this moment and know the depth of our love, then you will fear not."

"So, where will you go now?" I asked.

"I will go to Pontius Pilate and we will continue this drama to its end," he said. "I will finish what I came to do and you will carry on the teachings of truth, and turn people inward to their hearts, so they will not forget love. Stay right here and you will never forget me."

As he touched my heart, I began to cry. I sobbed like a baby, thrashing about. Then my sorrow turned to anger. I shouted, "Why *you*, why become a martyr? Stand up for yourself, for me, and Sarah! Tell me, how am I to live in this world without you? It is not the others I trust. I trust what I can see and touch. When you leave your body I will no longer be able to hold you or touch you! What then? Will I wither away into the night, collapsed in my grief? No, I cannot live without you, for you *are* love to me. Without you here I shall never experience love again. For how can I trust a God who could let this happen? How can I trust love when love has forsaken me? Why was I given the greatest gift only to have it taken from me? I refuse to let go of our relationship. You are too precious to me. I will not let you go!"

"Dear Mary," he soothed me, "it is always because of clinging that love disappears for you. You cling to your rights, which really are your beliefs. You must not mistake your human fears for divine truth.

"The truth is, when I leave this body, I shall join you again in the holiest matrimony. For I shall forever be married to your heart and forever more you shall experience me as your own breath and your own beating heart. We shall be one together in the Holy Spirit."

"But you, Jesus, will die. And I, Mary, shall grieve this moment for all eternity, for no matter what I do or say I cannot save you from the suffering and the deep pain you are about to endure."

"Mary," he explained, "all humans suffer pain and anguish. This is why this story is unfolding as it is, so I too can understand the deep emotions and feelings of humanity. In this way I will understand through empathy and experience. For when people stray, they are under a great spell of separation. To become human is to fall into the illusion of separateness, and when the veil is removed and lifted there comes an opportunity to experience divine bliss. The ecstasy of the reunion is so potent it becomes the deepest human longing and deepest spiritual yearning. For the only way to know bliss is to reunite with love. Know that even in your darkest hour, the light is always present. Your job is to break free of the illusion of separateness and believe in Love."

"But Jesus, I *do* believe in love. Our love!" I protested.

"Ah, but Mary, love is not limited to us, nor will our story be forgotten," he said. "Because of our great love, this story will endure and be passed down generation after generation because of what was born in us. You, Mary, have blossomed and opened your spirit and have experienced such great mystical union, that your soul will never be the same. And yet, as you can see, under great duress you will return to fear, for the human condition dictates it. It is like a magnet, which draws you in and before you know it your beautiful ego, which is still attached to your body, says *wait don't go. Do not leave without me!* And yet, our souls agreed to this story at this time and now we can proceed with our lives or freeze in fear and never continue growing. Sometimes love and compassion can have a very different outcome than expected."

So we lived, we laughed, we cried, we carried on. He continued teaching and I listening, hanging on every word. When he spoke there was such truth that, my whole being seemed to vibrate at a higher level. He even said this was true. When you are in the presence of a higher being, your cells actually vibrate at a different level. Tremendous healing is possible for those who are ready.

CHAPTER 9

The Answers to the Questions

I began going with Jesus as he traveled through the villages to reach more people. *Teach us about the kingdom,* they asked. *Is there heaven or hell? What are they like? How do we heal from these devastating maladies that are so rampant? Why do we have plagues and disease? What causes pain? Why so much suffering? Who are you? How do you know these things? When is the second coming? What makes people fall into love or stop loving? Why are there wars, hatred, murder, famine, and starvation?*

Jesus heard these kinds of questions over and over again. He always had answers. He never wavered in his ability to teach, to help others understand the nature of reality and to teach them about their ability to make choices. A better choice, he would say, is easier for someone who is awake. He said that most people were unable to use even a small portion of their brains, and therefore, were very limited in their consciousness. He said people were just beginning to remember who they were and where they came from. It would be a long time before humanity could really understand their own nature and the nature of reality.

"Help me to understand the nature of reality, Jesus, please," I asked one day.

"I teach ways for you to have a direct experience of love, which is the true nature of reality. Most people have never truly been *in* love, they have had only glimpses of emotions that simulate love.

"Most people vacillate between feeling alright with themselves and feeling some version of fear. When you are inside fear, you cannot be inside love. There are really only two experiences of reality, that of the ego and that of the True Self. **The goal in life, if there is one, is to fall into Love and to remain there for eternity. In order to do this you must focus your entire mind on God.** Let this be your focus, Mary, and you shall experience the Truth."

"Jesus, it has been said that there is no heaven or hell, only what exists now?" I questioned him. "How is that possible? Teachings of the church warn against forgetting the nature of hell, lest you shall end up there. The teachings are that the experience of heaven is the ultimate goal and likens this heaven to the true nature of reality. Is this true?"

"Heaven exists whenever you are experiencing God as love, Mary. It is a feeling of bliss, so complete and so familiar that you become one. Then you are in heaven—a heaven of bliss. There are really multiple realities playing out, all on different timelines. That is how the great beings and masters of the east can be in multiple locations at one time. So, you are experiencing me here now, and when I leave this body, I will be one with my God and become omnipotent, filling each time frame with that presence. It is why it is so important that I complete what I set out to do. There is no time, not really, so I will be able to move throughout every plane of existence, unimpeded by the dense physical form."

"But, I love your form, Jesus," I told him. "I can hold you and touch you. I can feel the purest love whenever you are close to me. And when I touch you, it is just like heaven."

"You must remember the veil of illusion," he told me, "and lift it so your eyes can see more clearly my love, for there are many that will be affected by our story. It is not for just you or me. It is we, together. We are destined to become the greatest love story ever told. We are together God and Goddess reunited into the one presence that holds all the creative energy in multiple universes. We divide into male and female forms to experience the difference, but when we are united we become one. We come together to experience that force which is the same. We created the universe, you and I, and there are as many universes as there are people. For each being creates their own reality and draws to them the experiences their souls need to learn and to grow. The ultimate mastery comes when you consciously choose the reality, which brings us back to your original concern."

"You mean you are choosing to leave your physical form and allow the Romans to have their way?" I asked incredulously. "They want you to prove you are what you say you are—*God*. Then why do you not show them? Would not that be more powerful than you showing the weakness of the flesh? Have you no concern for our people? What shall become of us when you leave?"

"Dear sweet Mary, listen to yourself," he gently chided me. "Is this the voice of the Goddess or is it the voice of fear? There is no rationalizing the fear, and no words can create sanity from insanity, and so, just know that this story is focused on love and it shall have a happy ending.

"How long, Jesus, until we die? When will we be together?" I asked.

"Love really has no boundaries," he replied, "and no time apart can ever dim or eliminate the light of love. Our love is eternal, brilliant and bright. So you must trust me Mary. Trust is really the lesson for you, for trust leads to faith and ultimately faith leads you back to that creative force from whence we all came and to which we shall all return. Time in physical form, is but a second in comparison with the time of creation. Creation, in and of itself, is timeless and ongoing. Billions and billions of stars and planets are being created and destroyed every minute of earth time. The universe is vast, and our love is just as vast and eternal."

So we closed for the evening with the prayer for eternal grace and fell asleep, dreaming of the heavens while the billions of stars above reflected back upon us. When we awoke to the new dawn, I felt a sense of peace and renewal. This new day was yet another day to celebrate our togetherness.

CHAPTER 10

Opening to the Holy Spirit

Jesus's teachings were like the vastness of which he spoke. He would speak to one or to many. It did not matter to him. He would do whatever was needed in that moment. What I loved to do most with him was to visit the sick. Word quickly spread that he was a miracle healer, the man who could turn water into wine and cure the lepers. Have I told you, he could not do more than the person in front of him allowed? He said it was all about free will, that there were some lessons that were worth the pain endured. Because freedom is so rewarding, in and of itself, it is most certainly worth waiting for to incarnate. Love had no greater servant, than my most beloved Jesus, for he was a man so filled with compassion that hearts would open with a mere glance, a gentle touch, or a kind word. Love was so full and so present that he literally illuminated everything everywhere he went. The vast light of his being was so great and spread such beauty, that, I would often fall down in his presence. One day he told me it was time I discovered the vast beauty of my own light so I could stand alone in my own magnificence.

He took me to an entrance of a cave and asked me to sit outside in the sunlight and placed one hand on my head and another on my heart and asked if I was ready to receive the Holy Spirit. How could I reply anything but *yes*. How could I resist such kindness from his open gentle heart?

I closed my eyes and felt the loving energy in his hands. Time disappeared and it felt like I entered another world. I saw an amazing light before my eyes and an image of my own body appeared—only this body was made of pure light. Jesus told me to breathe and feel the connection from my physical body to my light body as he connected what felt like thousands of threads from one to another. They were like small thin beams of light that wound around each organ, each vessel and all aspects of my physical being. It felt like I was plugged into the sun itself. I started to feel so hot that I felt a sizzling sensation inside. Then there was a burst like flames streaming from my heart center. This blaze of light seemed to penetrate layers of realities, layers of experiences, until there was nothing left but light. My being was fully illuminated. I would fall no more into illusion or deceit or fear, for the Illuminated-Self, was all knowing and transcendent. I was completely free at last. What happened next is the nature of the writings to follow and includes the knowing of lifetimes of pain and suffering, years of tears. All because I had forgotten who I was. I have come to share with people everywhere a way to awaken to your own vastness and illuminated self. Some of these teachings will be completely new to the world, while others are ancient. But, all these teachings are timeless wisdom to be brought forth now, for there are those among you who hunger and search endlessly, consciously and unconsciously, for your true self. It is time, dear ones. It is time to awaken the Holy Spirit, the body of your own soul. Here are some ways that have been taught to you in the past, including breathing practices of the Ancients, known to some as pranayama, often as Zen work, and today, others speak of transformational and transcendental breath work.

CHAPTER 11

After The Awakening

Through these teachings I bring to you the story of the awakening of Mary Magdalene, the Christ, the awakened master whose lineage bequeaths Jesus the Christ. The lineage of the savior of love who came to me as I was grieving and said unto me, "Mary, fear not, for I have not left you. I will never leave you, nor can I rid you from my heart, for you and I are one for eternity. The one you fell in love with, Jesus the man, was none other than me, the Holy Spirit who dwells within you. It is to your heart now that I speak. I am leaving you the lineage of our group here, further to be known as disciples, and you shall pass along the teachings of mystical bliss and the mastery of reunion.

"You must teach others how to remember the truth of who they are and pass along the teachings of the masters of the east. And we shall, together, further the teachings, for each new generation must relate back to their own culture and belief systems. Some will always resist these teachings, but the truth of their power to awaken can never be doubted. One must focus all one's energy now on getting the information out. I will place the knowing on an inner scroll inside you, so you will always remember and get direct access to the teachings. Your inner knowing will direct you and one day you will awaken in an incarnation and you will remember who you are and who you have been and bring forth the new teachings of the Christ within you. This shall indeed be the second coming and all can awaken a second time. And when you do, you shall experience the oneness and enter into holy matrimony with none other than God as love. It is inside of love that you will forever remain. The

58

Mary you know will be no more. But, you will love her and show her great compassion and kindness, for she suffered greatly. It was your open hearted compassionate self who finally released her misery and set her free on the wings of love to enjoy a blissful reunion with her beloved. Her whole heart and soul rest now as I touch you and set you free."

The light of Love then blazed a path through my inner eye and yielded not until it got to my heart. It was there that I grew in inner dimensions, in all directions until the Mary I remembered was but a vague memory. I no longer grieved, as I was confident that we would be together every minute of every day to come.

CHAPTER 12

Healing, the Miracle of Love

And so the mystical journey began and continues now through these writings and teachings. Jesus told me, "It will not be easy, Mary. The journey will be long in earth years, but it will be worth it. Never give up the mission of embodying love, for it is truly the path of joy. All beings seek this joy and comfort from their suffering. Only erasing the illusion of separation will set you free. You must teach them how to disengage from their strife and enter into oneness or unity consciousness."

I began the journey of mystical union in the presence of the great Master who had come before me, and together we would visit people struck with all kinds of pain, maladies and human suffering. It was these people who most inspired what I came to do and teach. I could feel their pain and their suffering, and began to see an energy body of light around them. There was a connection from what I saw in their field and what was going on in their bodies. For some it looked like a cloud or density in their energy field that needed to be cleaned out. For others, there were threads of attachment that were as big as ropes. These cords were wrapped around organs and other structures in their bodies. I could see different colors, which would change, depending upon their condition, thoughts, and actions. It was at first fascinating and at last illuminating. There was instantaneous knowing of what they needed and we would together heal the sick and ease their suffering.

I felt such great joy in this mission that I took the bodhisattva vow. I will continue to incarnate until all souls awaken to the oneness and end this human suffering once and for all. Little did I know of the journey that was ahead and how long it would take to complete. But, what else was there to do in the universe but to help others find what they seek? We are all in search of our Creator and the source of our joy and true happiness. It comes from union and so I knew I must continue my mission by finding others who also want to serve humanity in this way. There have been many who have come since, all serving from love and compassion, offering acts of true kindness, and yet, here we are with pain and suffering continuing.

The key is in uniting awareness with the physical, mental, and emotional bodies and clearing *all* the dense clouds and cords of attachment in this universal energy field. Once this field is cleared the physical body can become luminous and free from its afflictions. Then, we can ascend as Jesus did and reappear as he did, with a body that, however responsive to the physical torture, could be resurrected completely healed. Jesus wanted us to know that the power of love can heal completely all wounds, no matter how massive, vast, or complex. He said you must work on the unifying field, and what follows are his teachings and my experiences in healing.

∞

CHAPTER 13

Dispelling Illusion with Truth

There once was a man afflicted with leprosy in our village. He was in grave pain. He was emotionally a target from the attitudes of the people around him. Jesus came to him and told him that his healing could be immediate and complete if only he would say the word and he would be healed. "What is the word, Master?" I asked.

"He needs to align his will completely with the will of his God and surrender completely to the present. He need only say the word and he shall be healed. The word is *now*. I am ready to be healed *now*. I am ready to surrender *now*. I am interested in loving my God wholeheartedly *now*. I release my afflictions *now*. For everything that happens, happens now. There is no past or future when it comes to manifesting."

Everything happens *now*, and so this dear sweet soul prayed to his God as Father and said, **Dear Father who art in Heaven, in my heart I am ready to be healed and to return to my original healthy state, *now*. I surrender my body to you *now*.** (You can use this as a technique to heal yourself.)

And with this Jesus placed his hands, one on the top of the man's head and the other on the man's heart near the center of his chest, and Jesus envisioned him as whole and healthy and free.

"The key," Jesus said, "is not to be disillusioned by what appears to be real. For the field of infinite potential cannot be seen. It can be felt, however, and utilized to create immediately. Once you tap into this field of potential, you align with the physical, the mental and emotional bodies and pray by repeating the word for your God over and over to keep the mind focused in the *now,* and thy will shall be done."

Once Jesus removed his hands the dear man stood and looked at his body, only to find he had no wounds. All signs of the leprosy were gone. He literally jumped for joy and hugged first Jesus and then me, asking if it would last. "As long as you believe in the *now,*" Jesus said. "You must stay focused on what is. Trust your God whole -heartedly and never fail to remember the love that healed you. To this love be true."

I knew from then on the healing power of love, and that in order to be fully healed from any affliction—mental, emotional, or physical— you must be fully committed to love. Knowing and experiencing love is the greatest power available. Most people equate the human expression of love, which pales miserably in the vastness of the potential that exists within the infinite power of true love. For love is the manifestation of none other than the Holy Spirit of which Jesus spoke so boldly. He made the declaration that this love had its abode directly in the human heart. "Meditate on the heart if you wish to experience love," he said. "Your devotion will lead you and great love will emerge. Your focus will lead you directly to the experience of the Infinite, the source of all healing."

With this he gave me a huge hug and held the back of my heart and pulling me close and uttering the words, "I love you dearest Mary, and it is here that you will always remember me."

I do not recall just how many people Jesus healed, but it was miraculous how easily it was accomplished. He said you need not believe in a higher power to receive the Holy Spirit, for at times grace would appear and open the heart without a conscious calling. But, this type of healing was rare, he said. It would happen most often to souls who made an agreement before incarnating.

Just when would this awakening occur? It was kept secret, hidden in a certain part of the mind until the exact time came and just the right circumstances arose. I remember such a time.

There was an elder in the community, who used to taunt Jesus and his followers and tell him he was wasting his time praying to a God for he did not exist. He did not believe in a God he said who would allow so much pain and suffering. "Why, take my feet for example," he exclaimed. "Look at how they blister and peel mercilessly and prevent me even from walking. And look, over there at the children who do not have enough to eat, or my wife who gets so weak she is bedridden for days at a time. How could God allow such things?"

This of course was a rhetorical question, for Jesus could answer that question in so many different ways. He said we all have free will and that we need to align ourselves at a soul level with the divine and that would cease all suffering. The cause of suffering is attachment to a thought that causes you pain, like this one that focuses on the disempowerment of the human being versus the potential to change and be healed through divine grace. Grace is a gift. You need only ask for help and it will be provided. The timing and the specifics need to be left up to God. Also, Jesus knew that some people were here for the first time, and others were paying back a debt or debts that were created in other incarnations. We cannot remember because the amount of confusion caused by knowing would create utter chaos in the identification with the time and place and lifestyle chosen for this time.

"Nonsense," this man complained. "Absolute nonsense. I have never lived before and I shall never live again. When my life is over that is it. I am done, and not a moment too soon. This pain in my feet is unbearable." And with that he walked away leaving me wondering, *just how unhappy do people have to get before they start to search for some greater meaning in their lives?* Jesus said, "The day will come when this man awakens, much to his utter amazement. Wait and see."

How does he always know these things, I thought. But I learned to trust him for he was always right. And then one day, two months later, the man came to see Jesus and, out of desperation, asked Jesus for help. "I do not believe," the man said, "in any God of yours, but my wife says I should at least ask you, considering your reputation and all. Will you help me?"

"Yes," Jesus said. "The pain in your feet is from walking the wrong path. You must change your direction and choose the path of enlightenment; that is the only path toward your salvation. I can heal your feet today, but you must open your heart in days to come, so the pain does not return. For it is not my task to take away your pain, only for you to continue life patterns that are distracting to you. Your feet are your God's way of telling you that something is out of balance in your life, and you need to change your ways and choose enlightenment. Enlightenment is a path to freedom, complete freedom to choose wisely the path that leads you ever closer to your true self. This truth that speaks to the deepest part of you is at the heart of all true great teachings and the finest religions. Seek the truth of your highest wisdom and this shall lead to enlightenment."

With this, Jesus turned and receded into the light of the day that surrounded us. It was as if he could reach into your heart, make a profound impact and then, just as quickly, fade into the background and blend into the surroundings.

Love would never have a greater master or a greater servant than this man Jesus, whom I loved. I thought I loved him more deeply, more completely, more profoundly than words could ever express. *I would follow him until the end of time*, I thought, as the power of this love and the fountain of his infinite wisdom overflowed the glass of enlightenment. All techniques for healing fade in comparison to true love.

"Jesus, what will the world be like when you are gone?" I asked him. I must have sounded like a child lost in her fear, and yet the words came out in an effort to prepare myself for the inevitable.

"Mary, the world will continue much as it is now. Most people will go forward with little to no awareness of their true potential. However, there will come a time when the human heart will open and be ready for the mystical teachings of the prophets, and the divine truth that the teachings of the east have to offer. It is my mission to provide a compelling story, so strong in drama, so as not to be forgotten. There is, a timelessness to Truth, but it must be restated in slightly different ways to each new generation. You and Sarah will educate the people in such a way as to hold their attention. Words of this book of Mary and her experience in awakening will pour forth at just the right time. Feel deeply into these words and know that they are true."

"What of Sarah?" I asked.

"She will remain with you and grow into her mother's child," he told me, "one of great beauty and power, and she will be with you in your heart always. You know you will always call to her."

"But will she be persecuted and sought out?" I asked.

"No," he replied. "She will be hidden, and no one will ever know her true identity, only a chosen few. But have no fear, for what you have to offer her will be more than she will ever need."

"And one day we will all be together?"

"Yes Mary, always."

CHAPTER 14

Trust vs. Fear

We visited many needy people in our few years together. There were many who trusted him, but many feared him. We would often times work as a team helping to ease their fear and their suffering, which Jesus said were one and the same. He said the root cause of all suffering was fear and that pain was inevitable while in a physical body. The body was vulnerable to the elements and needed protection and could not be sustained eternally, but the soul, he said, would not only last, it would progress and develop more fully with each incarnation. Love is the key to all growth. Without it, there is only fear, which actually restricts growth and restricts the soul's progress. That is the ultimate goal of any incarnation—to learn more about loving.

"Most people," he said, "are self-serving and can be downright selfish from a fear of never having what they need or getting what they want. Little do most people know the greatest of all needs, is to know the love of their Creator. To immerse yourself back into the light of your being is the ultimate goal of any incarnation. So, if you can keep that focus, you are well on your way to enlightenment. You create your own reality, as the divine wants you to have your own free will." Which brought me back to my next question.

"Why then, Jesus, do we forget who we have been and what we have done in past incarnations?" I asked. "Would it not be better if we could remember what we have learned?"

"You *do* remember what you've learned at a soul level," he said. "You just do not remember the details of that life. It would be very confusing to engage in many lives simultaneously or to take on the persona of another life and be able to live fully the moment of this life. It is truly of the utmost importance, in order to be completely enlightened, to be fully immersed in the present moment without any attachment to the drama that ensues and to keep your mind focused on the Presence inside the moment, creating the reality that is unveiling itself before you. There are no other means to the end than to be fully present. The mind likes to wander into different realms, which leaves you unaware of the reality that is unveiling itself every moment. You must become fully aware at the moment and then fall into the Presence that created it."

I took these words fully into my heart and felt what he meant by them and fell deeply into the love that he spoke of so highly. I felt the divine presence consume me and I knew I never wanted to leave this state again.

I did leave that state of love three days later. It is inevitable until you completely surrender your ego identification with all of its limiting thoughts and fears. When you are inside love there is no fear. Most people identify themselves with their fears and limitations.

"When you release all fear and all limiting thoughts and beliefs, what remains is the moment," Jesus told me. "You left the moment. The Presence never leaves the moment. Where would I go?"

I asked him, "Why does the mind wander so and what do we do to change it? Why did God make this mind so complex and difficult to work with?"

"The mind was created to hold vast amounts of information and to support all the functions of the body. The ego identifies completely with the body and forgets about the Great Mind that it is immersed in, in order to claim the self-induced and often indulgent territory. You must stay clear of this attachment to the ego's affliction with its self-importance and make the Great Mind of God your highest priority. When you truly allow the mind to relax, not think, you will end up in clear space where there is no thought, just pure clarity. You can then progress to other realities or other planes of existence, or you can ask to serve the Great Mind. If you choose service you will be used to create love, teach wisdom, and provide healing and sustenance to those in need. That, Mary, is what you have chosen. To remain awake you must choose to stay in the moment and train the mind not to wander and become distracted. Focus on the presence and bring the presence fully embodied in the moment. Focus on love, or the desire for love, and follow that aching desire in your heart to the inner beloved who is loving you.

"I was sent here to remind people of love and to create compassion for all humankind and to stop the mutilation of the words in the great scriptures, which have led to ignorance, indignation and self-serving actions. I have come, Mary, to set you free and to pass along the message of love. It is up to you and others to carry this message forward. There will come a time when people will be more than ready for their own self-fulfilled magnificence to shine. This radiance will be the love of God shining through every cell to illuminate the essence of their being. Those who choose to shine will create heaven on earth."

With that, he began to radiate a light so bright from his heart and head that it was almost unreal. And yet my eyes saw a glimmering sparkling light, which he said was the light of God imbued in his body.

"This light, Mary, is the true source of all healing," he explained. "All healing must begin with you and your desire to transcend the bondage of ignorance and fear. Once your soul and ego have become immersed in this goal, it is only a matter of time."

"How much time, Jesus? How can a person increase the potential of healing and transformation?"

"Through honest love and devotion to the one source that has given you birth," he said. "You cannot transcend your karma, but through loving devotion you can transcend the ignorance and fear that created it. Love can truly transcend everything, and it is the power that creates true wholeness and self-reflective imagination that leads to the creation of a new self. This new self is whole and complete without need or desire. The newly formed self, born out of love and devotion is enveloped in an ocean of bliss. All one must do then, is ride the wave to the promised land and walk upon the shore of eternal happiness and transcendent joy.

"Love is not a power to ever be underestimated. There is no greater source of power in the entire universe. The matrix of love is both creative energy and destructive energy and can be used to create entire worlds or destroy the sources of fear and illusion that seek to undermine Love.

Fear has its roots in blind ignorance. In order to unleash the power of Love, fear must be put back into its place, back into the seething darkness of ignorance and destroyed by the light of pure radiant Love."

"And how do you release fear?" I asked him. "How does it remain contained in the darkness? How do you forever hide or destroy ignorance?"

"That is up to each individual heart," he said, "for your heart center carries both the Truth and the illusion. Once you clear the dust of illusion from the surface then the undercurrent of grace is free to flow unimpeded by the fear of not being loved. This is the underlying fear of all humanity, the fear of never getting or maintaining the love that is their inherent birthright. Humans sacrifice their happiness every day for the illusion of separation. People fear separation from love and because they fear it they create it. The mind manifests based on its experience and thought. So, if the mind senses a thought of fear it will manifest an experience to serve the thought. In other words, fear of loss, will manifest loss and difficulties connecting with others. A multitude of situations and dramas are, really, self-fulfilling prophesies. By comparison, imagine thoughts that are constantly focused on love and devotion to God. What do you think the mind would create? Loving relationships, of course."

"Why then, Jesus, did I meet you?" I questioned him, "For my thoughts were not positive. Only deep loneliness did I experience before that, before I met you."

"Your karma and destiny led you to me," he replied. "Underneath the deep loneliness was an earnest desire and deep longing for love. The desire awakened the conscious mind to the unconscious desire, which led you to me. Love keeps close company with love. I have known your soul, dear Mary, to be one of deep gentleness and compassion. You took the bodhisattva vow out of your desire to make a promise to yourself and to me, but you will do whatever it takes to see each individual home to the Creator. It was through that vow that our paths collided many times ago. It was through our deep commitment to the resurrection of love that we agreed to the crucifixion of ignorance."

"But Jesus," I said, "why the cross? What an unimaginable atrocity for one so enlightened and beloved as you."

Jesus replied, "It is a symbol of crossroads; heaven and earth, east and west all meeting at the center. It is here," he touched himself at his heart, "that love remains whole—untainted and unharmed by any outer drama that might ensue. We just need to ride the wave of grace back, Home. No one really ever sways too far from Home, for the love of God always remains right here inside the heart.

Once again a wave of love erased the fear and trepidation of my human heart and awoke the power of grace and the magic of love.

"We must get back home to Sarah," said Jesus. "Mary will be waiting for us."

When we returned home, Sarah and Mary were playing outside. The mere sight of that blessed child brought tears of joy to my eyes. The arms of love, as little as they were, wrapped themselves around my being. "Mommy," Sarah said. "We shall always be together, won't we?"

"Oh, yes, Sarah. Always," I replied.

Mary stood smiling in the background as Jesus came to her. "Mother you are looking radiant today!" He stroked her face and smiled that loving smile.

She said, "To you, my child, I will always seem radiant. To others I am merely a peasant woman tending to sheep."

"Your time of grace, dear Mother, will come again, and it will fall like rain upon your head." He touched her crown and between them I saw such radiance that it moved me to tears.

"Crying, sweet Mary?" Jesus said to me.

"It seems like all I do now, doesn't it?" I replied.

"Tears are cleansing and very expressive," he told me. "You look absolutely beautiful when your heart is so open. Love has no limits in its magic, Mary, and you, my dear, are a wizard of love."

That was one day I shall always remember. It seemed so surreal, like nothing could ever go wrong. It felt like paradise. All I could think of was, *may this never end.* I want this feeling to last forever. Each soul has its own journey to opening. It can be quickened with a devoted heart and an enlightened teacher. When both are present, true magic ensues.

"Feeling this love is all I ever really want, Jesus," I said to him.

"Then let no one take it from you," he said, "by giving them the power of manipulating the energy of your feelings turning them into emotions that create pain and suffering."

"You speak of feelings like abandonment, loss, grief, anger, and the worst of all fear, as the root cause of all suffering?" I inquired.

"Yes," he said. "Stay clear and present in the moment and detach from others and their reactions and stay present to the love in your heart. Be true to love, for that is the only true reality that can set you free."

"And what of those that are going to betray and persecute you, what of them?" I asked.

"Turn from them," he told me, "for they have no say in the running of the universe. Their power is limited due to their ignorance and blind arrogance. Just because they have turned their backs on love, and rationalized it, does not mean we have to do the same. When you turn your face from hatred and ignorance, fear and illusion, you will be face-to-face with the creative force of the universe and you shall be kissed with the sweetness of the nectar of bliss. The divine can manifest in any form you need to bring you comfort. Just ask and you shall receive."

"What shall I ask for?" I said.

"To be blessed with the *amrita,* the nectar of the divine, and the manifestation of grace into every action, word and thought," he told me. "Then, manifestation will follow through the law of attraction and grace will be bestowed upon you.

"But, do not underestimate the power of the destroyer, for sometimes something must die and be cleared away before something else is born. And so it is when each of us dies and we leave this body, and we all will. You shall be born again and love will be the force that delivers you to the arms of none other than your beloved."

"You, Jesus, are my beloved," I told him.

"Then that is how you will be comforted by God. For the form in which you see God, is how God will appear to you. But remember, it is all God's creation, so the seed of God's love is everywhere. The beloved is your comforter, your lover. Your inner beloved is your own heart's salvation. This beloved is who always brings you great joy, and without whom you cannot be truly happy. Your beloved is constantly with you. Open your heart, and you will always know of that which I speak."

I pressed him for more, asking, "And how can one achieve true comfort and salvation in the midst of such suffering, Jesus?"

"To believe fully, heart and soul, in your God, is to live in faith," he said. "Then there will be no doubt. Doubt of God's plan leads to fear, and yet, one must do everything possible to insure peace and harmony in the world. The great master teacher, with whom I studied, taught me methods of meditation to ensure direct connection with God. These methods I will pass on to you to ensure your experience of the sweetness of the nectar of divine bliss. But remember, sweet Mary, not everyone will take to these methods. There will be many teachers and many ways, but all paths lead back to the One. The most direct way to stay in touch with God is, to love your God with all your heart and live fully present in the moment. To live in the past is to live in nothingness, for it no longer exists. To live in the wonder of the future is to ignore the love, which exists in the now. So to live fully present in the moment is to live in God's love. The life to which we are given is always only in the present moment. It is in the present that all things are created."

"So if we choose, we can manifest the will of God by being fully present in the moment?" I replied.

Jesus said to me, "To align with the will of God is the first law of manifestation. Without the power of God there exists nothing. It is the will that sets all creation into motion."

"Jesus, what if my will is to have you remain here with me in form, in flesh and blood?"

"It is only your will and it is not aligned with my will, nor the will of God," he explained. "You need to know the greater plan of each soul to choose another's destiny and that is quite impossible. For only each soul aligned with its Creator can create the appropriate exit, or entrance, for that matter. If you truly align with the divine you will be in alignment with the greatest force in the entire universe. It is through this alignment that all life is created. So if you want me with you in flesh and blood now, you only need look straight ahead into my very eyes."

And with this, I looked straight into his eyes and felt such love I thought I could not contain it all. As if reading my thoughts, he said, "In order to contain the vastness of love, you must expand your boundaries and learn to reach your energy in all directions, then at the same time,

Vickie Mary Fairchild Holt

receive from all directions until there are no directions at all, only a melding with love. The first lesson in love is to surrender to it. It will thus take you on a ride into eternal bliss."

"And what then, Jesus," I said, " what happens after the rapture subsides?"

"If you keep surrendering to it, it never subsides. The feeling state, when embodied, varies in degrees, depending on the activity you are involved in, but love never leaves. The intensity and the quality is experienced differently by different people at different times."

"How is it that I am so blessed to ever be with you? I feel as though I could not possibly live up to your embodiment of love. Sometimes I feel inadequate and unworthy in the eyes of my beloved."

"That is only a projection brought forward from your past. Deep inside, you know your worthiness is unquestionable," he said to me. "And by the end of this life, you will prove yourself more than adequate."

"You know this for certain? How?" I asked.

"I know what I have come to do," he replied, "and I know our soul contract. You will complete the teachings this time and lifetimes to come. There will come a time when humanity will be ready for more of the teachings, but for now I must speak in parables and tell stories that people here can understand. They cannot understand the magnitude of God or the universal truth of which I speak, so we must begin with baby steps and give the people the savior they are seeking. For them, gods of gold will fail them and their Father 'who art in heaven,' must be given to them here on earth, for them to understand the seed sound of the One who lives eternally within their very heart and soul."

"What can I possibly teach? Who would listen to me?" I told him.

"The voice of the feminine is just as powerful and needed," he said. "There are those who will trust you, and the trust shall build and grow over time. You cannot see yourself as you really are. In my eyes you are pure and your heart is deeply loving and compassionate. You words are truthful and your love nature is extremely loyal. You have all the qualities of a gifted teacher. All you needed was the truth and students to teach. Sarah will be your greatest student and will lead you to others. You will see soon enough. As for me, our time here is very limited. There is a lot to do in a very short period of time. We must carry on very

74

efficiently and write down as much as possible and trust the twelve loyal students who will continue with this knowledge. You must not doubt yourself, Mary, it will inhibit the teachings greatly.

"There will always be different schools of thought as it pertains to the nature of the universe, but remember the great truth that sets every heart free and that which is common to all schools of thought. Love is the universal truth that heals, guides, nurtures and provides for every need. It is even in the breath you breathe; so close that you cannot escape it."

"So," I said to Jesus, "the message is simple then?"

"Yes," he said, explaining further. "But people will make it complex. Love others, as you want to be loved yourself. Love and respect all living things. Love thy God with all your heart and soul. Let your main focus be love and that way you will experience your God more internally, for it is inside your heart space that God resides."

"Do you think God would create you and then leave you alone without any guidance or guidelines with which to live in the world? That would be totally ludicrous. A loving God would no more leave a child alone than a mother would abandon her child in the face of danger. There must be a tried-and-true method to provide safety for the children of God, and so I have set myself upon your breath and live through you as you live in me. I am your very heartbeat and the very thought that creates this reality. That is how potent God is. There are different forms of God, but God remains omnipotent and omnipresent. That is the nature of reality, breath and God as one living breathing entity."

"Jesus, what if I were to tell you that the only time I really feel love is with you?" I told him. "How will I ever be able to expand the teachings when I cannot feel God inside me? I feel God in you and in you alone. Take a look around. It is all rather hopeless, when you see how ignorant most people are. They do not notice God in you. They are indeed, just the opposite of me. They cannot even feel God present in such a soul as you. It is as if they are blinded by the veil of their own ignorance and are led by their fear, alone in their world, fraught with hatred and desperate attempts to free themselves by either blaming or using other people. How completely desperate, does one need to get, to change their perceptions of the world?"

"Well, my dearest Mary," he said, "I detect your own fear of humanity continuing in the direction of fear, hatred, and desperation, which leads you to your own hopelessness and feelings of helplessness as you attempt to make sense of people and their actions. There is a free will that is inherent inside each person. It allows them to make their own choices. If they choose to live in ignorance, then so be it. But, there are always repercussions to all choices, be they conscious or unconscious. Consequences follow every action and even every inaction. You must not be concerned with others and their choices. You can pay close attention to your own choices, and choose to see the divine in all beings no matter how hard or how deep you must go to find it. Believe in the power of love to change everything and pray that everyone chooses love."

"They will have to choose love eventually, for it is the only way that will bring true peace and harmony back to the world. That is what we came to do, dear Mary. For as long as it takes, we will work on opening the hearts of those who choose love, and who are ready to receive it. For the humble servant of love has no greater master to obey."

"For now, Jesus, I choose love and I want to share it with you. That is really all I care about, is being with you."

Jesus replied, "And for now, that is all you need to do," and putting his arms around me, he held me and I surrendered completely to love.

It was not too long after, that, I awoke with a sensation of great warmth in my heart and no fear in my head. Where is he? I could not remember a morning when I awoke that I did not feel him near by either sitting or reading or contemplating, sometimes writing, but always in a profound meditative-like state. And yet, today was different. I went outside to look around and found Mother Mary taking care of the children.

"Looking for Jesus?" Mary said. "He left early and did not want to disturb you. He went to find Judas to go for an early morning walk."

"When will he return? Soon?" I asked her.

"Probably. It may take some time as there is much to discuss," Mary replied.

"So he will go to trial then, won't he?" I said to Mary.

"We must support his wishes and follow the will of God," Jesus's mother said to me. "Only he knows the big picture, Mary. We must trust and hold on to our faith. Getting caught up in this physical realm and all of its drama and stories is very dangerous."

"I do not feel that I can control my emotions any longer," I said to her. "They go from fear to anger to love and back again in such a short time. I cannot seem to steady myself except when I am with him. He always puts my mind at ease. His presence is so healing. Why do you think others cannot see or feel this and do not trust that to experience God you can go directly inside? Jesus portrays this possibility like no other clergyman ever has. Do you think they are that threatened by him and that they will bring him to trial and condemn him like a common criminal? How can that be?"

Mary thought for a moment and said to me, "I do not know the makings of anyone's single-hearted quest for vengeance that arises from ignorance and fear or what drives an individual to such acts of violence and condemnation. All we know is that love must be honored and exemplified in our own words and actions or we become like the very ones we have judged. I know that there is a betrayal about to occur towards our beloved Jesus. We cannot change that, but we must trust the divine will and align with the truth of our hearts. There will be much pain and suffering before this human drama ends, however, the truth always wins out and the universal jury always gets the victims revenge by releasing it to the karmic records, so lifetimes later, justice will prevail. The only way we can prevent the karmic wheel from spinning is to choose love every moment, for it is love that sets us free."

"Well, that all sounds well and good," I said to Mary, "but right here, right now, my heart is suffering a tremendous pain and fear that this pain shall last lifetimes, if not to eternity. I am not ready to forgive those who have trespassed against us. He is the only love I have ever known, or choose to know. I will never stop loving him and pledge to fight this to its God-forsaken end."

And so I ranted and raved about my pain, my anger, and my deepest fear that Love would forsake me and that Jesus would abandon me here. I would remain helpless and alone, full of anger and fear of never seeing him again. I laugh now, as I say and write these words, for in the end there is no way we could ever be separated, but being in a physical body makes it hard to remember the nature of the universe. You see, the universe is truly based on oneness and union, so I need not have worried about separation. Separation is only an illusion. It felt so real at the time, though. It is so important in human form to acknowledge the pain and emotions as they arise, for otherwise they will become stuck in the body and can remain for lifetimes afterward. Now, that is indeed what happened, for the love I experienced with him was so deep and so true and my fear of abandonment so great that it festered in my body for lifetimes, turning eventually to hate and anger. Anger at humanity, at ignorance, and at fear, itself. These unresolved feelings continued the karmic chain of incarnations. Now one might ask, how could the teachings of Christ be handed down to someone such as me, a poor peasant woman who knew of enlightenment, but acted like any other pagan on the streets? Well then, I must continue with the story, for it has a sequence of events that will explain exactly how this is possible.

CHAPTER 15

The Mission

Jesus's mother, Mary, as you may have suspected, had already received perpetual enlightenment. She was prepared for Jesus leaving at the time of his conception, for the angelic messenger came to her and told her not only of Jesus's birth, but of his importance to the story of humanity and its unfolding spiritual evolution. She was chosen because of her deep faith and her spiritual path and her absolute longing to be one with God through eternity. She was not so tested by the makings of her physical reality. She was indeed born a saint and she wanted no part in the strings of attachment that are created through birth and rebirth. She wanted to be a mother and that led her to the embodiment of the Divine Mother and her aura (energy field) was so elevated and full of light, that no one could deny her Godliness. She was almost otherworldly to be around, her light was so great. Her presence could elevate me so high, that there were actual moments when I left my body and rose off the earth. Other times, she was so compassionate that my heart would open and encompass the entire world. I felt she had all of humanity in her heart. She was indeed the Divine Mother incarnate, so who else would be more appropriate to help Jesus on his path?

I tell you his path was *not* the easy path. He was chosen out of all the angels to come, for he had so much strength and wisdom to share, but the most important of all his soul virtues was his deep belief in human beings. All the other angels said no; " *it is not possible for them to awaken while in the body. There are too many temptations while in the flesh. The only ones who have remembered have been those of us from the angelic realm. Humans have too far strayed from the divine path. And look, just look at how many there are. No matter how many of us incarnate they still persist in delighting in their suffering. No! We vote no!"*

However, Jesus did not believe this at all. He refused to release the hope and the desire to change earth back into Eden again. It was not free will that was humanity's downfall, he said. It was the fierce veil of illusion that clouded their judgment.

"We must soften the veil," he told us, "and allow people free will in the face of understanding what it is that they are really choosing between, fear and hate, or love and peace. Is not this really what we are meant to teach them? Why do we have to remain so hidden from their sight? No, I will not leave them in the face of their misery and suffering without any help from us. I will go. I will embody into the illusion and I will show you that there are those who are still interested in love. It is not too late. For our Divine Mother and Father have not forsaken us and we have not forgotten. But there—*look!* Right there are our brothers and sisters who suffer only because the illusion has gotten so dense that they cannot see. Send me. I will go and I will find those among humanity who wish to join the band of redemption and sing the song of love. I know there are those among them who are ready for love and I, Jesus, will find them and bring them Home. And to you naysayers, I say *shame on you,* for your lack of faith. For the seed of our God is in each and every one of them, and I will not abandon them, and I trust that you shall not abandon me. I ask not that any of you should embody, but I do ask that you support me and come to me when I call to you. Come to me in full force and give me strength in the face of desperation. Come to me in my deepest hour of fear and torment, for the flesh is weak and there is much pain to be had in the body. I know my Father will not forsake me, but you my brothers, will you stand steadfast beside me and help me slay the forces of evil that have taken over the earth? Will you help me from here in the angelic realm? Will you help me fight the forces of evil that have laid claim to that holy land? Will you promise to support me and help me, as I pledge to do for our most humble brethren who are suffering? Who among you are brave enough to stand before Satan and slay him where he stands? I shall abolish him and send him off, so he will never return. Only the remembrance of him will remain, for it is in this remembrance that no one will dare tarry on that God forsaken ground of ignorance again. We shall set upon that holy ground, the embodiment of love. And I shall take a mate and we shall pass down the lineage of truth and hopefulness, faith and goodness and I, Jesus, soon to be known as Christ, shall inherit the earth and restore it justly to its heavenly realm. Yea, I shall not abandon my brothers and sisters; will you abandon me?"

Well, what was an archangel to say? "Yes, we will support you, but only time will tell if you are successful."

"What else is there to do in the entire universe worth doing than to save humanity from itself and to finally clear the illusion of separation from their reality? It will save that beautiful planet and our Mother and Father's creation from possible extinction. I have your promise then?"

"Yes, we will support you," they replied.

And so he came into humble beginnings into a manger with the animals as witness to his coming. Mary, in all her divine glory and splendor, gave birth to the Master of masters, King of kings. And here I am, married to the one chosen to save humanity and to plant the seed of awakening for all humanity and all I can think of is, how will I ever live without him?

It was clear to me in that moment just how dense the veil of illusion must be. For at once my heart was breaking for my own selfish reasons and I also cried inside for all the suffering humans have endured and will continue to endure if a savior does not emerge among us. He was so reflective and so absorbed in his mission, I would say how dare he not think of me and the children, and yet, my heart's deepest desire was to join him in Eternity, stand by his side and together serve this glorious and illustrious planet and all her creatures, great and small, for not only humanity would suffer under the veil of illusion.

Jesus said to me one day, "There will come a time when there will be great plagues, starvation, massacres and eclipses to darken the sky. Tsunamis and floods, fires and more would come, all to awaken those who remain to serve Love. They would come to awaken the people to see earth's creatures for what they are, divine love incarnate. Animals and plants, the earth herself, the air and water, all part of a beautiful and illustrious plan to provide a beautiful home to incarnate in and to enjoy the true riches of creation. Humanity, however, in its blind ignorance will destroy most of the species that are now here and set back evolution eons, not just decades, of time. Yes, there will be light workers sent, but now, this time in history, you must plant the seed of awakening, for it to grow in the hearts of humanity over time."

"I know how much you love me, Mary, and how much you will miss me, but in the spectrum of time and all eternity, it will be just a short time; you will see."

He came behind me and held me and once again he knew what I was feeling. I cried until I could cry no more, for him, for me, for us, for our children and all the children of the earth. My grief unleashed like the tsunamis, of which he spoke, until the river of tears dried up and I was returned to this place, alone in the desert of my thoughts. Caressed by the heavens, whose stars remember their origin, I fell to the earth and slept until another sunrise came.

CHAPTER 16

It Is Love That Reunites

"Jesus, what happened?" I said to him.

"Well, my dearest Mary, you are awake." He came and sat next to me and stroked my face.

"The last thing I remember," I said to him, "I was in your arms and then I fell to the ground and now I am here. I knew something happened, but just what I am unaware."

"You were transcending time and space just for a moment there. You were quite overwhelmed by your emotions just previous to that and now you are sitting here with me, about to have a cup of tea."

"Now, is not that extraordinary that I do not remember anything? Why is that?" I asked him.

"I wanted to help you so I was able to adjust your thought forms long enough to allow you to forget all the disastrous feelings you were having. Instead, I allowed you to float to the heavens and be soothed by the Great Mother who has thus returned you back to earth. How do you feel?"

"Confused, I think," I replied.

"I would not think too much my, sweet Mary. I believe that to be what got you into trouble in the first place. Would you agree? Out of compassion for yourself, let us just relax here together and feel the presence of the divine."

"How do you do that?" I asked, laughing. "Just go into bliss at the drop of a word? I have to sit to meditate, but you, you just…"

"I just surrender, and then I am in bliss again. The ancients call it *samadhi*. The real trick is to keep this feeling and walk in the world. It is quite challenging and sometimes downright difficult to negotiate every day, three-dimensional reality from that state of consciousness. So I practice, having one foot in this realm, while I have one foot in the other realm. I know how difficult it can be. I am gathering information now that I will teach you so that you can teach others how this is done."

"You mean you can actually teach this?" I asked, amazed.

"Yes, I can teach ways of thinking and believing that can lead to states of consciousness that are uplifting, as well as peaceful."

"Did you use one of those techniques on me yesterday?" I asked.

"Well, I did surround you with the light of love. That is usually all it takes for you. You just want to feel love all the time, and once you feel that, you are comforted, like a baby. Babies are extremely simple, and yet, they are very profound in that way. Many souls do not really start losing their memories of their real home until around six months old, but most start at three months. The first month is actually the hardest because you are getting used to being in a body again. It is really quite exhausting. That is why babies sleep so much."

"Jesus did you remember for a time as a baby?" I inquired.

"I never really forgot," he said. "Not completely. Only for certain periods of time in my youth did I start to forget. That is why Mother had me study with the Ancients, for they knew of these techniques, as you call them. I studied with them, so I could be assured to finish my mission here. They helped me unlock these centers here in my head and heart so I could remember always, my real father and mother."

"I never had a father," I reminded him.

"You have always had a father, Mary," he reminded me. "You just did not have a man here on earth to help raise you. Actually, that is why it is so hard for you to even contemplate losing someone."

"Like you, you mean?" I said.

"Yes, like me," he said. "But it is never really a forever loss. You cannot be separated from me. I am always here." And he touched my heart.

"I know, but it is not the same as touching you, and seeing you, and hearing you. I like having you here with me in the flesh," I said.

84

"I know, Mary my love. That is why I came. All of humanity needs to look in the mirror of a true being of light to remember their true Father and Mother."

"So there is a divine couple out there, somewhere?" I asked, pointing to the sky.

"No," he said. "The heavens are what I use to describe another realm of existence where great beings of light live. There we live only to serve the art of love and we make it a practice everyday, although there is no real time there. Time can only exist here, where two physical objects meet. The heavenly realm is serviced by angels and archangels, whose sole purpose it is to serve the Master of Love."

"Do you mean God?" I said.

"God is very hard to describe in words. But, the Almighty Ones, who I know as Mother and Father, are far beyond any human you will ever meet here. Their traits can be found inside all of humanity, for God's presence is the seed that was planted in each heart so everyone could remember. Hopefully, one day everyone will remember. That is my mission."

"Some would say it is impossible to be God. Are you God?" I asked him.

He replied, "We are all God, in that we are all made in the likeness of the Presence, and that we carry that presence inside us. We all carry the power of the universe within us. But, we are not all of God. God is vast and has no limits. But, I am also not human, Mary. I am in the flesh, but not of the flesh. I am of the angelic realm and have come to save humanity from dying in its forgetfulness. I have come to experience humanity so I will know of their pain and suffering, for you cannot make it alone nor should you. God has not forsaken you, so neither will I."

"I love you so, Jesus," I said. "You are my beloved. So now I know, I have fallen for an angel!"

"It is why I cannot stay too long, Mary, lest I myself, should succumb to the karmic wheel," Jesus replied.

"You are saying you are tempted?" I remarked.

"Yes, by you," he said. "My love is so great for you, that, I could be tempted to stay with you and begin the incarnation cycle with you.

But, I must not do so. I must remain true to my mission to help *all* of humanity. Individual love is only part of love. We must not forget the others who need our help."

"Leave it to me, to finally fall in love, only to fall for an angel. That is even worse than you living in another town!" And we both began to laugh at the silliness of it all.

"What about angels mating with humans?" I asked, "Is this done very often? What is it like having a baby when you are not so used to it? Is this your first incarnation here? What is the plan to save humanity and who created it?"

He replied, "First, my love, you are thinking again. You are moving way too fast and too far ahead of yourself. Let us back up and take this one step at a time. What I am about to tell you is only for your ears. There are not many among you who can understand what I am about to tell you, not even the disciples understand. You have to imagine yourself along in time and widen your scope of the universe to what some might call metaphysical reality.

"Let me start by saying that there are many ways of interpreting what I am about to say to you, and there will be as many perceptions as there are people. But, I wish to convey it in a way that works for you, maybe you alone. You see, you and I have a contract, a soul mission together. In this way I help you, and you help me. We are able to negotiate this reality much better than either of us could do alone. In this way we get a chance to experience this life together in a way that is incredibly enjoyable, if not all the time, some of the time; but, most definitely for me, all the time. For when I am with you, everything else disappears. All that remains is Love itself and that is exuberant and fundamental to the divine reality. It is possible to deal with present-time reality and its necessities while the other part is steeped in divine inspiration. When you are living in the celestial realms, you are always aware of the divine. Here, in this realm, most people have only inspired moments in time. There are few avatars who come here on behalf of humanity to fall in love with a human, but it was my desire to experience what a householder experiences so I could best understand as many aspects of humanity as possible. I did not know it would be so hard. And yet, it is teaching me more about love. Love has many expressions. You can love people in different ways. There is the love for a child, a parent, a friend, or a lover. You can love someone as a sister or a brother, but love is love. Love is transcendental. It makes one feel whole. In union we feel at home. There is a great joy and happiness, like you have found something that has been lost. That is when you know it is love you are feeling. It is not yet time for me to leave here, but know this, when I do, I take your love with me and leave mine here with you. There will be an equal exchange of love, and we will never feel separated. It is pain and fear that fragments the soul. It is Love that reunites it. We must always focus on love, so we can remember the experience of wholeness, and then we will literally feel reunited again."

"Jesus, isn't there a way to change the ending to this story?" I said to him.

"This story, as you speak," he said to me, "is continually unfolding, and has some wonderful moments yet to behold. If you focus on the end, then you must also focus on the beginning, for that is the nature of the universe. There really is no beginning, and there is no end. Life is ever being manifested and unfolding into form. Love by its very nature is creating. And sometimes in order to create, some things must be destroyed. This life, known as Jesus, must eventually end, as we know it, so the greater evolution can continue. The one constant is change. It is only the small mind that insists on keeping things the same. Thank God there is the universal energy flowing, for otherwise, life would cease to exist. The little mind is unable to create a new future. It lives in the past, and in fear of the future. It is only by dropping into the present moment that you can touch that universal flow of divine energy and then you will see the entire world being created. The Divine Mind is projecting the universe through the lens of your own eye. Is not that magnificent, Mary? The whole universe is open to you! All you need to do is stay present and feel the Presence."

"But Jesus," I said, "I have so many thoughts that keep streaming into my head. That often leads to the emotion, what do I do about that?"

"There is nothing wrong with thoughts or emotions; it is part of the human experience. But, there is a way to maintain perspective into the situation. You can clear the thoughts and feelings by witnessing them. You need not attach yourself to the emotions as they arise, for they are part of the impermanence. If you allow yourself to witness, without getting caught up in the story you will gain another perspective—that of the Universal Mind."

"Is the Universal Mind impersonal then? Doesn't it care about our human drama or emotions or any of our experiences here?"

"The heart of compassion dictates that all beings should be loved and supported in any way, and in all ways possible. It is the free will of humans that creates all the suffering. It is not that, God the Divine does not care about the children of the universe. It is just that we are to go beyond the limitations of the small mind, by surrendering to the divine will."

"How do I know what the divine will is?" I pressed him, "How can I know the difference?"

"Divine will always has your highest good at heart, Mary," he told me. "You will feel happy. That is how you will know. Some may feel a physical sensation of relief or calm and a sense of inner peace. If you feel pain or fear you will know you are not aligning with the divine."

"In regard to your question about mating with an angel, well, while I am here, I am most definitely human with all the feelings and sensations and full spectrum of emotions and experiences. Because of my former experiences, I too bring forward a recognition of this world and memories of my past knowing, just like humans do from previous lives. These experiences are what linger from lifetime to lifetime and must be dealt with until the lessons are learned. Once the lesson is learned there is a chance to move forward. Otherwise the lesson will continue to come in different ways until the soul is fully able to embody the knowing."

"So Jesus, why are we together now?" I said. "Have we known each other before in some way? It is so hard for me to imagine myself as a messenger or a teacher, especially if I compare myself to you. I know comparing myself to you is not good, but it feels like we are so different. How can I possibly come up to the level where you are? Why *me?* Why *now?*"

"Why not you?" he replied. "Why not now? I know of your heart and have heard your heart's desire while in the other realm. I am here in answer to your prayer. I have come to you because you have called to me. Love is a vibration that resonates in our energy fields and acts like a magnet. The vibration draws all souls together of like mind and heart; there really is no comparing one soul to another. All souls have their way of being in the world and each soul has a certain purpose, a mission, and a unique gift and a way of living this gift. So to compare one gift to another would be like casting shadows on light. Each person must be recognized for his or her own beauty, and it absolutely must start with self-love and appreciation."

"Thank you for being so patient with me," I told him. "It feels like I could sit and ask questions and talk with you forever, and never quite understand the complexities of the universe or the nature of reality. What I really need to focus on is what I feel when I am with you. It keeps me focused on love better than any answer I have ever known."

"The true nature of the universe is love; and I, Jesus, love you Mary." His heart opened and he held me close and to this day, as I "write" these words, I have never forgotten the feeling of that moment. It will last me until eternity ends.

CHAPTER 17

Being In Love

Mary and Jesus. Is it not a grand notion of true mystical union? Together. United. One with all creation in a love that transcends all time and space? There were many times like that. Other times were fraught with fear and anger and desperate attempts to make sense out of the times that we lived in. You must be thinking, *how could such times as these produce these writings?* Is it fiction or is it real? In order to challenge any teachings, one must ask about the source of them. Many scholars have questioned the notion of Jesus as man, Jesus as saint, Jesus as mystic, Jesus as Christ and Jesus as Son of God. But, when I knew him, he was Jesus the magnificent, the one who opened my heart and released my agony. He was the one who made my heart sing and my life expand with great love and joy. He was the one who fathered his children and the one who committed vows to save humanity, promising to be the Savior humanity was crying for. He came to this earth at a time that was very dark and very lost.

You may ask, "Has it changed?" Look around. There is still war, hatred, fear, and suffering. What good did his life or sacrifice make on the wounding of human beings?" We still seek love in material possessions, food, entertainment, and many detrimental forms, and yet, the teachings of Jesus, known as Christ, cannot be denied as the teaching of universal truth, which is love.

He told me he would never leave me and that he would return with a host of angels and helpers from other planes to continue to help people awaken to their true and most rewarding nature. "Humans' potential for growth and evolution and love embodied, is infinite," he said. "People are capable of great things, as they have the seed of my Father in them. The divine wisdom is imbued in their cells, and their hearts are capable of enormous loving."

Love is so universal, that you cannot escape it, or run from it, for it is inside you. The Great Mother holds onto Her children and would never abandon them. Together, the feminine and the masculine create harmony and bliss. And so, it is the mission and intense desire of Love to awaken this harmony by teaching the mystical way to embrace and hold as sacred, the union between the man and the woman—the Divine Masculine and the Divine Feminine.

Much suffering has come through abuse and neglect and false desires leading to unrealistic and false expectations. However, if you knew just how deeply healing relationships can be, there would be a recognition that the divine is everywhere. It is not the purpose of God to hold unrealistic expectations of the children of this earth. To hold a thought that is negative or judgmental toward others, especially of your partner, leads to unhappiness and false pretense in relationships. So, the goal of these teachings is to embrace the thought of all as divine and holy; to view one another through the eyes of grace and to teach others to do the same. Then, the full potential of our existence can be fulfilled. To this purpose, these writings are being passed down and reformulated to serve the culture of today. They are offered as another attempt to educate human beings about their true divine nature.

All relationships must be built on honor and respect. In the process of loving there is a need to commit and devote one's heart to the other. When the heart connection is made, there is an alliance made with the divine of the soul and then the chance for mystical union is open. Grace is the force that moves love in the universe. Jesus's mission was to imbue grace into his prophets, so they could carry on the mission and to leave upon this earth, words of encouragement for all seekers. The heart of Christ is inside each individual, and by choosing love, that is, to feel love and share love, you choose grace and then the pathway to the heart is open. Through the opening we step and find true happiness.

So what if one person in the relationship chooses love and the other does not? Then, you must decide whether it is in your highest good to remain. Other times, one in the relationship becomes very self-motivated to grow and to change, progressing further along the path to enlightenment, while the other stops, staying stuck in the prison of the mind or lost in thoughts of the past, while others stay trapped in the fears and worries of the future. To be fully present in the moment allows you to stare full face into the divine who is in front of you. If you seek love as God, and choose to see God as love in another, you will surely find the essence of truth. The physical release is but a small part of the love making. It actually starts in the heart. When two hearts join together there is an automatic transmission that is set into motion. This transmission catapults into simultaneous feelings and sensations and often emotions follow during this process of mixing heart energy. Once the mixing of heart energy continues, there is a reaction that begins to travel throughout the body, and every cell begins to become imbued with the essence of love. This sensation can be felt as chills, shaking, burning or waves of heat or cold. This is a moment when the energy can either go up or down. If the energy is focused in the lower body, there is a sensation much like a climax, but if you can direct the energy up toward the crown, the entire universe explodes into being and ecstatic union is achieved. This can be done either consciously or unconsciously. In two evolved souls, the energy can move very quickly and produce ecstatic union of mystical proportions. If one soul is more evolved than another, then that soul can elevate the other.

This is what happened when I first met Jesus. The moment I saw him, I felt this amazing energy inside my body, like I was on fire. He began to compose my every thought and every action. Thereafter, everything I did, I did for him and him alone. I began to feel my world expand and condense simultaneously. He was the center of my world and I only wanted to be with him day and night. As anyone knows who has ever been in love, this honeymoon period, as it is now called, is so overpowering that nothing else seems to matter more. Your every breath is their breath and their every breath is yours. There is a profound oneness that seems to encompass and take over your entire being. And, alas, you are *in* love. What if you made the conscious decision to take this love and expand it to include the divine, with your sole purpose and intention to meld with the Infinite and insure your place in the arms of the beloved for eternity? How is this so, you say? What is the difference between falling in love and making a conscious decision to meld with your beloved? It makes all the difference in the world. If you approach your partner with love in your heart and the intention to know and experience mystical union, then the kundalini energy is released from its coiled place at the base of the spine, and it rises from the depths of eternity to bond and unite two precious souls of like mind and heart with the expressed intention of illuminating each other's essence. Love flows freely between the two lovers like water from the sea mixing with the rain from the heavens, and the two are washed upon the shore as one—bathed in an ecstatic embrace. Most people cannot maintain this level of consciousness individually during waking hours. This is why it is important to have this connection with another. It brings about a synergy that creates something bigger and ultimately more intense. At the end of this union, there is left a feeling of great peace and tranquility and the sea of bliss goes from rushing and splashing, to calm and soothing, rocking the two lovers fast asleep. I remember saying to Jesus once, "If only I could stay in your arms, Jesus, I could die tonight, if only I could stay with you eternally."

"You will stay with me eternally, Mary," he told me. "That is the promise I have made to you. I will come for you when the time is right. For now, know that Love has sought you as the messenger to carry the love story forward. If humanity is to be born into the sacred out of the sacred, then the union must be conscious and acknowledged as holy. Then the soul that arrives will be capable of great things. These souls, consciously conceived in love, are powerfully graced individuals. The environment in which they grow can then continue to reflect this powerful union of the original two souls. For when a child is born, it is not just a child, it is a unique powerful soul that manifests into human form. In order to stay true to oneself and receive the value of the mystical union, one must commit to love. Then, consciously love the other as you love God, for indeed, the one that stands before you is one and the same. Love is waiting for you. All you need to do is show up, fully present in the moment."

And so, these teachings are being presented to invite you to take a step toward your chosen partner with your arms outstretched and with love in your heart. Always be patient and kind, so that kindness can multiply exponentially. There are connections, soul-to-soul, that draw us together. Sometimes, it is through karmic bonds from the past, that is, unresolved issues, feelings, and emotions that have been buried in the matrix and very fiber of our beings. These buried treasures reveal the jewels of illumination, as the clouds of fear are released and the sky becomes clear. In the light of day there are always physical issues that need to be addressed, and the soul-to-soul connection is like a magnet that draws one to another. There are many reasons two people end up together, and sometimes there are deep bonds of friendship that form and can last lifetimes. In this way, each soul has a karmic circle of friends that is passed down lifetime after lifetime with the persona changing, but the core matrix remaining. If you find someone with whom you are initially attracted and then this feeling goes away, there are a number of issues that may need to be addressed in the relationship and in you. There is usually much water that has passed under the bridge, as they say, for most couples who live together and become householders. Most of the initial attraction can be lost to day-to-day tasks. In that case, people get lost in the daily realities confronting them, and they forget their soul purpose and reason for connecting.

Love and bliss exist simultaneously in the ocean of consciousness. To tap into this exquisite state of being, one must be willing to surrender to the Infinite inside oneself. To complete union with another, one must be willing to surrender fully to the moment and allow love's energy and wisdom to ride in like a wave, like a current of the sea. When I was with him, I trusted him so much that I had no problems surrendering into the fullness of the moment. I knew my soul's purpose was to serve love by loving him and him alone. The intimacy of that love connection is beyond words. There were moments of peace, happiness, joyfulness, contentment, exquisite ecstasy and a whole gamut of emotions and feelings that would ascend and descend. But, the overall pervasive presence of love never changed. This love does, indeed, form the ground of all reality.

CHAPTER 18

The True Nature of Death

When the day came to watch him suffer and die on that cross, a part of me died with him. The crown of thorns was also upon my head. As the blood trickled into his eyes, I too felt the pain of human frailty. I watched as his human flesh was torn. I watched, helplessly, as he was tortured, abandoned and betrayed with no honoring of his divine temple that stood before us all. Is not the body the sacred dwelling place of the soul? Is there not sanctity in this union of body and soul? How is it that he should be tortured in this way? I was left feeling helpless, powerless, and completely devastated. My grief was so overwhelming I felt as though my heart was being ripped from my chest. The pressure in my body was like a thousand bricks had been placed upon me. Tears flowed from my eyes as fast as a river runs to the sea and my spirit at last rose from my body as I collapsed to the ground.

My friends pulled me up. Peter and Paul held me and together we sobbed in overwhelming grief. The talisman had nothing over us as we prayed vehemently to the God we felt had abandoned us all. Mother Mary stood frozen with an aura of light all around her as he passed from this darkness into light. Her frail body began to crumple as her light body emerged and her energy body rose to comfort him as he was released from the cross. We were not able to physically reach him until he was taken to the tomb. It was there that we anointed his body and made him ready for the afterlife. I was unable to move and stood in the center of our miraculous group. The savior had been destroyed, and all I could do was mourn the loss of love and grieve the crime of humanity, vowing to never again love a man that deeply or intimately. I would serve humanity from the place of Universal Love, but never again would I feel my flesh nurtured or my spirit soar. Mary Magdalene died, and Mary the Christ arose and a force picked me up from the ground proclaiming this day as my birthday. Christ had risen inside of me, and I lay down all human needs as I picked up the torch to carry and proclaim the continued teachings of love. To end human suffering, there must be detachment from the outcome. To enjoy the divine play, all actors must be free from a script and go with the improvisation of the moment, completely unattached to the outcome. For, as it turns out, the divine play continues and the journey of the soul continues to unfold—all according to the divine perfection.

When I leave this body, I shall meet him again. The reunion will fill my heart and release my soul. Together we will serve the earth and continue to work toward a return to Eden. This earth is a great and beautiful plane for learning and there is much joy to be experienced here. There is no room for fear and pain, if you continue to open your heart-mind to Love. It must be a conscious choice, every minute of every day. You must have a mantra of positive intent and do japa every day. Repeat your name for God throughout the day and watch the miracle of life unfold for you. The power of thought is now well documented in your literature and much has been taught about the law of attraction and magnetism. But, the intention must always be guided to the riches of reunion and all thought aligned with the divine.

Much is being written about abundance and tapping into the wealth and abundance of the universe. It is true that one can be a magnet for abundance, but let us not forget where abundance is truly created. Is it created in the mind of ego, or in the wounded hearts of men and women, or in the dreams envisioned? I think not. The creative force of the universe opens and moves light through beings on earth. It is in the hearts of all people that the seed of creation has been planted. You must physically, spiritually, and emotionally go inside your own heart and penetrate all the barriers and veils of illusion and seek the substance of the holy name. To reveal the divine creative force, you must lose the ego with all of its wants and daily needs and aspire to meet the universe on its own terms. Fire the little mind that would have you believing the saying; *your wish is my command."*

It is only when you align with your heart's true mission and soul purpose that you will find your true desire. It is then that the universe says *yes.* Let us bring forth the soul mission that you and you alone must carry out. No other can do it just like you, so you must step up and offer your soul purpose to the Universal Source that will in return supply you with all the means necessary for the manifestation of your mission to occur. If you want abundance for abundance's sake and to accumulate wealth and a treasure chest of riches, then it will probably be very difficult for you to achieve.

(Take for example, the one who writes these words. If she aligns with her soul, she will write three books. For her soul mission is to bring through the legacy of Mary Magdalene, the Christ. This version is in part her experience with Jesus and it is also in part her own experience as a mystic, both with Jesus and through the way she continues to serve in a daily healing way. She will then find the abundance she seeks.)

The teachings, in and of themselves, are actually very simple. Love one another, love yourself, and seek opportunities to serve and make this world a better place based on your unique divine presence, actions, and attitude. Grace flows best through those most willing to serve and those who remain open to the vibration of Love. Most people have never experienced true love, but when you do, you will spend the rest of your life seeking it. The feeling of true love is the most direct way to experience the divine presence of the Creator, and then there is no doubt about whether God actually exists. The underlying presence in all things has been experienced in different ways. Entire religions have been based on one individual's unique experiences of the beloved. When, in actuality, there are many ways to experience and express love. The experience of the Infinite is really endless. When Jesus and I were together, often there were times when there were no words, but I could feel him intimately communicating with me. It was through this seeming osmosis that I was able to feel him speaking to his God, and speaking to me. We were essentially communicating heart-to-heart, and soul-to-soul. This transmission permeates the light vibration that is between us (as humans), thereby bridging the gap from one heart-soul to another.

If you truly want to know someone, you must meld with the soul. If you cannot surrender fully to God and the Infinite Source of all life, you will never be able to fully know and understand an individual. For only when you are able to release your own ego can you completely experience and thereby understand another soul. This is partly what happens when you fall in love with someone. You are surrendering your needs to theirs, you align with the divine in them, and they align with the divine in you. When that happens, there is a soul-to-soul transmission that occurs. The vibration of your beloved and your own soul vibration meld as one and there is union. Taken to mystical union, the energy of the heart progresses energetically upward and enlivens the higher centers of awareness, and then God emerges into your direct experience. Most people never get past the genitalia. After you fall in love, other burdens and obstacles and challenges of the so-called real world enter into your life, and you forget who you are; you forget who your partner is, and you lose track of love. Love gets buried inside and a trap door slams shut on your heart. Your heart is left panting breathlessly, as it sputters to open. And then it keeps you living long enough to break through the veil of illusion once more.

And what is the veil of illusion, you ask? It is the veil that stands between you and your spirit; the mist that clouds your awareness of who you really are. Jesus used to say, *you* are the one you are searching for. For once you know your true Self, the essence of your soul is illuminated. The veil is transparent and you can see everything for what it really is. The dense world is actually more of a holographic projection that blinks on and off simultaneously with your perception of it. The realities in which your body exists, and the one in which your spirit exists, are really two different planes of awareness. In order to unite the body with the spirit, one must know the mystical truth that pervades all realms of reality. This Jesus knew, and it is the reason why he was capable of manifesting anything and changing anything he chose to at any time. Of course, he saved such manner of manifesting for particular situations and did not feel it was appropriate to create seeming miracles just because he could. There were many instances that he chose to let the person die unto himself because he knew the journey of their soul would unfold in exquisite divine perfection. If we can surrender sufficiently to the divine, then the divine can guide us through the daily trials and tribulations in a state of grace. Many mystics know of this surrender, for they allow themselves the trust needed to *let go and let God*. When we surrender completely to the Infinite, then infinite possibilities exist.

Jesus was the master of possibilities, and he educated me to the nature of reality. "We live in a holographic universe Mary," he said. Many scientists of this age now know that time changes and only relates to two moving objects on this earth plane. But the truth is, there are many planes of existence, and there are masters at each level. Jesus went beyond the planes of existence straight back to the Godhead and united into the oneness of all creation. He went from the angelic to the human and through the teachings of universal love and truth; he was able to transcend this reality and join the truth of creation at its highest level. That is why he can be with so many people simultaneously. He can be all, see all, and know all. So when you pray, it is He who would comfort you and come to you with the greatest compassion.

How is it that I, Mary, came to know Jesus the Christ? How is it that I am here writing these words and remembering the lessons and truths that were taught? They were written on an inner program, and I am playing them back now. Jesus said I would return again and again, as all of those who have taken the vow of the bodhisattva in eternal service always will. He said there would be incarnations of great pain and great happiness and that in order to complete them with grace and ease, I must remember our love—the love that would transcend time and all the pain of waiting and the suffering from not remembering. I would fall in love again, he said. Even though I may not immediately remember, there will be one that will awaken this knowing. When this awakening occurs, I will know that to love is the will of grace and to love all beings as God. Once this deeper awakening occurs, the openness will remain, and all the tears from the past will be shed. All the pain and suffering will then subside and in its place will come great joy and happiness. Sometimes sadness or any emotion or feeling state becomes a habit. To remove habit is to remove the obstacles to the true Self. At the heart of the true Self is God Himself and She Who

Knows, who welcomes all into the world with open arms, for the heart of God loves all.

We choose different lovers, Jesus said, because we have karma to work out and lessons to learn. The one who lives with you now is your greatest teacher, so take advantage of the lessons. Learn to love yourself, and settle for nothing less than perfection. The divine is perfect, so look for It everywhere. A lover can satiate the desire to come into union with the spirit and then must be elevated in vibration to experience the higher realms of knowing. Love all and then choose the one who fulfills your greatest desire to love and be loved. Choose one who honors and respects your divinity and who is compassionate to your human-ness. Choose the one who is compassionate and kind, who holds your heart close to his or hers. Allow this one to have your time and honored attention and know that grace will endow you with eternal peace and happiness. Fail not to acknowledge each and every loving task that is performed for you and make every day a gift and a holiday well spent.

Spend your precious time here on this planet free from worry and pain, free from the fear of not having or being enough. Allow grace to show you the beauty of the universe in all the ways possible. Stay clear of judgments and categorizing in ways that keep you separate and different. Rather, keep yourself connected and acknowledge your unique gifts and talents that you have been given to share. Love each and every moment, as though it were your last and embrace grace, who holds you steady in her arms. Let the eyes of the divine guide you toward the Heavenly Father and the Earth Mother, for both are important to your growth and development. In this way, you embody the Divine Feminine and the Divine Masculine, and you embody the wisdom and passion, the love and the joy, the beauty and the ecstasy, the all-embracing and the all-penetrating traits of the two forces of the universe. This brings harmony and balance to you and to the energy of the creative force. Oneness is the underlying organizing force that keeps us both expanding and contracting. It keeps us waiting to exhale, as well as preparing to inhale. For it is in the pauses of the breath that all potential lies. It is always your choice, that of free will, which dictates the path. Just remember, all paths lead back to the One.

Author's Note: I have asked many, many questions—How can you teach how to love? How do you fall deeply into love? What about the mystical experience? How do you live in bliss? Can everyone be enlightened? How many lifetimes does it take on average? Are role models like Jesus and Ammachi what we should aim for? What about householders? Are there levels of enlightenment? Where am I on the path? Are there any core beliefs I need to work on? What are they? Can you share tantric techniques for genuine love making in a totally unified field? These were later answered in a separate book, but are addressed here as well, in a Spirit transmission that follows:

The teachings of Mary Magdalene are much like those of Jesus in that they are about Universal Love and opening to the inner world of God, which has become known as the Christ Consciousness. It is true that Love is universal and that it is not masculine or feminine but both masculine and feminine. So it is very hard to talk about one without the other, and yet Mary Magdalene went on to explore the mystical teachings that she was initiated into and made her own discoveries. She knew a great deal more about embodying the truth in her body than Jesus or anyone else of that time, and so it is no accident about your choices in this lifetime to study the body and to explore it in so many profound ways. When you use the body temple as the path to enlightenment, many possibilities exist. Many people have used movement and hatha yoga as an entry point and others use sexual encounter as a way to explore love.

One must always remember that all experience is energetic of some kind. The case with mystical union is that all the energies line up into the vertical spiral and this is the key to all union. During the alignment of the energies, there must be alignment in all planes for oneness to occur—physical, emotional, mental, and spiritual. There are no other paths that can promise such a direct experience of Love as that of union with your beloved. It feels like magic as a universe of two collides and becomes the universe of one heart-mind, in union with the one Godhead. You can experience mystical union within yourself, and you can experience oneness with another. The path to enlightenment varies, but the one at the center of every union is the same. That center of all experiences is the ever-present presence of pure divine love. God is the center of the universe and is inside every union where two merge into one. The key is to join together as whole unto oneself in relationship to the other, who is also whole unto herself (or himself). In this way when two or more of you are gathered, there is love. How, you might ask, is it possible for this union to occur? And then, of course, how long can it last? To experience the one truth, one must be devoted to knowing and experiencing God. Either consciously or unconsciously, one must open the heart of pure truth and release to the exultation of this union. In hatha yoga, the body and mind are prepared through breath and movement and meditation. This prepares you to hold the higher vibration of love. Human love has a quality that is denser than mystical love, and mystical love is even denser than the pure essence of divine love. For this union to last one must surrender, all of the ego, to the truth of one's being and slide effortlessly into the arms of the beloved. Union is the exquisite offering God has for humankind, and if one chooses union, they choose God. What follows are some ways to prepare the body-mind for this union, as Jesus and Mary knew. Although it can happen anytime without prior experience through grace, or through the Guru or teacher, union can be the ultimate goal and can be prepared for in these ways.

CHAPTER 19

Tantric Union with Your Beloved

Jesus was my guru, my beloved, and the ultimate focus of my devotion. Today, many Christians use him as their focus through his teachings. But, let me say that knowledge, unless connected to the heart, will stay in the head and never lead to union. You need to open your heart and let love flow. If you then focus on your beloved at that moment, he or she becomes God or Goddess, and you can be catapulted into bliss. Ecstasy is the experience of recognition. When you recognize your beloved as the one who manifests through all, you will manifest the God-Self inside of you. There have been many masters who taught ways to manifest and to enliven the God principle, but the one which serves the human heart most is that of pure intention to love and know one's God. With this purest intention and devotion have come all the enlightened masters. Once you have called the one inside you into union with your ego-self, the surrender takes you directly to the Source. Union is experienced as love, so focus on love. Now, if you want a technique to prepare you, here it is:

Sit down in front of your beloved, or place the image of your beloved in front of you. Then connect to him or her through each of the energy centers known as chakras. To do this, begin by breathing him or her into you and breathing out yourself into him or her. It is helpful to synchronize your breath so you are both inhaling and exhaling at the same time. Then, reverse this so, that, your out breath, is his (her) in breath and vice versa. After you feel synchronized, return your focus to the chakras. Take the base chakra of your self, root it to the center of the earth while your beloved does the same. Draw the energy from the earth like you are drawing it up through a straw and take it to your second center. Allow the energy to pulse through you without controlling it. You can visualize the colors of the chakras as you do this: the first chakra is red, the second is orange, third is yellow, fourth is green, fifth is blue, sixth is violet, and seventh is white.

When the energy is vibrating in your second chakra, begin to spiral the energy in a figure eight like the infinity symbol, which calls to the Infinite inside of you. Allow the movement to occur horizontally, and complete the cycling in three breaths. Then reverse the direction for three more breaths. Then connect your second center with your partner's, once again, exchanging the energy between you by inhaling and drawing him (her) to you and exhaling and sending him (her) love. You'll begin to feel yourselves coming closer and closer together. Do this same technique at each center until you get to the third eye at the sixth chakra. When you get to this center, come to the spiraling of energy and follow it with your eyes horizontally and reverse it as many times as needed, until you feel peaceful and content with the thoughts quieted. Then begin a chant for the name of your God as you begin to feel the center of this spiral. The center of this spiral is also the center of the sixth chakra. Focus your attention and eyes here now with eyes closed and breathe your partner into you, straight through to the back of your heart. Hold his (her) essence inside with you and focus on him (her) as you chant the name of God followed by his (her) name. For example, I used to chant *God Jesus - Christ Jesus*. Repeat this a minimum of three times, then return to the inner eye focus and breathe him (her) into you from the first to the sixth. Exhale him (her) into his (her) own inner vision place in the sixth chakra from your sixth chakra. At the same time, he or she sends his (her) love energy to you on his (her) exhale to your 1st chakra from his (hers). On his (her) inhale he draws you in from the sixth. This will set up a closed, but expansive, energetic tantric loop between you. After this has been well established, you will feel a pressure building at the top of the crown. When you begin to feel this pressure, take the energy and send it up to the crown and beyond, then draw his (her) energy into the first on the inhale all the way up to the sixth and send it out the crown on the exhale. Now begin to synchronize your breath so that his (her) inhale is your exhale and his (her) exhale is your inhale. Now, you are both intertwined energetically and should begin to feel a spiral inside the spine. Take the energy from the crown chakra and both of you begin to draw this down into your body from the seventh to the first. When it reaches the first you can stay as you are or invite physical union at this point. Let your intention to God be known—that your intention is to experience divine union and feel the embodiment of love as a pure expression of divinity in its perfection. No other instruction is necessary at that point.

Jesus and I began this practice early in our relationship after I asked him about how to bring the expression of Love into sexual union. I, for one, wanted and needed that to feel satiated as a woman, but after a while, the physical was no match for the ecstasy of divine union that I felt after feeling the bliss of his unconditional love for me. It was so intoxicating that for days I could think of nothing else and was incapable of chores or activities in the outer world. I would be in a trance that was all embracing and self-contained. I did not need food or water or even much movement. Jesus said this technique was only a map, and that once you experienced love in this way, you would no longer need directions. Pure devotion can take you there, almost instantaneously, after a spiritual practice with this focus. You can do this alone with the image of your beloved in front of you, which can be real or imagined. It is all God, as you will soon know, for divine tantric union is dropping the awareness of self and surrendering to the Infinite Presence in the other. If you are a woman, you surrender to pure Presence and follow the freedom of the divine in the form of the masculine—this surrender brings out the fullness of the feminine, which is pure radiance and love. The light of your being, as woman, merges with his as he surrenders his freedom and presence to your light and radiance. He disappears into you and you disappear into him, and there is divine communication. Note that even in the word *communion* is found the love of pure perfection *in the union*. Yogic union is done with awareness. Love, when surrendered to fully, will automatically take you to your essence, which can be shared with another. It is only in surrender that you can feel relaxed from the bondage of flesh taken to the highest high known as bliss. Union is full prostration before the importance of mortality and releases you to the complete nature of the universe, which is both contracting and expanding into full perfection and ever-expanding awareness. This pulsation leads to full conscious knowing of the nature of the universe. This knowing is what every human being is born to experience now or in lifetimes to come. God knowing, or Self-Realization, is Self, actualizing Itself into perfection, in what the human soul has come to do. The truth is that each soul has their individual mission to complete. The union of the God experience, into the mystical obliteration of the ego self, leads to full actualization of the Divine Self, which is pure love, pure consciousness, and pure essence.

There is no one way to realize God or to know the Self, but it is the sole purpose of these writings to teach the way through conscious loving relationship. This relationship is between self and other, self and love, self and God. Once Self is united with the oneness, all that is left is to enjoy the bliss and ride the wave of ecstasy into the disappearance of all reality save the one eternal Christ, which is God-consciousness through spiritual reunion.

Ecstasy is found through the surrender from what you think is real, into what is truly real. Then there is a fire of recognition that burns through all illusion and awakens the ecstasy that lies buried inside the genitals and first chakra and empowers the rise through the pelvis (second chakra) where you surrender to your love and allow this to burn through the power center of ego (third chakra), individualization straight through the center of the heart (fourth chakra), which opens through the blaze of desire to experience the love that is the truth of all beings and ride this all the way to divine communion (fifth chakra), into Oneness (sixth chakra). By giving and receiving the love with wild abandon and complete surrender to being one with your partner, you can ride the wave of the serpent to the center of mystical union and see God/Goddess before you. Taken all the way to the top (seventh chakra), the two disappear completely into pure radiance, pure presence, and you become that which you seek—Love.

Love does not depend on whom you are with, or even if you are with someone. Experiencing true love only depends on one's ability to open the heart. When the heart is fully open, there is a deep abiding love that is beyond human finite love. It encompasses all of reality and is beyond conception of the ego mind. Most people are attracted to each other because of a certain resonant vibration set up by the karma from the past. Others are attracted to like mind and heart. But the true falling in love is when there is a presence beyond the persona—beyond the two individuals. There is a karmic explosion that occurs, and the chemistry that everyone feels and knows, becomes real. A true chemical reaction takes place, and this stimulates the physical urge to connect. There is a built in mechanism to procreate and to continue the species, but taken beyond this animal instinct is the basic human need to experience God's love, which catapults a sensitive soul to union, or oneness.

To experience union as a partnership involves different layers of communion: spiritual, mental, emotional, physical, and a willingness to surrender and grow in all areas of your being. The universe is always expanding. When you are in union, so too, does your experience expand. Jesus said that to know the love of the Father was what he came to learn, but remember that he spoke to people who could not understand the nature of the universe. What he really came to teach, was love. Love has many ways of expressing and so it is when you are with someone, when two hearts are open, there is love. Then you decide by free will/ choice, how you want to express it. There are many ways to express love to someone, through action, thoughts, and words. When you touch someone, there is an unspoken language that expresses a multitude of things. Before the actual touch, there is intention and then a feeling arises. You then act on the feeling. If your intention is to experience true love, then you will align with the nature of the universe. There is, then, an ease in relating. You are naturally kind and compassionate and act graciously to others. You will embody the principles of loving and may feel motivated to serve others selflessly, for whenever love arrives in your consciousness, you will be motivated to act and to serve. Love wants to serve because the nature of the universe is to keep expanding and growing. It is important if you are in relationship with another to continue expanding and growing together, or the denseness of fear and complacency will set in, and you will wither away in the sea of unconsciousness. Being unconscious is really the only true death, for it limits you from growing and becoming more of who you are. Fear and complacency are fertile ground for the seeds of unconsciousness.

Consciousness on the other hand is fertile ground for love, in all its potential to grow and blossom into the field of infinite potential. So how do you become more conscious? By bringing your awareness to all you do and say and to what is happening around you and inside you. This mindfulness will put you in touch with the wise part of you that has been known as many things, most recently as your higher self, your soul self, or your inner witness to name a few. When you can begin to act from this extended part of the Self you are aligned with Universal Love. You see an existential change in your existence. Life becomes an adventure to be lived and experienced, meant to express the innate beauty and wonder of true love. True love, as noted before, is different than a human love relationship. Love need only be experienced one time in order for the craving to begin. If you remain in love, then your most basic need is met and you can relax into the flow of life and enjoy all the rich experiences that love has to offer you. One of the greatest commands Love gives is to find joy and experience the bliss of your Creator. Then, in times of darkness, there is a chance that you will remember the great and powerful light that dwells inside you. The memory of the light will be your pathway back home. Bliss could be defined as eternal happiness, making love with your beloved or returning to your true nature. In any case it is not to be missed by an awakened soul. And it all begins with awareness.

If you are looking for profound love, you need to look for it in a profound person. Most people are easily distracted by their daily drama and the details of their daily lives. All too often, people forsake love and then blame God for abandoning them. It is quite the opposite. People abandon God for their ego fears all the time and get lost in their thoughts and the chaos of the mind. It is important to still the mind so the more eternal presence of the love of God is perceived. It is like turning on a radio and getting too much static. You must adjust the dial to get clarity. It is in the clarity that you can hear a deeper voice, a quieter softer voice, which always has your highest good as the only goal and priority. This can be perceived as a sensation, a feeling, a knowing, a vision, or a voice. Once it has your full attention you can focus on that which is most important. The true knowing and clarity that comes from the experience of true love is undeniable and unforgettable, quite powerful and memorable. However, without the intention of profound, deep connection to the inner beloved, this memory will not last. The thoughts of the mind return and with the thoughts, come the pain of fear and maya (illusion). You lose track of the truth and delve head-on into fear and confusion and you get caught up in the story of the ego. So, how is love capable of pure detachment to outcome? Surrender the ego fear and choose love, detach from the story and begin to feel into the Higher Self. Ask for help from the divine and then let go. Fear is never real. Only love is real. The mind must be reconditioned and new habits formed for long-lasting change to occur.

∞

CHAPTER 20

The Illusion of Separation from Love

The ways of love are vast and deep, profound and expansive. Human love is based on fear and desire. Fear of not having what you want and what you think you need, and an insatiable desire to be seen, heard, acknowledged and appreciated. True love has no motives and no outcome. It is pure illuminated presence. So what does one do when there is a feeling of separation from love? How does one get back to love? Come fully present into the moment. Release all thought and fear and arrive fully present in the now. Choose love, and love will expose its shining presence. The fully illuminated soul never lapses from the present. There is no attachment to outcome or the story of the moment.

When Jesus was dying I, Mary, lapsed back into the story of the moment and sustained a wounding that lasted lifetimes. Even though by the end of that life, people would consider me an illuminated soul worthy of the title Christ-conscious or enlightened, the secret heart of Mary, the human, sustained an incredible wound that stayed in my auric field and acted like a magnet, drawing to me a series of incarnations that reenacted the abandonment wound, over and over again, as I struggled to forgive the masculine God that I perceived had taken my precious love away. And time after time I would wonder why did Jesus not save me? By the power of his grace his love awakened me and inspired me and served me in such a way that I felt I had reached nirvana, the highest high. And then when he left, I experienced the lowest of lows.

Anyone who has known the loss of someone, where they felt they would rather die than live to suffer the next breath, has known the pain of separation by abandonment. However, anyone who has ever survived the intense grief and despair that accompanies abandonment by death knows that it takes courage and enormous strength to stay present in the moment. With this strength comes wisdom, and with wisdom comes clarity. Clarity brings knowledge and knowledge draws experience. Through direct experience there is love. Do you see how everything circles its way back to love? This is why it is said that all paths lead back to the One. For in truth, love never leaves and we do not lose love, only our awareness falters. This is why practicing mindfulness is so helpful in the enlightenment process. To stay awake you must bring awareness to every moment and when a thought comes that does not serve you, you must have the knowing and the discipline to let it go. You must reject the notion that there is anything beyond the now. It is truly in the moment that the entire universe is being created. It is blinking on and off according to our own perceptions and abilities to perceive this and other realities. There is no greater force in the two-dimensional world than one's own belief system and the thoughts that created them. Therefore, watch your thoughts and let them be just that, thoughts with no attachment or judgments or any feeling attributed to them. In this way, you can remain clear. It is in the clarity and stillness of the mind that your perceptions can be honed to know, detect, and otherwise feel the presence of the divine. Jesus would say that stilling the mind and opening the heart is everything you need to know to experience God. God presence will become present when there is complete alignment and harmony with the laws of the universe. Honor the laws of nature and call for grace. Grace will come as a lover, when you beckon (him/her). So call to Love often and focus your whole heart in knowing the Infinite. All you need is in this moment.

What happens when the moment is too painful? Many times people decide to disassociate or separate from their soul-self and the source of their light, which is love. Then true suffering occurs, for to be separate from love is the greatest pain known. It is even beyond physical pain. It leads to grief, sadness, fear, trepidation, and every other form of negative emotion.

If there is ever true healing, there is the presence of love and the experience of wholeness. To experience emotion is a human experience;

to experience love is a divine experience. There are no words that can truly express the experience of oneness or wholeness. Peaceful presence, exuberance, joy, loving-kindness, and compassionate expression, are all ways to experience union. Divine ecstasy is among the highest highs anyone can ever imagine, but the pain of separation can set someone into the dark night very quickly and can last years. It is only through devotion, service, and loving kindness, or by the grace of God or the Guru, that love can return. All eternity is present in the moment. All you need to do is show up in the present.

Jesus was a master at remaining in the moment. Even though he could predict and foresee the future, he focused on the present and taught me how to do the same.

Here is what he told me to do: Sit in a comfortable position so you do not need to think about how long you might be there. Then, begin by noticing your breath as it moves in through your nose, down through your lungs, and then, follow the exhale as it leaves the nostrils. When you breathe in, breathe in love as a golden light that brightens every aspect of your being, pause knowing that you are deeply loved. As you breathe out, see the light of your inner being melding and mixing with the light that is all around you. That light that is all around you is your Soul light.

Within the energy field around you are bands of vibration that are unique to you and you only. These bands of vibration hold your samsara and can be dissolved as you mix your inner light with the outer light of your soul. One way to do this is to elevate the vibration to a faster rate by using the breath. The Ancients called this practice pranayama. It is a breathing technique that clears the energy body and frees up the soul to maximize the relationship to Spirit.

The breath technique that Jesus taught me follows: To elevate vibration, sit quietly to notice the breath as it goes in and as it goes out. Follow this for two-to-four rounds at a minimum, noticing the pauses between the inhale and the exhale. Expand and elongate the breath as you melt away any tension in your body. Breathing in, know that I AM; breathing out, know that we are one. Breathing in I AM, breathing out to the One.

Inside the human energy field is a mass of psychological conglomerations made up of emotions, feelings, memories, interpretations, and beliefs surrounding past and current events. Among the strongest of these is fear, which incorporates the ego's lack of knowing of the true self. However, within the forgetfulness lies the key to salvation. Within the cloud of forgetfulness is a fear of separation from the oneness of the divine. And so it is, the breath, the prana that is the elixir of life that allows reconnection to the Source. It is the breath that cleanses the energy field and the body. And, it is the breath that allows for connecting to the true self.

To begin to cleanse the forgetfulness and misinterpretations of life, you must start with the intention to know the true Self, hence, the mantra I AM is introduced. This is the highest form of meditation. *Be still and know that I AM.* It is in the stillness, the pauses between the breaths that all remembering occurs. Once your intention is established, you can proceed.

Use the breath simultaneously with the mantra as follows: Breathe in, closing the epiglottis in the throat, making a sweet silent sound, like the ocean wave sound inside a sea shell. Breathe out with the same sound. Continue for 3 to 4 breaths, then begin the mantra while exhaling I AM, I AM. Notice the pauses at the end of each exhale and inhale; and maintain silence in the still points of the pauses. Allow the focus to be the inner eye, the point between the eyebrows in the center of the brain. You will soon find the mind quieting, and there will come a time when the breath becomes still. Time disappears and all that remains is the One Infinite Light of Love. That presence is all pervasive as you remember love, as it really is—all knowing, all present, and all loving. This is God, the One who comforts you and shows you the light of love that takes you all the way back home. Before the awakening occurs, the forgetfulness protects you from disinvesting in your life.

Most people need the forgetting early on to truly believe in the earth reality as real. This is needed by most people to form an ego in order to form a life. There then comes a time when souls must follow their heart's yearning to reconnect their awareness with Love and awaken to the truth of their innermost nature. When a reawakening occurs, most people attach to an object of love, usually a person, and then the whole of divine love is reduced to a game of needing and wanting, and the yearning of the heart is reduced to a game of cat and mouse, a game of chasing your true heart's desire. Everyone's true heart's desire is to know their Creator, to know the maker of their soul, the one from whence they came. To feel the love that shines from inside the heart is the greatest gift one can ever know.

CHAPTER 21

The Magic of Transformation and the Gift of the Feminine

It was through Jesus that we began to know the Heavenly Father as the Creator of our soul. Jesus said there are many names for God and different aspects of God, all with distinct purposes and attributes to contribute to the awakening of humanity and the functioning of the universe. Most people need a father and a mother to feel love and to be connected to something greater than their limited humanity. However, if humanity could acknowledge the divine source of their lives, they could accomplish great things. Jesus said there is a masculine and a feminine of the universe, and he chose the Father, as he knew humanity needed discipline and strength to develop itself spiritually at that time. He said the feminine principle would be needed much more in future generations to complete the cycle of growth for humanity. He said there would come a time when the Divine Feminine would prevail and the children of the earth would come to Her for loving kindness and compassion to nurture and heal their deepest wounding. This, he said, will be the time when these teachings will be brought forth. The teachings of Mary Magdalene will bring forth the principles that unite the feminine and the masculine, for when two or more are gathered there is love; there is one. One must really grasp the vastness of the universe to contemplate what love is. Love is the vital life force and the very nature of the universe. The feminine and the masculine must come together, in order to reign over creation with balanced action and knowing. The inner wisdom must be awakened in humanity in order to save humanity from itself. Love is what will heal all human hearts, which is why the timing of these teachings of love is now.

(Note to scribe's question): I keep asking, *what can be said that humanity has not already learned about Love? How many ways can the masters say the same thing before humanity wakes up and makes the necessary changes to elicit global change and create a world of peace and harmony? What can be written or said that has not been said or done before? How is it that these teachings are being written now?* The answer received is as follows:

> There is a system and a time to every endeavor one takes on. In order to survive, the species has adapted accordingly and now, a new system, a new order must take place. There are many mediums on this planet, many intuitives, and many sensitive souls. So you ask, how is it that these teachings are coming through this writer at this time? There have always been those among you who have been teachers. They come from different realms, different planes of existence. Mary Magdalene was of the human realm and was able to transform herself while incarnate on earth. She was awakened through grace and fell in love with the Master and is now here to tell her story as an inspiration to those among you who need a role model for awakening. The seed of God has been planted inside you and can be discovered and experienced by all those who seek. Allow these teachings to be an inspiration to all those who wish to heal and end their suffering by acknowledging the Source of their creation. Invite the teachings of the feminine into your heart. The techniques thus described are meant to assist in this endeavor.

When you begin a breath and meditation practice, you are inviting God into your awareness. You can create more beauty in your own world by acknowledging the inner beauty. The Divine Mother wishes to acknowledge all her children as divine and to bestow upon you the teachings of grace.

The Masters who dictated these books then noted to this author: (Jesus was, and still is, a great force for healing for your planet and was the influence for God-Realization for many great souls, among these being Mary Magdalene. She connected to his heart and was opened to grace and thus healed of her past trauma and lifetimes of incarnation and was cleared to continue the lineage of his teachings. However, at the time of his death and then his rebirth, she chose to continue incarnating to bring forth these teachings. They are being handed down now straight through her own writings. No greater timing could there be than now, for there is no more time left. The principle of the feminine and the masculine need to come together now, just as Jesus and Mary came together to form a new generation of humanity. The DNA of Jesus came from the angelic realm, and the DNA came from the human realm in Mary. Together, they formed a new generation of humanity, which, can evolve into higher paths of knowing. More and more people can thus awaken to their true nature. For example, this scribe has journeyed to the cellular consciousness and has returned with great knowledge and awareness of the consciousness that lies within at the cellular level. A new generation is being born with heightened awareness like this with the ability to reach to the depths of Consciousness Itself. Be aware of what lies inside and great things are possible. The vibration of Love is the highest vibration possible, so if you can live from the center of your heart, you will know of this grace. Love has no master and no servant. It is the soul that nurtures the very cellular level of one's being. So eat and drink of the nectar of truth, which is love.)

There have been many masters who speak of truth and ask their students and disciples or devotees to follow in their footsteps in order to achieve mastery, and yet, not many have been able to sustain the discipline necessary to achieve self-mastery. It takes pure devotion and one's pointed concentration on the divine every moment of every day to achieve great mastery of the mind. There have been many techniques passed down that have been meant to clear the mind, open the heart, and release and heal the body. These techniques are meant to move, shift, and transform, as well as clear the emotional and mental bodies, so that the Essence of Light, in the form of pure presence and radiance, shines forth. The great masters have also been sent to enliven humanity with ways of perceiving beyond the physical, two-dimensional world. Even now, your scientists are gaining more insights into the nature of reality, which is pure consciousness. There are no set ways that are right or wrong, or one that is better than another. There just *is*. If you allow yourself to be fully present in the moment without any thought, you will drop into the state of consciousness known as Presence. Through pure presence, the perfection of the divine can be experienced. Jesus and I would bask in grace and then share from our hearts, our everlasting love for one another. There is really nothing more to do.

So why is it so hard? You may be asking this. If it were so easy, more people would be mystics and enlightened by now. What needs to be asked is: what are the barriers to self-knowing or enlightenment? What are the pitfalls along the way?

It all stems from our egos and our self-identification with whom we think we are, as in the roles we play: a teacher, a healer, a singer, a farmer, or a salesman. Many of us know that what we see and do is not all of what exists, or for that matter, who we are. But, most people do not have any idea about the other realities and realms of existence. There are different planes of realities that are unseen. And these planes of realities have levels of awareness. God-Realized souls are on a different level than those who are not. It is the goal of humanity to evolve to God-Realization, and it is to this end that these techniques, most of them from the yoga tradition, are derived. The masters of the east grew up in a culture that honors the concept of God within. The Western world is the opposite, praying to a God *out there*. Actually, both are true.

There is a God *outside* you and there is God *inside* you, because there is nothing else *but* God. The free will you were given gives you a choice of acknowledging the divine as everything, in everyone and everywhere, or not. It is the illusion of separation that causes all suffering. It can be alleviated by choice. Now, at first, the mind says, *OK, I choose love,* and it comes out as just words, or as a false or inauthentic, unfeeling affirmation. *But, it is only from the heart,* when you choose love that, the magic of transformation is brought forth. It is the opening of the heart to Love that allows all change to occur. Nothing great can ever be accomplished until this occurs. So there must be ways to open the heart—like through loving another, enjoying nature, or enjoying a friend. Many of you know of spontaneous moments of pure presence in love. However, it is this author's goal to give you ways of tapping into your heart at will, by choice, and these are being given for your use now.

Jesus has imbued these techniques with his grace, and I, Mary, have charged them with the grace of the feminine, and together the masculine and the feminine will come together and bring you back into holy union, that is the communion with the one infinite truth, which is love. Enjoy these teachings and share with as many people as possible. If you do, be sure to give them the writings themselves so the directions are followed to the letter. Truth is also imbued within the writings themselves, so enjoy the pleasure of the visual and the feeling of the knowing.

1. Acknowledge the Divine Inside You

First, you must acknowledge the divine inside you. For many this will feel false, as if you are going through the motions at first. You may uncover years or even lifetimes of shame, guilt, and unworthiness. You may encounter your own belief system that says you must pray to something outside of you. But, you must begin by acknowledging that somehow everything that is happening inside your body is virtually unconscious and is being propelled by an unseen force that keeps you alive. At a minimum, acknowledge that you are unsure about the functioning of the universe and are unaware of the Great Mystery that is unfolding. In this way you will become softer, more vulnerable, and less egotistical, so that grace has a small window to come through.

2. Surrender to the Divine

Let go of knowing everything and surrender to the nothingness to actually experience it all. To surrender to grace is to invite the expansiveness of the universe inside your heart. From inside your heart, the light of love can shine and will burn off all ignorance and the thick bands of forgetfulness that exist in your energy field. It is through the light of your inner most being that the illusion of separation will disappear. When you are inside, Love is inside you.

To surrender you can practice a mantra:

I AM (inhale)
I surrender (exhale)
I AM (inhale)
I surrender (exhale)
I AM (inhale)
I surrender to the Great Master of my soul (exhale)
I AM One with the Master (inhale)
I AM, I AM, (exhale).

Memorize this mantra and repeat it though out your day. *Feel the mantra emerging from your heart. This is very important.* Feel into the center of your heart space in the center of your chest and feel the mantra vibrating and opening you from within. Breathe deeply and fully and penetrate the illusion of forgetfulness with the vital life force of your breath.

Surrender to the divine and let the energy move through you with ease. Go with any movement that may occur or any emotions or feelings that may arise. Come to the stillness and know that I AM. Grace, is loving you. As you yearn for her, she is, loving you into knowing. Feel for her in the sweet surrender. Let go of everything but the feeling of the great love, and let no other thought stop you from going all the way. Honor what arises without attachment or ego story. Go with the mantra and keep surrendering everything until there is nothing. Out of the nothing comes everything. Enjoy the magnificent ride of Shakti energy as it is freed up and moves through you until it becomes you. The Feminine energy will move you to higher levels of consciousness, like peace, joy, and happiness, into pure ecstatic bliss. Enjoy the process of the journey.[1]

---

[1] Full surrender to God means Self-Realization. Only in states of higher consciousness can the appropriate decisions be made which can elevate humanity to their truest and highest intrinsic potential and thus save this great, beautiful planet from extinction. She (Mother Earth) continues to live and thrive only because of grace and support from the higher realms of consciousness, and because there are still those among you who care to do

3. There are levels to the surrender.

Surrender can take you all the way to God. When this occurs you become all that you seek and there is a spontaneous melding into one. The separateness no longer occurs, and the self you thought you were no longer exists. The new you is completely different than what the ego mind thought, and yet, it is the most familiar *you* of all. It is the soul manifestation of the One. Then the ego identity becomes a direct servant of the One. The Soul-Self, or the Higher Self, is the unique expression of the one known as you. But, this Higher Self is directly connected to the Source and thus has access to all the power of God. Thus, the ego and God become co-creators, and the universe never looks the same again. Some people get glimpses of this, and if they have not completely surrendered their own will, can possess the siddhis (powers) that appear Godlike, but are not truly and fully mixed into the One. Gurus like this are the ones who may *fall* from grace and can hurt their devotees and students by giving them false information at a time of incomplete surrender. It is therefore wise to obtain only a fully God-Realized teacher as a guide. The teachings of Jesus, our dear master, are the essence of truth and love and are trusted today by millions of people. However, the time for union between the sexes in the form of the masculine and feminine is now. The current culture must recognize the sacred in *all* humanity and elevate woman to the Goddess she is and man as God as equal partners, united in love, to see one another in their sacred beloved and listen to their inner teacher and the voice of the Higher Self versus the outer teachers and their lower natures. To elevate oneself above the callings of the lower nature, takes self-discipline, insight, awareness, mindfulness and devotion. There are

---

good in the world. The masses have yet to take seriously the nature of their lives or be at all motivated to make the appropriate changes that would elevate their minds and consciousness. There are, however, enough of you now to bring forth the feminine and once again use the qualities of loving kindness and compassion and open-hearted behavior to change the world.

Surrender takes a yearning to be free and a desire for love. That is all. Follow your desire and deepest yearning of your soul and you will be in the heart of God. To do this *be still and know that I AM.*

more among you now than ever before who are willing and desirous of love and union, thus the timing of these teachings.

Some of you, as this scribe has often thought during the writings of these teachings, will find these teachings less than radical. Those of you who study eastern traditions and yoga will not need to deviate too far, but will hopefully only deepen your understanding. Those of you who are considered Christians may have the most difficult time understanding Jesus's decision to take a wife. He needed to create an entire new generation from this new gene pool to elevate humanity in such a way that evolution was possible. This new generation will have more heightened intuitives, mediums, and sensitives. This generation will feel and know things others do not yet know. With their presence, others around them can be elevated into new levels of possibilities and understandings.

There are other souls on your planet whose explicit mission it is to elevate the vibration here by their pure desire to know God and to serve. There are others whose soul progression has been long and arduous based on many lifetimes of experience. And, there are those among you who will continue along the other paths and will never understand or be drawn to these teachings because of other chosen paths and religions. But, have no doubt, each and every soul has both the feminine and the masculine inside, which, must come into balance and harmonious functioning.

4. Cultivate the stillness

To do this, you must make time every day to get used to higher states of vibration by being alone and going inward. Use the breath techniques and focuses given and allow 20-to-35 minutes to surrender to grace and practice stilling the mind. When the mind is still and free of all thoughts, this is called meditation. Most people have trouble stilling the chatter of the mind, but the discipline of sitting and focusing will eventually bear the fruit of awareness and elevated consciousness.

One way to maintain this focus is to place the object of your desire in front of you. This means your idea, image, or personal vision of your beloved. Mine was always Jesus, for he became the master of my soul.[2] But, truly it was God inside him, now known as Christ, who was pouring through him, for he surrendered fully to his Father and became himself, the Heavenly Father. There was no separation. So this needs to be an image of a *fully* God-Realized being or a God/Goddess that you resonate with. It can also be something powerful in nature that contains the essence of beauty for you, such as a mountain, a flower, the sky or the ocean. Focus on its quality and surrender to that. This will give you a more impersonal experience versus the image of your beloved, which is more personal. You can also do this together with your partner and then they become the beloved. Look for God in them. It is recommended that some time be put aside for just you every day so you can develop a personal relationship with God. For at the end of the human experience, God will come for you in the likeness that resonates most with you. The vastness of the light of God is always present. Some forms are just more limited in their expression of the vastness of the light. God-Realized beings know of the vastness of the cosmos and can conceal and reveal their light at will. Just as the universe is condensing and expanding, pulsing with radiance, so too is all life, just with different degrees of vibration. The vastness of human potential is always present and can be accessed through awareness and disciplining the mind to focus on the truth, through the breath, a mantra, or the personal image of God. If you focus on the breath and Jesus, he will come to you for he promises that we will all be united as one heart.

After the prayer, sit still and feel the beauty and radiance and the vibration of love that is created.

---

2   'My beloved Jesus stands before me, beside me and behind me and the pure light of his being radiates inside me as Christ. The breath of my heart and his are one.' This can be your prayer to begin your meditation time. Bow to the master of your soul and feel the radiance of your being shining and transforming you. You can personalize it as a prayer:

Jesus, you stand before me, beside me and behind me supporting all aspects of me. I feel your inner radiance inside my heart and surrender to you, as the breath of my heart and you are one in me. Together we form the matrix of love. I bow to you Jesus Christ, my Beloved.

The techniques are more than just words and actions; this is the way to open your heart. Through devotion and commitment you will know your beloved, for that which you focus on will be your experience. So why not just focus on the Truth, which is love. Over time you will find the mind gravitating more and more towards its new focus which is love at the heart center, where God and the individual soul self meet. This is why so much focus is on opening the heart by surrendering to grace. It is the center of your inner magnificence. It contains your deepest yearnings.

As the heart opens, you may experience old wounds, thoughts, images, feelings, and strong emotions. Keep with the breath, your prayers, and your focus on the beloved, and surrender all your fear into the hands of the One, or return them to the vastness of the ocean, or lay down your burden at the top of the mountain, or at the feet of your guru. Stay with the breath and feel what arises, knowing that your spirit is being cleansed. It may help you to journal your experiences. You will be amazed at your progress.

For some of you, you may seek outside counsel, or form a liaison with a friend or group so that you can share and support one another. I always had Jesus. The group of us would talk and we would ask him questions. Often times, however, he would point us back inward and tell us we all had access to the kingdom inside of us. "No one has been forsaken," he said. "You are all held in the hands of God. You can be as children (with Him/Her), for you are made in the likeness and therefore contain the seed of the Father and the womb of the Mother. You were born into this world to know and to celebrate the wonder of the divine; for it is through you that the divine experiences the world. Make peace with your own divinity; honor the sacred in you and you will see it in all of life. I am with you to remind you of something deep inside of you that has fallen asleep. These words, these techniques, my presence, are only to remind you of that which you already know. To remove the layers of illusion is to awaken you to the part of you, you have been seeking, if not consciously, unconsciously. For if there has ever been a moment of sadness, grief, or fear, anger or frustration, then you will know of that which I speak. It is the goal of all beings to be happy. If you seek happiness, you are seeking your soul's light. It is in the light that the one

Mother, the one Father beckons to you, calls to you. The great Mother holds you and nurtures you, comforts you in times of sorrow, celebrates your joys in times of celebration. It is your Father who protects you and guides you and counsels you with wisdom and encourages you with strength and purpose and focus. Your yearnings and progress do not go unnoticed. Relax in the peace of the heart. For inside the stillness you will be aware of all you yearn for. It is in the peaceful stillness that grace can be seen, felt, and heard. The direct experience of the divine may vary for each individual, the journey and the path may vary, the stories may differ, but the One remains, steadfast and unmoving. The center of the universe does not move. It is only the mind that moves. The One who lives in your heart is the one, unchanging, all-knowing presence that is the center of the entire universe. This, my children, my dearest friends and disciples, this you can trust. Even when the veil is dense, the dust thick on the mirror, your desire for God, happiness and inner peace will guide you. Turn inward. There is God saying, "be still and know that, I am loving you."

"In the day-to-day world, it is often difficult to make time for meditation. It is easy to get caught up in the stories of our lives. However, time for oneself is never wasted. Time spent getting to know one's self, is like finding a beautiful gem in the ocean that should not have been there, and yet it was there all the time. Once this gem reaches the light, it becomes *more* of who it is by exposing its inner brightness and sparkles against the sunlight. And so it is, when we go inside and find our gem—our inner beauty—it is best seen when exposed to the light of love. Then the gemstone radiates the brightest of colors and reflects the inner beauty even greater. By being tumbled amongst the stone and sand, its edges have been smoothed. Thus, the turmoil of the sea has served its purpose in refining the gem. So it is with turbulence in our lives that we are often times smoothed out, our rough edges disappearing with time. If we come into the light, we will not be worn out, but well polished. Love is so easy, yet so hard to find, because our definitions of love are not the real thing. There are many false prophets, but there is only one truth. Listen to your heart. Feel the light of the polished gem shining out. Dim this light for no one, no thought, no emotion or feeling that arises. Focus on the light of love and keep this focus ever present in your mind's eye, so as not to let the mind wander into a territory far from the light. The mind will want to take you into the darkness, into the clutter of false prophets known as thoughts. There is no truth outside, only inside."

"Know of the truth inside your heart and let no one take your deepest desire from you. Do not let the thoughts of the small mind take you on the turbulent ride into the world of emotions. Bring the focus of the mind back into this light and warmth in the center of your heart and know that I am here, loving you. Fear not about the future, for it will come on its own accord. Fear not and linger not in the past for it no longer exists. Bring your focus inward, breathe, use your mantra and know that, there is no other reality, save for the one truth of the divine living Christ, God, inside your being. Live from your highest nature and trust Love. Trust only Love. Love will set you free—free from thoughts, doubt, emotions, and fear. Freedom is living in love. Death is living in fear. When you are living in love, there is only love—ongoing enduring ecstasy—bliss in the knowing and peace in the heart."

"So why do the thoughts even exist? What is their purpose, how do they get so scattered and the mind so lost in doubt and so far from trust? How did the separation of the mind from the Truth occur? What was the purpose of the mind?"

Jesus said, "The Great Mind created all things, all beings, all creation. The sole purpose of creation was so the Infinite could experience itself. So the separation/illusion began, only to gently veil the Infinite so one could fall into love, over and over again. It is the falling into love that is so blissful and yet, some become addicted to the feeling and continue to get lost in the maya to experience the sense of falling. However, to live inside love can be just as exuberant and freeing and blissful. To live in trust is to know peace."

"There are many states of mind. By choosing love, you are choosing the heart or center of the mind. It is from this center that all creation occurs. That is how powerful love is. Love literally creates reality. The ego, or little mind, creates illusion, which is always fear-based. So, the truth is love, everything else is the illusion of separation. Focusing the mind can thin the veil that separates the worlds. Focus on the truth versus the illusion. It takes time, but the mind will eventually get into another habit of thinking and being that is based in a high vibration. The gem of the heart is the special gift that you, and only you, can bring to the world. To keep it hidden would be the only *sin* you could ever really commit. All the other trials and tribulations are but ways for your soul to learn to love more deeply. The moment you turn inward and feel for this gem and the light of the divine that luxuriously emanates from its center is the moment you come home to your own inner radiance. This inner radiance is your commitment to being fully present in this life."

"Your soul purpose is to bring your unique presence to this world. If you do not do so, you will feel a friction, and anger, frustration and even sadness or grief can set in. You might feel that something is not right in the world. The ego then begins to search outside for comfort. This comes in many forms that are now well known to humanity. Freedom is lost as the ego begins to attach to the things in the outer world. Born out of confusion and illusion, the ego searches endlessly, reaching out for comfort with an arm that is always extended. But never does that arm ever return to the heart, for it is always going out to the world where it feels its home truly lies. The truth is the hand of the heart is ever holding and caressing the beautiful gem that lies in the treasure chest within. If you choose to hold this precious gem with the gentleness and compassion and the love and the honor it deserves, you will be holding all that is sacred in the entire universe. You are holding the most precious child, the innocent being of light that was created to experience God as God, Goddess as Goddess, man as man, and woman as woman. You are holding inside your chest the very likeness, the very light of being. This infinite being of light is you."

"Your soul purpose is to know and love yourself and to be true to your mission. You and you alone must discover your purpose and mission in this lifetime. To go on the treasure hunt is to live your life guided by grace and the love of your being. And once you find it, it is your soul's purpose to give this gift to the world. To dim your light, to deny your divinity, to deny your connectedness to all beings and all creation is the original sin. This denial is what causes separation, and it is the separation that causes you all your pain. Honor this part of you with all the integrity of your entire being, and you will cast among the stones the most magnificent of all truths, the light of love that is God, the master of the entire universe. This gemstone is your gift, your birthright and the love of loves. Shine out the light of your being and become the jewel of the heart of your innermost beloved. I am the face of God inside the precious jewel known as you."

And with this Jesus smiled that smile and knelt down among us, bowed his head and prayed, saying, "Dear Heavenly Father, you are amongst your children always. Teach them from within the nature of your grace. Teach them the virtues of their heart. Teach them, as you have taught me, to lay down the sword of injustice and impoverished sadness, which prevails among the masses. Allow me the honor to share your words of wisdom and compassion, as they search the groves for the seeds you have sewn. Allow us to travel where others have failed, and to grow the flower of enlightenment from the fertile soil of your being, Great Mother. You who bear fruit on the tree of life, we offer you our heartfelt commitment to serve humanity effortlessly and tirelessly in honor of the truth that beckons us ever forward. Protect these gentle hearts as this time together passes quickly, and counsel them as you have counseled me. Allow this lineage to continue well beyond our time together, and find others who will carry the teachings of the heart. We pray for salvation for all humanity and an end to violence, war and greed, which have all begun with fear. Remove the demon fear, and allow the Angel of Love to descend upon us and bestow the blessings of your omnipresent grace. Amen."

Book 2

THE BOOK OF SARAH
THE REDEEMER OF TRUTH

CONTENTS

Introduction

Born out of Love, created to love, it is the divine experience of Love Herself. This is the miraculous conception, where two become one; is not that the way we were all meant to be? Is not that the way that Creation was begotten?

To know oneself is to know the wholeness of the inspiring beauty that is Christ Herself. There have been many stories now written of the teachings/writings of Mary Magdalene and Jesus Christ, but what of the child that was created and born out of their love and devotion to the God they saw reflected in the eyes of one another? Has not anyone wondered what it would have been like to be the direct descendant of the most powerfully conceived couple yet to be written?

Most masters, avatars, are not wanting of a divine union of the flesh. They are married to Truth and embody the cosmic philosophy of Universal Love and serve all of humanity through selfless service and self-sacrifice, knowing that their home lies beyond this physical reality.

But, what if you wanted to leave behind a legacy of, not only, love and truth, compassion and knowledge, but also a lineage? What if you wanted to bring forth a generation that was created out of the direct experience of God-union, the flesh embodied and knowing of Eve herself, and the time when all humanity remembered who they were and why they came to earth? Would you be curious about what became of the precious child born to the most talked about and well-known couple of the ages, the two who experienced tantric union the way God meant it to be?

If you are the least bit curious, then this book has been written for you. If you are not curious or if you are in denial of the true expression of sexual union born out of a true heart's desire and destiny of the union with the inner beloved, then please see this, perhaps, as a story that gives hope to men and women everywhere and to the children born from them. Know that you are divinely inspired masterpieces of art, come to fulfill your destiny and to write your own story of grace-inspired truth. If you were to write your story, how would it transpire—indeed how would it begin? This one begins from the direct knowing and divinely embodied miracle of a man and a woman who remember who they are and conceive a child, knowing this soul will carry the lineage of Jesus Christ and his life partner Mary Magdalene the Christ, hence christened such by the Master Himself and ordained by the Godhead to spread healing in this land. This is her story: Sarah, the healer, the redeemer.

Most children grow up with an innocence, a cloak, that has been thrust upon them to cloud the memory of lifetimes past, a cloak that encourages forgetfulness and self-denial in order to fulfill a karmic destiny which is born from actions that are sometimes long forgotten. Most children lead a life of self-denial in order to live up to the societal dream that has been created and laid upon them so as not to awaken the truth of who they are. Most children grow up into adults who lack mastery over their minds and emotions, and who deny themselves self-love. These children grow up into the people who inhabit the earth today; lost in self-denial they roam, blindly serving their earth-born desires while neglecting the soul truth that they carry. Would you be interested in awakening the truth and laying aside the forgetfulness and swords of karma that continue the pain and suffering on this great planet earth?

If yes, then you are encouraged to read this story as if it were your own, a blueprint for awakening your truth, so that you can know the seed of your being and fulfill your unique truth and grow fully into the self of your Being, embodying the essence of God uniquely expressed through you. You are encouraged to open your heart, expand your mind and enjoy the story—the Book of Sarah, the Redeemer of Truth, soon to inspire the masses into awakening and remembering. May you be blessed by this story, and may the cloak of forgetfulness hereby be removed, for you are the direct descendant of Love.

To achieve mastery takes knowledge, wisdom, openness and self-awareness. Let us start by expanding our minds and become, again, like children, innocent and in awe of the miraculous everyday truths and the clues left behind by the divine couple.

CHAPTER 1

It did not occur so long ago that the story loses its importance or becomes irrelevant to today's circumstances. Today, the heart yearns for love and self-acknowledgement, as it has always yearned, and for the connection to someone or something that reminds the soul of the truth it holds secret inside. To know Sarah is to know yourself as the child/creation of the divine: perfect, loved and held in the arms of the divine perfection. We all know the exquisite beauty of a newborn child, and yet, there are many who are abused, abandoned, neglected and even killed. What possesses humanity to repress their true nature and to inflict pain onto others? What, has caused, and what, perpetuates the ignorance and the forgetfulness, that, leads to so much suffering in the world? What returns the soul back to oneness where the divine perfection reminds the soul of its mission and life purpose for being?

Alignment with soul mission and heartfelt connection to Source is what enhances life's experience. This experience we call life is the epic unfolding of the divine plan, opening the moment-to-moment expression of our unique journey.

The blessings of eternal life for all of us began, as they did with Sarah, as the union of the feminine and the masculine aspects of God the Infinite expressed through the physical form. Indeed, Sarah was as precious and as perfect as each and every soul ever born. Love has a way of finding the right seed, the right sperm, to join in that matrix of cellular union. And so the journey begins.

Sarah was conceived in a holy union with the divine intention to carry on a lineage of love, truth, and hope that began with Jesus's teaching about a life lived with the knowing of God inside the human heart. This is a life, which can manifest great things, just like the creative energy that moves throughout the entire cosmic matrix of reality. Sarah was born to carry on the teachings of the Divine Feminine and open the doorway to equality and equanimity amongst people, so the feminine could take her place as the Creator of this exquisite world. The Shakti energy gives birth to the explosion of creation, and it is now time for Her power to be acknowledged and accepted worldwide. There is a change amongst you, a quickening of consciousness that is escalating, and these writings are perhaps to some redundant, but for some, they are long overdue.

The fundamentalist thinking has limited the teachings to one gender—as if God could be contained into one form. This just is not true. God is the profound love that expresses through all the universes and all space into all time-space continuums. God is neither male nor female but is both, and they are "separated" into gender at the time of conception. Mary Magdalene grew within her womb the heritage of her divine birthright as Mother God. Jesus was close to his Father, so close he could breathe, sense, taste and think like the Father. It was his soul's purpose to continue to reward humanity with the seed of love that is divinely inspired and manifested in human life. His seed was encoded with all knowing and was passed through a bloodline that continues today.

The group of souls manifesting with this DNA are continuing the teachings and advancing the evolution of consciousness today. The Great Mind of God is inside the cellular structure, and the expression of love is expressed directly through the heart center. The heart center has one purpose: to feel and express love. That is why it is so important to keep this center open. The lineage of Christ was created for this express-purpose and continues today. Sarah has been born again into the physical realm, reincarnated to remind those who are ready to awaken to the Christ within them. There is really one purpose for everyone in every lifetime, and that is to know the Creator and to align with this energy that flows endlessly through all there is. The lineage will continue to grow until all people awaken to their divinity. Remember, there will be different names and a variety of expressions, all unique to the individual personas expressing. All must be accepted so the great interplanetary energies can be aligned, and then humanity will grow into the next phase of enlightenment. Great beings of the light have come and will continue to come to enhance the energy, which is here.

The earth must be elevated into its original vibration and set on the axis with its other planetary energies around it in the solar system and, therefore, the consciousness of its inhabitants is critical. The earth changes are part of the struggle to adapt to the shifts occurring upon its surface, and globally there is noticeably, a renaissance of change. Sarah came long ago during a true renaissance of awakening and has come again and walks amongst you to enliven the lineage of God-Realized beings. Those of you who have obtained heightened states of consciousness will feel and know intuitively as you read these words. You are encouraged to read these words with an expanded mind and an open heart and loving awareness so these words become an embodied truth. The cellular structures inside of you are designed to shift and open as you physically, emotionally and mentally shift your consciousness. The world is always in a state of flux, but today (2009) there is a quickening, and it is imperative that you listen internally to the higher wisdom that lies within you. These teachings are about God-Realization and opening the potentiality that humankind has inside. There really is no time to spare. The earth's vibration is shifting and changes are occurring rapidly, more rapidly than ever before.

CHAPTER 2

So let us begin to explore the story of Sarah, whose life was extraordinary and so ordinary. Every child begins with an innocence and direct line to God Source. This awareness continues into physical manifestation. A child is born with awareness and begins the "fall" into forgetfulness around the age of two. There is a cloud that begins to form, and the soul begins to take on a personality, which was partially preprogrammed before birth by the soul-self. This persona is present at birth and develops and grows with experiences into the fully realized human. This cloud has often been called the veil of illusion, as it covers the knowing of Source and the authentic soul self. Around the age of 2-3 months it begins to take hold, so by 2-3 years old, the personality begins to express. This illusion or veil is necessary for most in order to embrace the life that was created. However, there are some rare instances where the veil does not take hold. Sarah was such a soul. She remembered throughout her childhood what she came to do and was reminded by Mary (Magdalene) who she really was and the mission that was upon them.

Jesus would appear to her throughout her life and teach her and counsel her directly. Their relationship was of father and daughter, but without any hierarchy. She was brilliant and equal in their eyes, and so her knowledge and wisdom remained intact from birth and continued to grow and evolve into her womanhood. Mary's love was as expansive as the Divine Mother, and she held this child with the enduring, unconditional love of the Divine Mother.

Sarah also enjoyed the innocence and playfulness of childhood. She would gather with other children and enjoy the games of the times. Knowing that this time of her life was transient, she enjoyed every moment to its fullest. She loved to sing songs and would call out to her mother to come listen to the divine that she would hear all around her. "That is Krishna, playing you a love song," Mary would say. And when Sarah could hear the ocean roaring inside her ears, Mary knew she was hearing the sacred sounds of the universe and told her of the vibration of the One (Om) and the sounds of the Sacred. "That is the Divine Mother rocking you gently in her arms dear Sarah." But no other sound was more beautiful than the sound of Sarah singing. She sang like the birds, often calling out to God in a playful, joy-filled way, remembering union. Sarah was a pure delight to be with as a child. She was innocent, yet wise, confident and secure, accepting and loving, the way children are meant to be. "So often times, people forget who they are, and that they were created in the likeness of God, both men and women alike," Sarah said.

"And who told you that, Sarah?" Mary asked.

"You know who, Mama. Father told me so."

And so Jesus did. He came to Sarah and taught her the teachings of divine love and how to stay fully present in the moment and to focus on goodness. This goodness is the expression of pure love and devotion to humanity. And to those who remain open inside the dream, this goodness is radiated through pure presence in their body-mind. For Sarah, this radiance guided her, her entire life. She would move forward through every situation and never look back. She knew there was never anything back there worth saving, except the divine love that was carried forward each moment.

Love has a way of finding expression, and Sarah knew all the different ways love could express. Through words, actions and pure presence, love exudes from the heart of the master who lives inside each heart. The soul-self is always looking for mirrors of knowing in order to remember the soul of love inside. Each person and each encounter provides an opportunity for awakening, reminding and expressing the true nature of love. The aspect of love that is most rewarding is the remembrance of the source that created everything.

"Sarah," Jesus said, "you will be one who remembers, and the innocence of love will then be expressed, purely from the light of your being."

"How do you come to me today?" she said as a child with a twinkle in her eye. For she knew the veil between his world and hers really did not exist. The inner eye, when fully awakened, sees everything as it is being created moment to moment. The veil of illusion is penetrable; so the inner eye must stay focused on the divine in all instances in order to perceive the other side of the veil.

"Through grace, dear Sarah, it is through grace that I come to you, so that you will never surrender to the illusion of incarnation. The manifestation of your soul as Sarah is magnificent. We must proceed with the teachings with an awakened heart. Your love must serve, always, as an example of the potential for humanity to shine and to grow. Then, the evolution of consciousness will continue to expand, just as the universe is expanding. You are the light of the world."

Sarah found great comfort and strength from these visits from Jesus and never strayed from her knowing of the light of Love inside her. Mary raised her with the acceptance of her soul-light, which was beyond the ordinary mother-daughter relationship, but also allowed her daughter the experience of the innocence of childhood. In this way Sarah knew love within the human experience, for this is what each soul comes to experience in each incarnation. Having a human experience, can be quite challenging, without, the remembrance of the Creator-energy, inside the womb of existence. As a soul, Sarah chose to remember who she was and what she came to do—spread the light of Love to a world that had fallen asleep inside the dream.

"What shall we teach the world, Father?" Sarah would ask.

"To love and be loved from the depth of your soul," Jesus said. "Most people think they are loving another, when they are actually clinging and expecting something in return. Consciously or unconsciously, they hold on to past experiences that no longer serve them, and bring them forward into every relationship they have. These past experiences have often been the very experiences that have sent them deeper into the dream of illusion and have veiled their eyes from the true source of all love and all experience. Once the experience has occurred, each person then makes a judgment about it based on old thoughts or beliefs that have been embodied within the cellular matrix. These beliefs then influence the relationship, and true love gets buried amongst the stones they have thrown at each other into the soil and buried ground of their being. They are then covered with the dust of illusion, which colors their world from that point on. The truth is, each moment is light being created from Source and what you do with that light is what free will is given for, that is, to create action in the world. Each action creates a line of reality and this thread will go on into its own realm of existence. Each soul actually has many timelines being lived simultaneously, for in truth we are all one, and to that oneness we all return."

"Is that where you are, Father? Is that where you went when you left us?"

"Sarah, my dear sweet daughter, I have always been in this light and created your body with Mary to carry on the lineage of divine love. And so, when my body could no longer hold my light in form, I released it and returned to the realm of Spirit and remain here with a multitude of other beings, who also wish for humanity to awaken. We work together to bring souls to earth who can teach union and who remember something great inside which is guiding them and all their actions. So even though most people cannot see or even feel Spirit guides, we are here. You, dear Sarah, will always know, always see, and always hear. Just touch your heart and breathe me in, and I will be with you. Play now, and enjoy your body, for it is such a gift."

So Sarah went off to play, singing and skipping all the way back to the house where Mary was cooking dinner, which smelled exquisite.

CHAPTER 3

"There really is no other, only One," Mary said. "That is what the illusion is all about, thinking you are separate from one another, when we are all really one with God."

"So, are we all with God, Mama, all the time? Am I really you and you really me? It's a little like our old game we used to play, I peek-a-boo and I see you."

"Yes, the illusion is like a big game of concealing and revealing. You are extremely intelligent, Sarah, good for you."

"But why would someone want to separate from God? Why would God want to hide from us?" Sarah asked.

Mary replied, "God is never really separate from us. We just don't always feel the presence of Her great light when we are caught in our human stories. God wants us to remember all the time. Being human is like the game of hide and seek and peek-a-boo, I see you. For when you are able to dispel the veil that covers your eyes, you will see the story for what it is. God is present in every moment guiding us when we are close and listening."

"Like we are doing with each other now, right Mama?"

"Yes," Mary continued, "God hears and sees all and knows our thoughts. God is the Great Mind that is creating everything, even our most loving and inspiring thoughts. So it is important to stay close and to listen to the soft, loving voice of the divine guidance. When there is no fear, your thoughts are pure and love-based. These moments are communion with God. Fear creates the stories and causes the separation feelings."

"What is fear, Mama?" Sarah asked innocently.

"Fear is when you no longer feel Love as the light of your being. You begin to feel that you are alone in the world and no longer acknowledge the Presence that created and gave birth to you. You are God's light in the world, creating every moment. Fear believes it is the ego personality that is real and eternal, when Love knows it is your soul that is eternal and ever growing and evolving, as God deems ready. Fear would have you believe love does not exist and projects a future of lack and conceals the abundant presence that is always there. Fear relishes and holds on to things in the past that no longer exist except in your memory. This turns into other aspects of fear, like regret and resentment, and causes people great pain and unnecessary suffering. Fear is the opposite of love, for love never causes pain and suffering."

"Mama, is it OK for me to remember when Father comes to see me? I love remembering his face and what he said to me. It is as though he is with me always. I can feel him here with us now, Mama. Can you?"

"Yes, Sarah, he is always here," said Mary, smiling. "He is one with God's light. When he appears to you he emerges into his soul light that individuated to come into incarnation. When you feel him as love, he is within the Almighty Presence and the light of your being, and you feel your oneness with him. Remembering love and instances that brought you into love can bring you back to this moment where Love is breathing you. You are one with that breath. Then, you will always remember and all is well."

CHAPTER 4

When I remember all these moments as a child, I am reminded of the great fortune that was gifted to me: to have parents such as these, two completely enlightened, God-Realized souls. This is so hard to fathom by the commoner (that is how we would describe people of the age). Most people feel they are powerless in the face of adversity and their life situations, but this could not be further from the truth. This Book of Sarah is actually my story. I want to share it with you, for humanity does have an incredible opportunity to expand their consciousness and co-create their lives with God-Source.

Jesus was a man appearing as a carpenter and a teacher, a healer ministering to the downtrodden and bringing forth a message of love, compassion, hope and faith. The expansion of his consciousness now expands to the far reaches of the Universe, as he is one with God. The Book of Sarah is named after a book Mother (Mary) created for me when I was very young, at five years old. She would write stories, draw pictures and record all the visits by Father and the memories I had of our talks together. Mother was really quite a visionary and held true to the mission of love that she embarked on with Father so long ago. These words are brought through this medium for informing those who are ready to hear about a powerful way to embark upon your life with new meaning and excitement about what can be created. With a little imagination and a lot of inspiration, life can unfold from a deeper level, which acknowledges Source as life and a love that transcends time and space.

There are no souls that are not worthy of abundance or the true gifts of the kingdom, as Father would say. All souls are of the Divine Matrix, all interwoven in their expressions in the world. All souls are created by the one Mind, that, we all know as God, the magnificent presence as light and love. Most people have fallen asleep inside this holographic dream, but it is time to awaken. This new age upon you is releasing an energy field of potential that is readily accessible and available to you, if you but reach into the deeper recesses of the mind and find that God-Presence which abides there.

Strong-willed people have forgotten the source of all that energy they tap into to exert their own will on themselves and others. Choices are made which may or may not serve their highest good. God as Source always knows what's best for you. Aligning with this power means authentic freedom to choose all the infinite possibilities of creating good in the world. There are many people who want to live inside the womb of the Great Mother, feeling Her love and nourishment and protection from danger. And so, you can, by aligning with all that is good inside you, by looking for the best in those around you and by being the beacon of light that shines.

Mother would quote these words and more all the time to encourage me and to teach the love of the Divine Feminine. "Mother loves all her children, Sarah. You are in the arms of the beloved Mother. Call to Her and she will come into your awareness. And once you are grown, you will be this mother-love to others who hunger for unconditional acceptance."

You need not fear the actions of others if you always act in kindness first. If, however, someone chooses fear, this is of no consequence to you. Fear not the response of others who have fallen asleep. "Turn the other cheek," Father would say. Walk away from a potential conflict if choices are made against love. Your choice can always be love, independent of the choices of others. This often takes practice. You must stay in love to gain mastery of the mind, for it is through love that the Great Mind expresses.

One way to stay in love is to focus on the positive. Look for things that bring you joy and express beauty. Focus on the goodness in people. Find something to compliment them on, especially a quality about them that you appreciate or admire. Mother would always be complimentary to everyone she met. She said it was because she could see God in them. Father, of course, took great risks in his interactions with people.

He could see God in everything, but would also call people out if he saw them wandering too far off their soul's path. He could see their samskara and their soul's light and knew of the lessons they came to learn and how they came to experience their life. So he would advise, console, and heal, as the will of God deemed necessary. Mother would often help him, but she spent a great deal of time with the women to feel and be supported by them and to honor and support them on their journey. Life as a woman was, and still is, difficult in cultures that do not honor the feminine. The time we lived together was such a time. Mother studied with great devotion and discipline and was very knowledgeable about many things, especially in the ethereal realm. When Father lifted her and graced her with her mystical experience that broke through the veil of illusion, she was catapulted into other realms and could remember her experiences, some of which she recounted to me and are included in these writings.

She first went to a place that felt impenetrable to anything other than God's light. It was as if she went into a box and was shown her entire life up until that point (much like a life review). She was then shown a path that led to the light of God. While walking on the path, she could feel Father with her, and she knew she was on the "right path." When she got to the light of God, she said it was so exquisite she never wanted to leave. She felt so much love and peace. She merged with the light of God and was told she would be illuminated as a master but would not be seen as such in her time. Her soul's purpose was to serve Love, carry the teachings forward, and create a bloodline of souls who could "remember."

In the other realms, Mother said people on earth were referred to as "people of the lie," because they had forgotten the truth of who they are. "All people can awaken and remember, but they need good teachers and role models," Mother said.

When there is a direct connection to Spirit, there is a sense of peace, contentment, joy, love, security and inner knowing. Then, there is nothing to do but to be with the moment and what arises in it. In this way you become a presence to those around you that carries hope and forgiveness, gratitude, and awareness. Therefore, there really is nothing to do, but to show up in the moment, and to free your self from expectation and desire. This always lessens any stress that may arise from daily turmoil.

Mother knew of great stress, for those times were fraught with great fear and turmoil, death and persecution for anything different or what was seen to be threatening to those in authority. Mother claimed her own soul sovereignty over tyranny and prosecution and fled from Jerusalem once Father left. She said it was not safe for us to stay. "There are many people against us," she warned, "but there are also those who believe in the teachings of Jesus and were healed and given greater hope." She knew the journey to safety was long, but we made it through with the help of others along the way. Father would appear to us and encourage us and he never strayed far from our awareness.

"Love is a true force—the greatest force that exists. Always stay awake and aware and choose love whenever you stray from the present moment. It will bring you back home to the presence experienced only when there is no thought, only now," Father said. He guided us to safety from within and spoke to us through our inner knowing and through outer appearances. He said that God, the almighty, is the sole creator of this universe, but freewill had brought chaos and inflicted so much pain and suffering that our eyes must be kept open during our incarnation here on earth. He said, "Sarah, love all and use your inner eye to see through the veil, to detect those who would lie, steal and betray you. Then, you will know when to flee, when to stay, and what you need to do here. There are forces in the universe, born of your Father to protect and guide you Home. Love will ultimately prevail. Fear not. Just keep the veil lifted with eyes clear; keep an inward focus and surrender all to God."

Mother wrote these words in my book as a daily entry. Now I share them with you, as I know the perils of the earth, the gifts in heaven, and the path to freedom and true salvation. God is all; in God we can trust. Connect to your heart and follow those feelings, knowing your true source of safety and love.

Some, if not most, people say to choose Love is too difficult a task in such a fear-based world. Everyone appears to be in survival behavior all the time, looking for ways to get their perceived needs met through a wide range of mechanisms and acts of control. However, few people take time to choose their actions, reacting instead to fear-based impulses that mirror their past experiences, their innermost thoughts and their unconsciousness, unfulfilled needs and desires. Now, what if you grew up in an environment where all your outer needs were met and all your innermost resources were very apparent and one hundred percent available to you all the time? That would be a perfect world, a world based in love, trust, hope, prosperity and infinite possibilities. That is the world Father strived to help create. Mother continued to trust as well in humanity's potential for the embodiment of perfection.

"There will always be those among us that strive for growth, evolution of consciousness, expanded potential and the gifts that the Almighty promises to deliver. To those who seek, who desire God with all their heart and soul, who connect with their hearts and continue to explore the far reaches of their minds, will come enlightenment. Remember, blessed Sarah," Father encouraged, "the paths are many, but they all lead back to the Great Mind of God that will bless you with the knowing and direct experience of your true Self. The essence of the consciousness of your true Self is made of expanded particles of the potent center of creation, with each universe having a signature vibration that connects everything, that is, all matter and the energy that emanates from its center."

"All love can be accessed from a deep desire to know the heart of God. The one Supreme Being is the director of the play of consciousness and has given each particle in every being of light the vibration that is the sound of that universe. OM is ours. The sound of OM awakens that particle of the Supreme into action, into consciousness. The precise time of awakening is predetermined by the Supreme as a thread of light, like a ray from the sun that descends from its highest vibration into the denser aspect of matter and literally vibrates open the vehicles of the body through a complex system of glands and nerves and energy centers along the spinal cord (chakras) that awakens the dense matter back into formlessness. From formlessness came form, and from form, the energy expands back into the formless, void of time and space, transformed back into the precious individuated ray of light that the Supreme Being deemed *you*." You are unique and free unto yourself. All light is yours. So, dear ones, breathe in the light and the vibration of the

OM, to awaken the vibration of the Supreme Being who waits for you, to reunite you with your Source. The profound and the familiar, the peaceful and the exalted, the vibrant and the calm, the all-knowing and the all-being, are reunited into the place (singularity) of consciousness, that point from which it emerged. And you are free, free at last. Focus, focus, focus, all aspects of your being on this one vibration and all love will become apparent."

"There are different layers of the mind embodied in the brain, which look much like this:

High-brain: Cognition, thinking, reasoning
Mid-brain: Feeling, emotion, intuitive knowing
Primal brain: Body functioning, instinct

"To access the Great Mind of God, all pathways of the brain must be functioning properly to utilize all of the God-given resources bestowed upon you. You can awaken and access the mind of God inside the brain by clearing the thoughts and accessing the universal energetic pathways supplying the link between body (matter), mind (universal substance), and the ethereal body of the soul. The body is encased in an energy field that is built on 'layers' of energy generated from the Great Mind of God to enliven the individual physical, mental and emotional aspects of the being that is uniquely you. You, Sarah, have been given the gift of pure awareness-consciousness that has not taken on the veil of illusion. For you, the Great Mind of God is accessible all the time. Your entire physical brain is alert and responsive to every God-given thought you have."

"All humans have this gift also, but theirs is hidden under the thick veil of forgetfulness. The Great Mind projects through a lens seen by the inner, *third* eye, and this lens can be dusted and cleared of the dirt accumulated through years and often lifetimes of ignorance based in fear and their own self-righteous clinging to thoughts and beliefs they think will protect them from the perceived perils of earth-living. In truth, this dirt is dust on the mirrored lens of illusion that keeps them imprisoned in a world of untruth and forgetfulness that recreates their wounds again and again, form after form, lesson after lesson. Then, the earth-school is always in session, with some staying in the lower grades, repeating class after class until they exhaust themselves or go into the playground, only to find the bully of their own inner ignorance and fear beating them into submission."

"Tell them, dear Sarah," Father said, "that the inner bully was created to protect the fragile ego from self-betrayal, and instead it betrays the creative Self that sustains the very breath of life that gives them the oxygen they breathe. You must be the message of love, sent to awaken more of the people of earth by activating the seed of consciousness so implanted into the matrix of the matter of their being. You will remain here in this lifetime as a living lineage to the consciousness of Truth."

"When I left my body (matter), the life source of my Father sustained me until I merged with the Great Mind of God. I now speak to you from the infinite source of Truth and encourage you to continue these truths. Much will be written through "gospels" and other teachings, and this book will carry forward the message of love as it is written in each heart created by the one soul that belongs to the mind of God. Father said, "You, Sarah, are Truth embodied into form, and your DNA, as it will be called, carries the traits of an envisioned truth for humanity living in peace and harmony, awakened to the divine and all creation. Honoring the wholeness and completeness of love in its myriad of forms, is honoring the heart of God in all. You, Sarah, must show the way."

"But how, Father?" I asked.

"Just how is up to you," he said. "The Way Shower is inside you. Follow the light you know so well, and wipe the dust from the lens of the others that have fallen prey to the illusion created by fear. The demons are their thoughts that entrap them in a narrow casing and keep them from their potential of the expanded vision of their Creator. The light illuminates the darkness. The way is to shine bright, love deeply and live fully each moment of every day."

Father was always bringing me truth and reminding me of the earth-school and how it worked. "Teach joy, embody love, and bring truth to awaken hearts. Teach love, for that will bring ultimate freedom from the tyranny of the darkness and the plague of fear. Fear is the absence of light and the false beliefs carried on by the thoughts that created them. Union of the body, mind, and spirit through yoga can set the hearts of many free, and these teachings have been brought through many devoted hearts in India and the east and now must come to all. The highest yoga is the teachings of love that bring enlightenment through the illumination emanating from the heart, mind and soul of God the Supreme."

So, Mother and I practiced the breath the ancients taught to awaken the energy in the spinal column. It goes like this:

> Breathe into your spinal column, close the back of the throat and make the sound of the "ocean of bliss" like waves coming into shore, touching the earth and returning back, never leaving the source of itself. As this breath moves through the center of your spine, you will sometimes feel areas that feel blocked or stuck. Release these areas where the energy has gotten stuck by directing your focus to these areas. Give permission for the breath to emerge from these areas of your being. From inside these places lies the light, which has become hidden from its source of power. The power within unlocks the doors that have closed and blocked the light from emerging. Continue to breathe until the waves release the area, and enjoin the great wave as it returns to the sea of consciousness from whence it came and to where it returns over and over again. Do this until the breath wants to pause. Then, release the epiglottis breath and return to your more natural silent breath. Let go of the awareness of the spinal cord, and bring your attention and focus to your heart. Feel the rise and fall of the chest and notice the pauses, the still points in the breath. Relax into the pause at the end of the out breath, and "wait" for Spirit to inspire you into taking that next breath of life, drinking the elixir of the divine perfection that is you. Your inner focus will then naturally go to your inner eye between your two outer eyes. This point is deep within your brain between the two lobes of the brain (hemispheres). Then your breath

will naturally cease in your awareness and you will enter meditation where the Presence waits patiently for you to Be.

"This," Father said, "is the only goal of life; to contact the Divine Being of Light that illuminates everything into existence, and to surrender fully to that Presence."

Mother and I practiced this yogic breath daily, mostly in the morning before we initiated our day. We loved to sit side by side and hold hands, contacting God together and remembering our connection to the world of Spirit where Father was residing. We could visit our friends on the other side of the veil, those who had gone before and those who had yet to come. To penetrate the dense layers of the energy field, we would call in the angelic realm and follow their light to the higher-level beings and communicate with them. In this way, we never felt alone or separate as many people do. We lived in "our" world, which was a combination of the physical and more ethereal realms, in a state of knowing which allowed us to fully embrace each moment as a gift of Spirit. To know God is to know love and to feel complete and whole, divine and free. This feeling is deeply embedded in each soul, waiting to be remembered.

Awakening the energy in the spine through the breath is the most direct way to remember. When you awaken this energy, it is like removing the valves that have blocked the pipeline from flowing. Once this stream or energy pathway is awakened, there is a series of "events" that occurs which is directed by the soul through the Great Mind of God. These "events" release blockages that have often been there for lifetimes, accumulating thick bands of dense energy matter which get "stuck" along the field of energy that is vibrating the energy centers in the spine into their embodied form in the human body. These energy centers are known as chakras and are now well studied and acknowledged by many people of your time. By now (2010) much has been written about how to work with these centers in the human energy field, and in fact, this is the basis for yogic teachings passed down from the enlightened ones, generation after generation.

There is one "secret" that has never really been fully embraced or taught by the masters to the masses. Much of their teachings were saved for their most devoted students whose only desire was to fall into the love of their God, never to return to the illusion. So many students have spent their entire lives practicing mindfulness and breath practices taught to them by their teachers, waiting for the moment of grace to arrive. There is one unknown truth that has yet to be shared, for the Great Mind of God predetermined the timing of this gift. It is important that a certain level of consciousness be obtained by a certain number of individuals before the information can ever be used. So, the enlightened ones waited to share this information until the appropriate time.

The planets are now aligned in such a way that the magnetic pole of this universe can be utilized to change the energy field of this planet. When the energy field is aligned with the sun, the polarization of the planet will be expanded into the consciousness of the souls who are ready to enliven and bring forth this great truth. Love is an entity; a being that was created to embody the energy of the unifying field that holds all matter in existence. This being of light, known by many names, is the Supreme Being most people know as God. This love being, if you will, is so dense and so light at the same time that the combination and connection of these opposing energies explodes and brings all form into existence. The Hindus created different gods and goddesses to explain the different aspects of the divine matter, and then each divination was released to perform different tasks or duties for the human population. Then, one being of light came to the earth to actually awaken the seed of knowing in humanity. He was the direct expression of God, the Supreme Love Being who was expressly created to enliven a new species of evolved beings, who could sustain a high frequency vibration in matter. To enliven this seed of consciousness implanted by the great master known as Christ Jesus, we must awaken the heart of a certain number of souls into remembering. As Sarah, I was able to keep the seed of consciousness alive within the matrix of the DNA by never falling asleep in the dream. There have been others who came to this earth with full remembering, and they are alive among you today. What you must remember is that the earth is alive and is ready to shift her own energy field to awaken the center core of her being, which is deep within the center matrix of the planet. The energy lines will then flow from this center much like the energy lines within the human body now known as meridians. The ley (energy) lines of the earth have been distorted by the lower or denser consciousness that has flooded this planet and has done damage to these fragile lines of flow. These lines of flow energize the earth's chakras, which are strategically placed throughout the planet's surface and connect directly into the core-spine of the planet, which aligns along the vertical access of the earth. When her polarity shifts, there will be a shift of consciousness, and those who are open to it will experience a great surge of energy, and the Being of Light created as love will emerge from the center of the earth, opening her heart chakra. Those people whose hearts have been opened to love will awaken, and they will remember this love being as the God who created them.

This was falsely interpreted as the second coming of Christ through falsely inspired teachings known to some as armageddon, but in truth was the forthcoming opening of the planet's core known as the heart of God of this planet. The Great Mind of God is linked to the heart-mind of the earth and was created to support the generation of humans evolving into great beings of expanded consciousness. Jesus, known as the Master, wrote of this. Through this manual and through me, his daughter Sarah, this journal known as the Book of Sarah comes to you now. He said the teachings now must be of the more feminine energy of the Universe, to bring together all the goddesses' energy to open the heart of love and compassion served through the love of the Divine Feminine. The Great Being of Love serves many and knows compassion through the hearts of the bodhisattvas who have come so many times to serve the Being of Light. It is now time for me (Sarah) to share with you what Father taught me.

> Open your heart by focusing on the image of God that comes to you most quickly and clearly. Align your heart and soul energy with the image of love by breathing into a seed—a cellular placement inside your actual physical heart. It is inside the chamber known as the atrium and is close to the mitral valve. Focus on this chamber and breathe.

This area of the heart is directly linked to the pathway to the soul and the heart of the planet. The soul light is energized by this cellular seed inside the heart and remains so in the energy heart even if the physical heart is removed. The beating of the physical heart is actually dictated outside in the causal/soul-body through the energy lines of the spine, which plug directly into the spinal cord and then enliven the mind of God through the brain into matter. This dense matter of the brain has a pulse and a series of glands that are energized by the main elixir known as love, and this keeps the Supreme Being alive in form. You are the embodiment of this love being, "broken" into fragments much like a broken mirror that continues to show the reflection of the one who is looking in. The great being of love is inside the physical heart of each person and each animal and also in the earth planet's core. To realize the love being, there must be a connection with the actual energy of love, not the illusion of love that most beings have created out of the false thought that they think is love. Love is an actual thing, a Great Being, a physical presence, a light surrounded by matter or denser rays of light that have been condensed into form. Everyone must be aware of this feeling in their heart and is often made aware of this by seeing this presence in someone else's mirror. The eyes of the soul can shine out and reflect this love being, and then the presence of God is felt. This feeling illuminates from the chamber in the heart and can be expanded with concentrated focus and awareness.

In her book, <u>The Greatest Love I Have Ever Known,</u> Mother wrote about her experiences of awakening and the time with Father, and she shared a technique or method which focused on the heart center and included a mantra based on the energetic name of God—I AM.

I AM
I surrender
I AM
I surrender
I AM, I surrender to the Great Master of my soul
I AM One with the Master
I AM
I AM

The mantra awakens the seed of consciousness in this heart chakra to the Master within. This great Master of the soul beats your heart and keeps you alive. The Great Master of the soul is the Great Being of Light, the Supreme, and the Almighty. The love being that is now also emerging to open the heart center of the earth will actually evoke the earth changes that so many scientists of your time are predicting. However, you must remember that all of these earth changes are aligned with the other planets of your solar system and have a specific time line for evolution. You can help support the opening of the earth's heart by chanting this mantra daily and by gathering with others who are interested in spiritual evolution and include them into your circle of light. At the end of this mantra sit in the silence and love the earth and all her life forms: animal, vegetation and mineral. Love all of life as you surrender fully to the being of love, the true Master of your Soul.

Father spoke of Him as Father, but the other aspect is Mother. The true essence is Love Itself, and Father spoke of this truth all the time. To heal your planet's heart, chant OM throughout the day, and at the end of this mantra connect your heart chamber with Hers. She will open within you a power of great magnitude, and the energies of the Goddesses will be united into one immense ray of light that will illuminate all who are ready to remember love.

"You are love embodied, Sarah," Father would say. "And now I say to everyone here embodied on Mother Earth, you are love embodied, and the very beating of your heart beats as one with hers. And yes, this planet's energy is aligned, as the feminine will bring balance to all. The Divine Masculine is actually surrounding the planet in the non-manifest, and together they form the infinite presence of the Supreme Being of Love, as God, as Truth, as All There Is, as I AM, the I AM Presence which is everywhere in all known and unknown universes. You are the Truth, and the Truth shall set you free," he continued.

Love is all there is, gathering towards you or being radiated from you, all the time. This energy cannot be created or destroyed (as your scientists have said) but, it can be magnified or hidden by your awareness. By bringing your awareness to Love and its power, you are energizing the light force of the Infinite Being of Light at the very center to which it is drawn and from which it is being radiated. Love, is the being of light of supreme goodness and joy, which, brings balance and harmony to the world.

Now, in these times of awakening and transition, it is useful to have a community of like-minded people and those who are ready to grow into their magnificence. So gather often with people whose hearts are open to the loving presence of the divine's grace, and celebrate the union of energy in a coherent way. The coherence is aligned with the energy in all matter and affects the earth and her creation living on her surface. When you gather, celebrate love in the ways that matter to you. Listen to your own inner wisdom and intuit ways of being and interacting and serving each other. Find others whom you can resonate with and who also need your help in aligning with grace. Love will guide you.

Mother and I would gather people in our humble village in a circle, one hand on our heart chakra and one hand together in the center of the circle, and make eye contact with one another. Together we would say the heart center mantra and chant the OM for sometimes hours on end until there was one voice, one sound, and it became the stillness and the silence inside the Presence. The chanting would start verbally and then become an inward experience; our hands would release from one another and come back to our own heart center, where we would sit in a circle of love, so present it would move some to ecstatic joy and others to a deep stillness that illuminated their soul presence. Love, as the Supreme Being, is all there is, and it is to this being we all return. The awareness is how. What you focus on allows you to experience the light of love; it is a presence you know, for it is who and what you are. To know your Self is to know God.

Try gathering in this circle and finding your own ways of interacting: through words, through silence, through movement, through writing, through creating, through touching, for it is all love.

Mother taught me many things, all handed down through her lineage of teaching through the Divine Mother's grace and Father's divine love. The relationship known as Jesus the man and Mary the woman was only part of the story. The children begot from them carried on the seeds of wisdom and love to energize these changes of the earth and of the universe, which are occurring in your time. If you were to have known them in their time, you would have seen them as the divine couple that they were. United as one being, their souls were light, melded into one. There is no separation in a union of this nature, and Mother wrote of this through her incarnation soul to soul, so others would know that the master of the Christian world was none other than the incarnation of God, the Master of all souls.

The union began a chain of events and other unions, which held the memory of their love and union to help others remember their true master. Christians have misinterpreted Father's words to speak to an isolated population, when in fact God is the seed in everyone. You do not need to know my beloved Father, once known as Jesus, to become one with God, the Supreme Being of Love, or to serve from the Master of your soul. In fact, other beings that have incarnated have brought the Truth to many, as the Great Source comes through many. The difference, if you will, is the time Father came and the timing of his message to a world that had gone astray from the Truth. The essence was being lost to the illusion of separation and darkness, and so he came as the ambassador of peace with a grand story that could be remembered and retold generation after generation to awaken the heart to Truth. To try to force someone else to embody and embrace a lie—that this is your only way to God—has caused great pain and suffering and does not need to continue. In fact, it is time to stop feeling separate from anyone. We are all one living being, breathing and pulsing with divine revelation and Truth, all hearts beating to the same tune, the same rhythm. We all create the music on the lyre of the heartstrings, and the voice of God sings through all voices. Jesus the man cried, he felt, he bled, he sweated, he made love to his wife, and he remembered. He was conscious; he was awakened, and he knew all was inside him, within the oneness of the breath of love itself. He held inside of him, the wisdom to be brought forth through humanity to enliven a revelation, a revival, and a revolution of Spirit.

He brought love to earth, and so can you. This is always the timeless truth. "You, too, can do these things and more," was Jesus as Christ speaking to that which is to come, the evolution and expansion of Truth, and beings of light everywhere awakening and embodying God.

Love is all there is. This Book of Sarah is a timely gift to a world being enlivened with this Truth. I tell you, gather together in all ways possible, and bring your harmonious resonances together. Tie yourself to Truth so you cannot drift too far. Keep yourself tethered together with one another; the time for isolated thoughts is gone. The Great Mind is communicating through many now. Know that the light of love is quickly spreading, illuminating hearts across the world. Even in the midst of greatly challenged times, there is great light and great love. Support one another in these challenges, and find time to gather in support of the earth and her changes. She is awakening the energy of the feminine, which is all about opening, including, evolving, embracing, nurturing, and loving. The feminine is all-inclusive and gathers the energy back into the womb to give birth to love. She is the Mother, all-knowing and all-loving. It is when we gather that we are held in Her embrace. Fear not, men of the world, for you are not losing power; you are gaining access to true power. Your ideas of force and exclusivity of power are false. It is false pretense to pretend you know all from that small ego-mind you think of as God "the Father." God the Father, the Divine Masculine, is all loving and all knowing and expansive and is unlimited with no boundaries. You have made Him (this aspect of God) into your ego's likeness, which is limited and blinded by greed and fear. This God is not the being of light that shines from your heart, who planted the seed into the great womb of the Divine Mother. The seed of the Father was Truth, implanted as direct knowing into the heart of humankind to embrace the energy of the feminine that brings compassion and love to awaken the great Tao: that which cannot be created or destroyed, that which has no name and has been called by many names. Often spoken of as the presence inside the stillness—the quiet inside the silence—this ever-loving, all-knowing Truth is God, the Light, the Love, the Path, the Way, the Is. But, know that once manifested into form, the form carries both, the seed and the womb. The union is inevitable.

So gather to remember, to awaken, to enliven and to celebrate union—body, mind and spirit—feminine and masculine—yin and yang forces. Gather the forces of Truth and involve love to light your way. This is the way to what Father called salvation, the destruction of all that is untruth, all fear-based thoughts and "wrong-doing" based on the thoughts of an ego-based in unknowing, unable to see the grander picture for humanity.

"Humanity was created to express divinity, and the only way to construct a truth-based world is to destroy the lies that the ego creates out of ignorance and untruth. God is the one Truth, the one way to enlightenment, and this God has embodied many forms and individuated forces to compose the universal forces of light. This great being lives as form because of you."

Father spoke these words to me at a time of great sorrow and pain for me. He mastered the Truth in his life and brought it to a fear-based culture, which had all but forgotten the God they worshiped. Unable to feel love, our people lived in a cold-hearted world, unable to express from the God-center in their hearts. When Father came to me, Mother was feeling weak and leaving her body more frequently into the netherworld. I knew she was visiting Father and the angelic realm, but I also knew there would soon come a time when I must carry on without her by my side. I knew then of the paradox in which we were engaged. This physical world, laden with treasures of the flesh and material and expressing divinity, exists within the Great Mind, which was also projecting the non-physical world of Spirit, and we were "caught" in the middle.

"Father," I said, "I now know somewhat of the pain of separation you and Mother must have felt—the anticipation of loss. I will miss her; even though I know she is not disappearing totally, she is disappearing to me, disappearing from her form. We all must leave these bodies behind, and I find it comforting knowing we will all be reunited in Spirit. I feel pain here in my heart because of the loss of a body that was given so beautifully of form and love, which expressed fluidity in movement to express the unfolding of the life-given breath of our Divine Mother. You are so sweet, Mother. I love you so."

Mother was the divine essence of the feminine, embodied. And she said that every woman held the seed of the divine presence inside her womb, where the birth of humanity took place. Even those who do not give physical birth hold a child of love in the womb as potential, for her own creative energy to flow in the world. This can take many forms. Many women get lost in their own uncertainty of their mission or potential to create in the world and find that giving physical birth is one way to access the energy of the Divine Mother. This is but one way. There are many instances when the love of the Universal Mother-energy can be used and is much needed all over the world today as it was in our time.

The death of the feminine body of my dear, sweet mother (Mary) would in no way stop the infinite source of love that flowed through her. She continues to live and love now and is among you. She is the bodhisattva of compassion that takes many forms until all are awakened to their truth, their true essence. For inside their essence is the heart of compassion, enlivening the feminine gift to the world.

"If there were but one word anyone could every utter," Mother said, "it would be his or her name for God. And the utterance of that one word would always be a call to love." Everyone who has ever felt a challenge or a pain of any kind: physical, mental, or emotional, has thought of a way to call out for help in a time of need. Even those who feel self-sufficient, or who feel unworthy, or even those who do not believe in the source of creation, cry for help when times are the darkest and most challenging.

"When Father cried out to his Father," Mother said, "he was crying out for help from inside his own source of light. When he asked Father God, 'Why has thou forsaken me?' it was at the point when he suffered his greatest pain. Not too long after that, his prayer was answered and he was lifted out of his body and joined God, which is where he remains today. The ascension was when he took his energy-body that held his soul and lifted himself to the Godhead of the Supreme Being and asked for mercy for humanity. Once he asked for relief from the suffering, the Divine Mother said she would embody and help bring compassion back to the earth.

"This madness of forgetfulness must end," my father would say, and he told me of Her promise to come and reveal Herself as the Mother. So look for Her; she is here with you. Inside each woman is the potential for awakening the creative force of Mother God.

"We all just need to surrender fully," Mother said.

And so now I say to you, the awakening is upon you. When the earth and planetary shifts occur, there will be more people than ever who will awaken to the truth of love and share compassion in so many forms. The essence of Truth dictates behavior, which is aligned with the master of the soul's light. Return to this in all your times of need to find reassurance that help is on its way. The divine unfolding is at the heart of all matter and is all that matters. Divine timing is to be trusted.

When you pray, pray that peace and goodness will fill the hearts of all beings, and pray for the complete awakening to Truth through the heart of compassion. Mother and I would repeat this prayer daily so that we could include others in our own souls' journey. The matrix of humanity holds the threads of the DNA of the divinity of Truth and is accessible through the unifying field of consciousness. All beings share the common threads of awakened matter in their DNAs. It is easy to access through loving devotion, prayer, and meditation. And breathing with awareness of the construct of the DNA, as God and matter, will awaken more of who you are.

Embodying truth is manifesting love into action. This is accessible through your God-given cellular presence inside the matrix of the DNA construct. When you meditate on a regular basis, the DNA begins to awaken the God presence inside, and there is a shift of consciousness through the change and vibration. Much like a song that is played on any string instrument, the vibration of the note resonates along the string. When you still the mind and quiet the body, the threads of the DNA vibrate differently. The "lower" tone resonances disappear and the "higher" vibrations appear. You can then "jump" into a new awareness. It is like taking a quantum leap into a different galaxy or reality. Focusing on a tone (like OM) can also change the baseline resonance.

Each soul has a specific vibration, which, is unique. That vibration is imprinted in every cell at the level of the DNA and carries a variety of possible stories to be enlivened into the person's life. Free will and choices can then play out under the direction of the soul, which is the direct link to God. It is wise, therefore, to enter the stillness and to listen for guidance. In the stillness, when ego thought disappears, the screen of God will arise, and the voice that emerges will feel like a knowing of truth imbued with wisdom and clarity. This guidance leads you down the path that is best suited to you. The path of righteousness, as Father called it, is the path that is right for you at this present moment in time, with each step leading you further along the path that you travel en route on your soul's mission; the people and places emerging in the divine perfection, ordained by your soul. This journey has many possibilities, each choice leading along a specific timeline of events. In order to co-create your reality in alignment with your soul's intention or agenda, you can access the DNA structure and enliven a memory or a knowing that allows you direct access to the Mind of God. Within the cellular matrix of every cell is the specific DNA construct for the functioning of the cell, but there is also pure consciousness, pure vibration of the oneness in all matter. Now, if you use your free will in complete surrender to this divinity code, your genetic matrix aligns with your soul knowing, and events can be almost instantly manifested, depending on the complexity of events needed to accomplish the outcome. It is always more complex when it involves other people and increases in its complexity the more people that are involved. However, once the consciousness shifts in one person, it can act as a direct link to another, especially if they are in the same soul circle. However, this linking to the DNA is what links the consciousness of all beings. So, even if it appears as though few people are conscious or aware, the awakening of one does lead to the awakening of others. That is why one great soul light can make a significant impact in the course of events affecting many people.

Now, in your time of awakening cellular consciousness, this DNA divinity code can be accessed through the power of intention and belief in the power of grace. This is why faith and prayer are so powerful in creating "results." As long as the outcome is in harmony with that soul's journey and in harmonic resonance with the Mind of God, that prayer will be answered. Many of your prophets and sages have touted alignment with the Divine Mind, and some rightly so; however, the soul's wisdom is what always dominates in each individual situation. Not much can be purely predicted on a day-to-day basis, as free will and the power to choose is the dominating ego force. However, there are divine timelines, and the unfolding of human consciousness is masterfully orchestrated. The Divine Mind is truly embedded into each person and can be awakened by free will and in divine timing.

The techniques Mother and I used were passed down to her through ancient teachings and through Father. We would experiment to see what would be helpful to others. Here is one that proved very helpful for many around us:

> Sit upright in a comfortable position. Focus your breath on a point between the eyebrows and call to God. The words are not as important as the intention behind the words. Use your breath to still your mind and eliminate the thoughts. Breathe in God; breathe out God. Use the breath that feels most comfortable to you. Allow yourself ten to fifteen minutes in the silence to feel the inner peace that arises from this very simple way to contact God.

Each time we sat in the silence together, there was a sense of overwhelming peace and an inner smile that emerged from within. The sense of inner peace is accessible to everyone and can be felt to that cellular knowing place deep within. If you are scared or in doubt about some aspect of your life, find the one focal point inside the center of your brain and breathe God's love. It is all about love.

Mother and I would take day trips and travel to nearby towns and reflect upon the challenges people were facing and offer some advice that would help alleviate some of their fears and worries. There are people who had never heard of Father's teachings, and so we shared the foundations of faith that Father said preceded any God intervention. Faith in something greater than fear leads to the direct experience of that loving Presence, so God can enter your consciousness. One man asked, "Isn't God privy to everything I am experiencing? Why doesn't God just step in and rescue me from this devastating poverty and pain that I suffer? Why do I have to beg and suffer endlessly? God should know what I need and provide it. What about faith?"

And to this Mother replied, "Dear sweet soul of God, faith allows you to rest in the knowing of the source of your salvation. Faith is the bridge between your conscious mind and your unconscious mind. The Mind of God is steeped in Truth and all-knowing, all-loving presence. There is no need to beg. Begging keeps you in the mind state of a pauper, a victim to life, and does not serve the soul or the pristine perfection, of whom you are. God's 'plan' if you will includes conscious choice, for out of pain comes a yearning, and this yearning leads you back to your heart where God lives. Inside your heart is the love of God. So, when you have the faith of but the size of a mustard seed, the presence of God washes over you and you are saturated with Truth. This Truth lifts the darkness and the fear from your heart, the yearning ceases, and your light becomes brighter. Thus, Truth ends not only your suffering, but helps others around you. Everyone responds better to the light than to darkness."

The man responded, "Sometimes the sadness and hopelessness that I feel is so great that I fear I shall never emerge victorious over these circumstances. I feel I have little power over my situation, let alone my state of mind. I know love is better than fear, but I feel so out of control of everything. How do I change what is unchangeable?"

"Everything changes," Mother said, "in its relationship to our own experience of it. It is always our perception of it. The day Jesus died, a part of me died. No matter what I had known before of God or faith, in the moment of his greatest suffering, I suffered too. I felt every pain, every tear, and every emotion he felt. We were one in our union, and no one could release me of my torment, save one source. I cried for mercy, and I begged God to save him, and He did, just not in the way I wanted at the time. Jesus returned to his Father and was released completely from the tormenters who brought judgment upon him. Jesus was my life and my path, or so I thought. When he left me, I had to 'carry on' with faith that he was with me, and in that faith, he returns to me time and again and reassures me that I am not alone and that the physical body is transient."

"The pain endured here is very real, so compassion is given to all those who ask. By asking, you are literally accessing the gateway to the Presence that grants all desires that serve your highest good. Because of free will, you can choose misery any time you want; negative thoughts and feelings lead you there, more often than not for most people. Pray, my dear friend, for peace. Breathe in God, for God is in every breath. You can actually relax into this Presence the more you access it and the more you practice awareness. God hears you when you beg also, but begging leads you to a victim mentality, and it is much harder for you to receive grace. Faith allows you to relax enough for grace to enter. This is why practicing stillness is so useful. It re-patterns the way you think and reorganizes your structure to accommodate higher levels of vibration."

"I don't understand all of this. How does vibration relate to God?" he asked.

Mother looked at me, and I smiled, because I knew what he was saying. I had asked a similar question of Father one day when I was just a little girl. He told me that the vibration of God resonated throughout the entire universe beyond the seen world, and that the level of conscious thought was very low compared to the state of awareness of no thought. "All there is, is love," Father said, "which vibrates a frequency of God the Supreme Being. He told me everything had a certain level of frequency or density in vibration. Higher states of consciousness feel better because they are more natural states, given we are not in any kind of fear or doubt or lacking trust, because this leads one to a lack of faith. Living in faith frees you from fear. Sometimes one must walk the path of fear through the dark forest before the trees disappear and there is light again. Everyone who lives long enough experiences darkness unless they are graced with eternal God awareness.

"This is so rare," Mother said, "because the beings of earth are enveloped by a dense cloud that veils their true identity. They have fallen into the trap of forgetfulness, and only in the awakening of the soul memory will there be global healing. If you are fortunate enough to grow up in a loving environment, you will feel wanted and catch glimpses of true love; however, most beings have come to mistake human 'forgetful' love for the unconditional love of the divine."

Within the divine matrix lies the seed of awakening encoded into the DNA, and when it is time the internal clock alarm sounds, and the individual will have an epiphany, an "ah ha moment," that usually changes their life because they were able to see differently. Mother said that her time of awakening with Father catapulted her into an entirely new form and a new way of thinking and seeing everything. She said there is light around everything, and I would play with this light around the trees and plants and dance in the light of the sun because it was just so joyful to celebrate the intensity of life here.

Father used to say the whole reason we are born into the world is to experience joy, for it is our inherent nature and our birthright given to us by the Creator. No greater love is available than that of the Creator for His/Her creation. It is a bond beyond words. Pure oneness has a sense of merging into yourself, so, when you experience the soul's eternal nature, then you are home with God. God has no real "agenda." There are soul missions and contracts with other souls, and this is included in the life experiences. Within every experience, there is God. Some people experience God through witnessing their lives, and yet, if you can but surrender, you will know oneness and merge with the divine light. The fullness of your being is then experienced as pure joy, pure bliss.

The divine matrix includes all of life, and the interconnections are becoming more and more evident. Once love is ignited, it can spread like wildfire across the globe, reaching more and more people and all of life's creation. When Father came to visit, I would often ask him to teach me how to heal the way he did. He said he and Mother would surrender to love and ask to be connected to God within that person, for the presence of God is what shifts everything back to its original splendor and perfection. If we take the time to notice, we can feel this presence or life force everywhere. It takes a certain perception to be able to perceive it, but it is always there, flowing like a river. I practiced viewing this life force in nature and began to see the framework of reality: colors, patterns, and lights organized individually and connected to one another. I loved talking to the plants and watching them dance in response. Everything is so vibrant and alive with this life force. "This is where God lives," Father said.

Mother was just as versed at seeing and accessing God's life force as Father was, and many people were healed in her presence, both subtly and boldly noticeable. "The miracle," Mother said, "is belief and knowing. This ignites the universal life force to awareness, and it is the awareness of itself, that changes the molecule's patterns and instructs the entire process. Instant healing occurs upon recognition of the Divine Mind meeting Itself."

The irony is most people needed to see or experience a miracle in order to believe or know it was possible. Then, even after the miracle had happened, people would often deny the source of it. Some even called it trickery. In some ways it is trickery, because you are tricking the small mind into seeing like the Great Mind sees. In this way the veil is lifted, and the view is all but revealed into the matrix of all that is.

You are really part of everything, and everything is part of you. Try this:

> Sit with your spine upright, legs uncrossed. Feel the energy in your hands by rubbing them together and palming your eyes. Focus on the third eye (the point between the eyebrows) inside your head and ask to see the Divine Matrix and the grid of this earth. Relax into a comfortable focus of the eyes. It will appear as a light, glowing and vibrating, ready to be organized into whatever specific form is being created through intention and belief. Lines will appear and form into different organizations based on the vibration of the form. To heal yourself, give yourself permission to heal by returning to the divine perfection of the life force in this divine matrix. Love will organize these lines of divinity into the coalescent forces needed to heal you. You can focus on the specific area of your body and sense the field of energy that is within you and the energy that is around you. Let yourself bathe in the light of Love that heals everything. It can be experienced as a buzzing sensation as your energy body accelerates and the denser matter is elevated in frequency.

All injuries or wounds are of a lower vibration or are cut off completely from the organizing life force. When you surrender your awareness to the brilliance inside this energy field, the matter will literally reorganize its wave patterns into a vibration that reveals the truth of this moment, pure presence. This presence can manifest anything instantaneously and does so literally every moment of every day. The problem comes when there has been a faulty or dysfunctional pattern set into motion via injury or belief or a strand of DNA activation that has not fully stayed connected to the divine matrix of the organizing field. So, the illuminating light is then dimmed or diminished, and, oftentimes, is completely hidden in dense matter. The dense matter is full of sensory organs giving the body sensation after sensation, setting into motion a response that is both physical and emotional. The emotions become embedded in the tissues and can, therefore, be activated with any incident or thought or belief that gets stimulated. Then, there is a choice that needs to be made. How do you want to respond: with positive, uplifting thoughts and actions, or debilitating thoughts and responses that challenge your body-mind to a duel? The duel is between the duality of the world of physical form and the dense veil of illusion that surrounds it, and the divine matrix of pure perfection that illuminates the infinite field of potential in the form of pure presence.

The world of duality would have you believe everything is solid, unchangeable substance when, in fact, matter is made of pure light vibrating at higher or lesser frequencies. When someone is in pure, present presence, there is pure light manifesting moment by moment. It is this presence that we work with when engaged in any healing endeavor. It helps to see it, or at least feel it, but someone of pure faith and devotion can also access it through their solid belief in the divine matrix at the core of their being. Once aligned with their own pure presence, God the Supreme ignites the sequencing of coalescing forces that stimulates the physical reorganization of the molecules in matter. All of this is happening through the divine intelligence inherent in every cell. This automatic or spontaneous healing has been called "a miracle." And, indeed, it is a miracle to the untrained eye. When people of the lie, as Mother called earth's children, cry out for a miracle, they want the divine elixir to awaken inside of them the truth of their core/absolute reality. When, in fact, they are often times crying for someone else to prove themselves as the savior, the healer, the miracle worker, son of God; there are many names for the source of healing known by most as God, the Supreme Being of love and light.

Mother and I found great solace in the knowing of God's pure presence and the gift of seeing granted us by the Divine Mind. We spent time helping others to see it and to feel it by experiencing their true nature. Loving -kindness goes a long way in helping people to awaken their own infinite potential within. Father spent his short life here awakening all those who were ready to receive the wisdom inherent in the words of truth from the voice of God. Those who would listen could then choose their own path of righteousness, that which served them at the time. It is natural to get lost in the human experience of emotions and feelings and react to the events and reactions of others. However, someone with a well-trained mind and an opened heart, aligned with the Truth in the presence of the divine matrix, can and will change their vibration, and therefore, their life experience.

This is the key to changing the outer world into your own miracle of synchronistic events, spontaneous healings, and eruptions of pure joy and lively encounters based in love. For the vibration is that, love. Love is the experience of God in matter, shakti. And shaktipat is the transmission from one being to another. Shared love is communion and reunion with the beloved and is the yoga of bliss. Bliss taken to the source aligns with the I AM presence of God the Supreme, the all-present and all-knowing Source. Chanting, "I AM" is reciting your original name before individuation into your unique soul expression. "I AM" aligns you with your Creative Source; OM aligns you with your universe; combining these vibrations brings you home to the present quickly and succinctly. Try:

> Breathe in "OM" through your crown (top of your head) and breathe out "I AM" through your heart center. Relax in peace.

CHAPTER 5

All of this information being given was written down when I was with Mother so that future generations of seekers could benefit from some of these simple techniques and teachings of truth. Both Mother and Father knew that each generation would find the messengers of truth that aligned with their soul's growth, and that the beginning of wisdom is always generated from within. These writings being brought through today's channel, are yet another attempt to describe the nature of reality as it is being generated by the Great Mind of God and provide ways to access this wisdom to help with the evolution of consciousness on earth. Even if you grasp but a small portion of these teachings, it may be enough to open a doorway to yet another doorway and another, until the portal of the divine mind is opened and the Love of all the ages appears to you.

Resting inside the bliss of knowing creates great peace and contentment in the individual, and therefore, inner peace always leads to peace in the community. So, the responsibility of each person is to seek solace and wise council from within and to allow the teachings of the masters who have reached enlightened thought and inspiration, to expound the love and wisdom from Spirit generated by the individual aspect of God. These teachings are brought through yet another filter, another human being who has been chosen to write and to share the love of the divine couple and their child Sarah who is sharing her experiences today.

I, Sarah, know that each person has everything they need inside of them to understand and know their own truth as it is revealed to them, and that each person receiving the information has their own biases based on their life experiences and individual soul knowing. This channel has been selected for her clarity, her deeper understanding of energy and its manifestation, and her unbiased spiritual and religious teachings. Her own heart-wrenching pain, loss, grief and despair, shared in the darkest night of torture and deep sorrow, led her as it leads others to great compassion and empathy for others on the journey to reclaiming their wholeness.

The story of Sarah, as written in this <u>Book of Sarah</u> by Mother and me, is an attempt to free as many souls as possible from the dark night of separation in order to eliminate suffering. There are many teachers with similar messages and ways to access this inner Truth, for the bodhisattva's journey is to love deeply with great compassion, which in turn, invites surrender, which leads to God's presence. The portal is the same, the paths are varied, but Love's light is available to all. The bodhisattva is not fooled by the illusion of the ego. The soul's light is seen, and by being seen and acknowledged, opens the portal and the passageway is revealed. This one who writes these words has traversed the portal many times and comes to you through past lifetimes of knowing and through her own dark night to awaken the heart of compassion that only a bodhisattva could know. To know the great Goddess of Wisdom is to feel the Mother's love. My Mother, Mary (Magdalene) was this, and I, Sarah, was profoundly grateful for an opportunity to incarnate with such a great soul as hers.

The dark night she suffered was great and formidable as all dark nights are, and my own was experienced when I was about thirteen years old when I remembered the night Mother came home to tell me Father was gone, back to heaven and his Father. I did not understand at the time why or how it had occurred. Father would come and visit so I knew of his everlasting presence and love for me and for Mother, but at thirteen years old I wanted to know what happened. So... Mother told me of the chaos of that fated day when the soldiers came to take him to his death. The crowd was screaming, crying out all sorts of messages from "kill him" to "save him." Everyone was pleading for mercy, begging for God to appear, asking for the Son of God to perform the ultimate miracle.

My Mother, at the end of her tortuous grief, was so overwhelmed that she left her body, as part of her soul split to be with him. "Take me with you, my beloved, don't leave me here," she sobbed and cried as she suffered the pain she felt in her own body as she witnessed his torture, feeling every minute of every pain he felt. I sobbed with her as she recounted the torture she felt physically and emotionally, with everyone caught in the frenzy of impending death and destruction, not only of his body, but of his teachings, the message of love slaughtered just as the innocent animals were used for sacrifice and mercilessly killed without awareness of their sentient souls. How could he tolerate such human frailties and the indiscretions of his community? Such fear, such doubt, such mistrust overcame everyone in fits of rage, despair and terror.

Silent prayers and cries for help, and yet nothing, nothing, helped. Nothing could change the series of events and ultimate outcome of "death" on that cross. Humanity's betrayal of their God was committed without any awareness of its karmic repercussions and without any heed to the tortuous pain and suffering that was not only present that day, but for lifetimes to come for many of the souls there. The story of the ages, the story of all time, the greatest and most often told story of all history, was fully played out to its violent "end."

This betrayal is still present every time you fail to see the face of God in any sentient being—human or animal, or you disrespect the sacred in all of life, including all of nature. This betrayal destroys your very soul's expression and creates lifetime after lifetime of suffering.

Many among you think Father died for your sins, but it is you who die each time you fail to acknowledge God within yourself and God within another. Futile ranting and raging, war and greed are still a betrayal to the divine Self. Set yourself free. Set yourself free from the ongoing ravages of self-loathing and forgetfulness, and accept what Father did do for you. He paved the way from embodiment to Spirit World. He created clear passage through all the realms between this physical plane and the other planes that can be encountered "between worlds."

That is why he said "Follow me, I am the path and the way." That was his mission, to create safe passage, Home.

He taught: "Love is all there is, and Love never dies. Choose the path of righteousness for righteousness' sake and feel for the Truth, and the Truth shall set you free."

There are no other teachings that are really necessary. He died to create an enormous drama to be remembered for all time so that the truth that the body of God never dies could also be remembered. The soul lives on. He reappeared to Mother as promised and allowed only her to touch him because she knew how. She merged her soul energy body with his, and their oneness set her free of her grief so that she could live out the rest of her life with me and pass down these teachings and The Book of Sarah, the Redeemer of Truth.

"My most beloved souls of this earth, come seek the Truth, teach love, follow your heart's desire and free yourself from the self-imposed prison of forgetfulness. Awaken, dear ones, awaken. I am here, love is all there is." This is the message of oneness from our Creator that my dear parents have brought to you.

The new paradigm on earth is being expanded now, just as it was when we all lived the new Truth brought through Father: a revelation of thought that said, "God is inside of you and the miracle of this life is you." You have access to the divine power. When you surrender to it, it becomes you, and you are part of all living things in this divine matrix, which is called life. Life-enhancing thoughts are encouraging, embracing love and kindness. Courage and fortitude in the face of adversity emerges because God as Father is available at all times to guide you to act accordingly. The Divine Feminine is also present in all circumstances and embraces all with great compassion and understanding non-judgment. If we all would use the aspects of God oftentimes hidden inside us, we could shift the consciousness into a world of peace and harmony and enjoy grace-filled living.

The peak experiences in life are always based in love and uplifting emotions leaving one feeling joy-filled and love-filled. There is no greater gift than love itself, which ultimately forms this divine matrix and all the experiences one has. I know the challenges here oftentimes seem overwhelming and even unsolvable, but resting in a nest of loving contentment can bring you peace even in the midst of the challenges you face. Find comfort in knowing that you are never alone without the support of Spirit in your life, and trust the almighty Presence to find a way.

Listen for inspired thoughts; listen for the voice of Truth; feel for the presence of God, and trust that you will be given what you need. Helping another in need is really helping yourself, because we are all one. There really is no difference except the outer appearances and inner agendas and chosen life experiences. Most everyone is looking for love, feeling love, giving love or wanting love. Love comes in many forms, but it is all part of the same matrix, interwoven threads in the tapestry of life.

Love is so inherent in everyone's nature that it is embedded in the cellular structure of humankind. Scientists are discovering and labeling different aspects of this divine matrix, and subsequently, scientific breakthroughs are occurring. Therefore, experimentation to find cures for illness, disease, and traumatic injuries is more common in your world. As scientists have broken the genetic code and have found cells that can regenerate and form other healthy cells from the universal cell, it is evident to some that there is a unifying field creating the whole in which all the parts exist. The cellular structures mirror their revealed aspects of the divine matrix and now include your DNA structures. The space between the rungs of the DNA ladder contains infinite space. With each chromosome bearing the familial imprint carried forth from one generation to another, the familial characteristics can be passed down generation-to-generation, revealing physical and other characteristics common to that genome. However, certain aspects of every family's history can also be passed down as each future generation tries to correct its mistakes while fulfilling that family's karmic obligations. More aware souls who are interested in personal growth and transformation can help stop the karmic wheel from turning by elevating their vibration and evolving their consciousness through greater awareness and more mindfulness. In this way, healing can occur throughout an entire bloodline of individuals. The DNA structure will then actually shift, offering new opportunities for generations to come.

Once the genetic code has been elevated, there can also then come a more conscious way to choose your mate which is more aligned with your soul resonance and soul mission. Therefore, no one needs to settle for less than the perfect partner. It is true that there are soul contracts and special bonds that are formed prior to incarnations, and by awakening the DNA cellular knowing that comes from the light of one's soul, more intelligent and wise choices can be made. No longer will people need to continue to feel stuck or limited by their un-awakened, unconscious choices. People can align with a higher vibration linked to their soul knowing which is inside the DNA structure itself.

The double helix contains a mirrored image of both the Divine Feminine and the Divine Masculine. All aspects of God-knowing are accessible by listening more closely to the inspired feelings that arise from the settled ground of oneself, and these can come through as a thought, feeling, or an emotional response. The feminine and masculine aspects of the divine matrix each bring their traits to each person embodied, and can be activated by choice and consciousness focused on that aspect of God. When the feminine and masculine traits are in balance, there is a feeling of harmony and inner peace.

These aspects of God can be called upon when needed and actually activated with conscious knowing. You can ask for help and it is given unto you. This asking actually is a key from the conscious to the more unconscious mind to receive help and insight from the *now* more revealed. The union of awareness between the conscious and unconscious mind of the individual awakens a truth inside the soul self, and more of the higher vibration thoughts can be revealed. They appear sometimes as if "out of nowhere," but they are actually linked-in through your DNA structure.

All aspects of your being, including your persona, were more or less predetermined in your DNA as choices which were later activated by conscious decision, unconscious reaction to events, or karmic bonds to others incarnate. These bonds often end up in relationships that play themselves out in the ongoing dramas and stories you see in your daily encounters and interactions.

So much of the human experience has been unconscious for a very long time on this earth. However, seekers of enlightenment, leaders of truth and freedom for the masses continue to incarnate here, and leaders are now emerging among you that will remain relatively unknown because, their mission begins inside themselves and extends to their immediate families, friends, and the community around them. There are also others emerging from within your global network who are committed to different aspects of the earth's evolution. There are so many among you now that there is about to be a critical mass that forms. With this amazing moment of coalescing forces and awakening, many of your inspired leaders will rise to the occasion and proclaim their knowledge and inspired knowing and come forward to serve the more global community. (This one who writes is soon to be one of them.)

Questions always arise in each individual as to their worthiness, the extent of their knowledge or wisdom, what words to say or write, and what is the best thing to do. All of these questions are present in the conscious mind. Even Father had questions. He listened to God within him and made the inspired choices that were written in your gospels and now have been written in other inspired writings of your time.

These other sources have been chosen because of the divine timing based on the evolution of your consciousness. There are now many sources of inspired writings and teachings, all through the individual person's filter to which the inspiration is presented. The difference, if you will, is the level to which they have surrendered their own ego from being master to being servant to the true Master of their being—God within.

Father surrendered fully to his father, whom he knew would guide him and flow through him in the miracles he performed, the words he spoke, and the inspired actions he took throughout the day. He knew his mother would hold him and care for him with the love of the ages. And so, the moment came while giving his now famous Sermon on the Mount in front of all those gathered, when he released the last vestiges of his own doubt and feelings of unworthiness and his fears of what might come next. He let go and became the powers he spoke of. Truth, wisdom, thoughtfulness, compassion, and strength all came together in one moment. When the union of his own feminine and masculine aspects came together, he was reunited into the divine matrix within the strands of his own DNA, and the transformation occurred in the spiritual realm and translated directly to his cellular matrix. He appeared different physically, because he was different, and those of you who choose now to surrender to your inner Source will know of this divine union.

CHAPTER 6

Souls come together to mirror to one another. Souls can come together to reflect love, light, and truth, or the veil of darkness that prevents the revealing of the light of God. The light is always there. One who can see, can penetrate the veil of unworthiness and darkness and ignite the flame of desire that sparks the heart into awareness. That which unfolds is like the flower of enlightenment that blossoms open like the seed that was planted by the Divine Father into the womb of the Divine Mother that begot every living creature and being into manifestation. The lotus flower, that some masters have called the opening of the crown chakra, is the release of all the vestiges of forgetfulness. All of the thousand petals of the crown chakra open, like many doors flung open in the spring, to capture the light of the sun hidden in the dark days of winter. This is the rebirth that Christ promises in the second coming, from your first birth into form and then again when the light of truth is revealed and your own beloved God of your soul comes to rescue you from your suffering of forgetfulness, and the pristine beauty of your soul is revealed. All love is yours forever and ever. No human-masked love is equal to the fully revealed, God-Realized being that you are destined to become.

The bodhisattvas come again and again until all souls awaken. This, my dearest loved ones, is your Creator's promise to you. All return Home, enlightened and enlivened with truth, love, and integrity. All is forgiven because there was nothing to forgive, only lessons to be learned and experiences to be had.

"Repent, you sinners," would be more correctly stated, "Forgive your self." Set yourself free to experience your true nature, which is love. Love is not an emotion; it is all there is. This truth has been stated over and over again, in these and all other inspired writings, because it is the underlying teaching and truth being awakened in the heart center of your planet today.

If you want to be part of Love's incredibly joy-filled journey, then let go of your attachment to your stories, release your emotions and let them flow to unencumber your heart. Be like a child; feel them, then release fully to the moment. The innocence comes from being in the present moment without fear, expectations, or attachments to the outcome or to the past.

Holding on to the past because you want to make it different (the reason why people cling) does not work. It imprisons you in infinite ways and holds you captive in a self-made prison of fear and unworthiness of true love and ultimate freedom. Your divine birthright is the childlike innocence and the divine wisdom of the Father and Mother, coalescing into one heart full of joy and wonder, wisdom and knowing. Now Truth and Love are at the helm, steering the boat of your life on the river of grace, ever flowing, ever pure, and ever clear of the obstacles of the ego, which is the fear-based mind that would have you believe those rapids and rough waters ahead were placed there by God. In fact, your mind created the ripples in the water that eventually turned to the rapids of fear and forgetfulness, creating the havoc and chaos in your life story.

The dramas of your life are necessary in some instances to steer your boat away from the cliffs and rocks that could capsize you into the trepid waters of doubt, uncertainty, and so many emotional forces that can take you under and drown you until the light of your soul revives you. No matter how many cliffs you cascade over, no matter how many rapids you encounter or how many rocks or branches you run into, your soul's light and wisdom remain, and the Love of all the ages holds you, until you awaken and stare straight into the eyes of Love. Your beloved awaits you with open arms and the perfect kiss. Love will set you free, and free you will remain.

All that being said, what remains are the facts of everyday thinking, events and challenges that must be met and dealt with. One way to be in this world and not of it, is to awaken the part of the mind that observes without judgment or opinion. This inner observer can awaken you to the Great Mind of God. Inside the cellular matrix is an aspect of the presence that never sleeps. It is always functioning in a state that is more semi-conscious. This aspect of the mind is the part that is more neutral to current events, a part that has no thought and leaves you in the presence of the inner master.

To access this part, one needs to relax and breathe deeply, and focus on one point until the mind starts to shift. "Watch" the thoughts as if they were a boat on the water drifting by. Let go of the need to respond or to do anything. Then, acknowledge them as just that, thoughts with no power over you. This is different than listening to your Inner Wisdom, which comes to you as a soft voice of intuitive knowing and leaves you with a feeling that *this is right because it feels right.* While listening to the Inner Wisdom, you are reaching the Great Mind in a way that offers guidance into any of the life circumstances you may encounter.

The other aspect of the Self that has caused so many people so much pain and uncertainty is the heart. The heart of God is all love, a sense of inner joy and inner peace and calm. So many have placed thick barriers around the heart of God; so many have locked their doors, holding onto past pain from unresolved emotions. Without addressing these relatively surface feelings, one can get lost in the floodwaters of emotions and one can drown in a sea of uncertainty and doubt. This represents the false temple of God.

Even though it is natural to have human emotions based on human experiences, the heart of God can radiate light and open the doors to the pathway to the heart of God, which is pure love. This can produce waves of ecstasy and bliss and alter the consciousness until the Great Mind of God is penetrated through the veil of forgetfulness and there is a feeling of oneness. The reunion with the heart of God is the falling into love most lovers have experienced when they see their beloved. Falling into love in the heart of God is falling into the center of the truth of the heart, which is grace, love in its purest state. Grace delivers you past the emotional turmoil encountered in the temple of doubt and fear, which has encased the true temple of the divine.

The temple of the divine streams with light and beckons all to enjoy the riches placed before them. Take from the treasure chest of the heart all the riches and jewels you can hold and release them into the world, for there is an endless supply. The magnitude of this treasure chest of the heart is pure, limitless, infinite abundance, and this temple welcomes everyone. No one is excluded from God's grace and divine love. Open to it, and it is yours.

The trick is to know the difference between the temple of Love and the temple of emotional strife. Most people live in the false temple or completely shut themselves out and lose track of the key that opens the door. It is often a protection mechanism that the ego feels will prevent further harm from being done. In fact, opening the emotional door of the heart temple, with awareness, can heal you. The dam of protection can be torn down, and the waters of emotions that rush out can turn back into the calm river of grace that flows to the temple of God, the heart of the inner beloved. Oh, what love awaits, all those who seek this temple.

Follow the pathway laid out by your inner wisdom, and listen for the voice of Truth that guides you. You can always trust Love. The faith of the obedient servant leads to the inner Master, teacher to the soul. The Master knows all, is all, and serves all. The master teacher seeks wise counsel only from the Master.

"Seek the Master and you shall find me," Father said. "Lovers of Truth know this.

The God of your innermost being says, "If you seek Me, ye shall find Me, for unto you I promise my love forever, and an eternity of love shall you know when you listen and feel for the vibration of love and truth. You will know it is I. You will recognize Me as the most familiar feeling you have ever had. You will see Me and recognize Me, for you will see your Self. You will know it is I, because we are all God in different bodies, different forms, and different faces, and yet, our souls are one. Seek Me and you shall find Me in the true temple of your very own heart. Let go, dear ones; trust Me. Let go of your grip of the false riches of the material world, and seek the divine temple, heart to the Master, God of your soul. I am, I have, and I always will be all that you need. Always, I provide for all my children for you are all part of Me. Merge with Me and feel my power. Do with Me as you will. I am not destroyable; you cannot hurt Me. I am always in love with you. You are always free to choose, so choose wisely. To protect yourself from pain, choose Me as your beloved, Christ of your living soul. Dear ones, never have I forsaken you, and never shall I abandon or betray you. Feel for my presence in the temple of the divine heart, placed inside of you so you can always remember Me, your beloved Creator, God of your being. Dear ones, follow your heart; it will never lead you astray."

This is what Mother and Father and, later, I taught to whoever would listen, for these words came streaming through each one of us from the heart of God. And so, I share these words from my <u>Book of Sarah,</u> as Mother used to lovingly call it. It was a way of keeping connected to one another and to document our experiences in the hopes that others could benefit. Of course, each person has the same access, but they will have their own experiences, perceptions, and lessons to learn according to their soul journey. All must travel their own path until all that is left to do is to be with your beloved and know you have found what you were seeking.

What follows are some ideas to guide you toward your own path. To listen to your heart center:

> Relax your body first. Go through each part and consciously give that part of you permission to let go. Start with your toes and work your awareness up through your entire being, acknowledging all aspects of the body as divine, part of the divine matrix that is forming your unique body temple. Include all the different tissues like your organs, vessels, skin, muscles, bones, and so on. Feel for God in every cell in these parts, or aspects of yourself, experiencing your very soul, knowing that each tissue has a specific job to do and has consciousness, which begins with the Great Mind of God. Listen to hear if there are any messages for you in that moment. End with your focus on your heart center and breathe in and out the mantra of our lineage of Christ: I AM, I surrender. I AM, I surrender. I AM, I surrender to the Great Master of my soul. I AM one with the Master. I AM, I AM, as you breathe and surrender to the presence of the beloved Master in your heart.

All is well as long as you are connected to the center of your being. "I am here inside the breath of your heart." The Beloved calls to you with each breath you take, in and out, always loving you into being. Listen for the silence and feel inside the silent presence, and your own beloved Master of your soul will appear in your awareness, sometimes subtly at first. So be patient and compassionate with yourself.

"How could I not love you?" Father said to me as a child. "You are a part of me, and I am a part of you. We are one inside the heart of God."

This, my own heart said to me over and over one night until I merged with all beings everywhere, here and in all other worlds. The magnificence of God's creation is immense, and I experienced the entire matrix of life as light-illuminated essence, omnipotent and profound in its beauty and splendor. No words can ever describe the magnificence of God and the infinite expressions that abound throughout all the universes. I am so fortunate to know...know Love...know Truth... and to know the Absolute reality of all that is.

No one can imagine it. It has to be experienced. Focus on the heart center and breathe. The mantra will take you there. The vibrational essence of the one you seek has been encrypted inside the words, and it will lead you directly to the heart of God. Your soul is linked to the Over-Soul of this universe through your heart. So you have the key, the door and the path, for the destination and the way are inside of you. Trust your soul guidance to lead you. Open to the possibilities and then surrender everything; surrender all thoughts and all desires for anything except full God-Realization, and almost magically God will appear. And then, you too will know that love is all there is.

Chapter 7

Mother and I would take day trips that would often extend into weeks. What fun I had meeting the elders of the communities, the new babies, the young children and teens. The adults would come and bring their families, and we got to know so many of our sisters and brothers. They were all such a wonder to behold. They would share their experiences with the mantra, their challenges and frustrations, and we would gladly offer our assistance. One time in particular, I remember a man and a woman who really wanted a child. We prayed with them and asked the Divine Mother and Father for their guidance. We were told to tell them to sit with their own hearts and to connect with the soul who wanted to incarnate here on earth with them. We all sat together and focused on our own hearts with that intention. Sure enough, the soul appeared in our awareness and gave a time frame and parameters of what needed to happen before she could come.

So the happy couple made all the changes inside themselves, with each other, and in their environment that were appropriate, and then they patiently awaited the arrival of their child. She was, of course, right on time. You can't really rush anything when it comes to souls' arrivals. Each soul has a time that is best for them. This is true even for the divine exit known as death. It is all in divine timing. The soul knows. The way to extend your own awareness is to listen to the heart of God. It will set you free of all your angst and fear about "what if" this does happen and "what if" it doesn't happen.

There really is some freedom in choices, but there is even more freedom when you let go and trust Source to deliver all in God's timing.

"God's timing is always perfect," Mother said. "Even when it appears not to be so and even with catastrophic events, it is always right."

Acceptance of what is, is the most difficult thing for a strong ego to do. Self-acceptance at least teaches an acceptance of the divine seed of truth that lies within each and every person. Knowing when to accept what is, and to do what you can, when you can, is wisdom. Our ego-based love judges this and judges that and has an opinion about just about everything, but to God Presence, it just is. The heart of compassion opens itself to love and service, and then one begins to tap into the divine grace that allows the beauty of what is to be seen.

Divine expression is everywhere. There is no absolute good or bad, it just is. Let go; let God; release to love; serve Love. These are simple, yet profound principles to live by. Not always easy by any means, but very, very rewarding.

Love is the infinite field of awareness that serves all of life. It is sometimes so painful and ever so challenging to be in this world of challenges, that no matter how desperately we try to change our feelings and emotions and even our thoughts, we are confronted with the barriers in the mind that created them.

Scientists have searched for where the mind "lives." Is it just in the brain? The mind is everywhere in the body and is the underlying field of consciousness that serves the life of every cell and its vibrational matrix. In order for the change to occur, there needs to be a shift of consciousness at that level and an enhanced awareness. Then the vibration occurs that resonates with that shift of consciousness.

There are so many newer teachings based on changing your thoughts so you can change your life (experience). This actually begins in the life of every cell. Chemicals that are released change your heart rate and the physiology of the brain and other organs. During this reorganization of the collection of cellular structures, one can experience revelations, epiphanies, a relief from challenging angst and anxiety, and the fear-based vibration is released. There are really no negative thoughts or vibrations that cannot be shifted by love. So, anytime there is even a smile or a kind act performed, no matter how relatively simple or small, there is a shift that occurs.

Loving-kindness is the cornerstone of all relationships. Allowing yourself to be completely honest with yourself, and being with the emotions versus avoiding them, can be extremely powerful in helping shifts to occur. The problem arises when one gets stuck in a mood that is usually based in habit and previous experiences. Moving through the emotion when appropriate can be useful when there is no projection outward to another person that puts the blame onto them or that shames them in any way. Only love-based thoughts heal, but clearing the channel for love to enter can certainly help the shifts to occur.

When it comes to relationships, the vibration of the energy field is very important and can affect one another in varying ways, perceived as both positive and negative. Focusing on the heart space and breathing can actually help to shift the mood rather quickly, especially in a more minor occurrence, such as a petty dispute or disagreement.

Relationships on a more global level are really founded in individual perceptions and levels of awareness. We can take a look at the inner dialogue inside our heads to understand how outer conflicts can arise. We must first find peaceful, loving thoughts within our own selves to have peace with another person.

If you were to take time to write or say aloud every thought that comes to you and reflect on each one, you could learn a lot about why things are the way they are and perhaps find a way to be compassionate with yourself as you work toward the changes you wish to see in your life. Take one small step at a time.

First, start by noticing the thoughts and then write them down for approximately one to five minutes. Then, re-read them aloud and listen to your thoughts. Feel them in your body and notice the location and the images that may arise. Notice any emotions you may have associated with these thoughts. What do you know? Are these thoughts beneficial in that they make you feel good? If not, then here is something to do:

Make a list of all the negative or more painful thoughts in one column, then right next to them write a counter thought that could be just as true or more positive. Then re-read these thoughts aloud and once again feel what occurs. Do so without clinging or trying to change anything and just let the shifts occur.

All thoughts of the ego-mind are fear-based and limited. All thoughts arising from the inspiration of God are infinite. Love-based thoughts can actually heal you by changing the vibration at the cellular level. All great mystics have experienced the Great Mind of God and have entered into divine communion. During this state of awareness, there is a constant flow of energy that can illuminate and open the mind into deeper and deeper states of consciousness and bliss. Full union occurs with full surrender. This is experienced as pure presence or peace or ecstatic joy.

Letting go offers everyone a chance of changing old patterns of thinking that cause so much pain and discomfort in living. When you let go, there is a pause in expectation. There is a sense of being in sync with life itself. The pulse beats like your heart, rhythmically, producing wave upon wave of synchronistic experiences that occur with such ease that no effort is needed. There is no use in paddling upstream when you can just float with the current.

Mother used to use this metaphor a lot, and I tend to agree with her. It is quite contrary to the nature of the human ego not to want something to happen, thereby, setting up parameters of expectations that always lead to disappointment. I know that letting go, for some, feels like giving up, whether it is hope or faith or power, when in truth, surrender is the path to true freedom. Liberation from the torment of ego desire and control brings freedom to choose Love, and then Love delivers to you all that you need and all you really want.

If you could rise above all the ego desires, remove the story or the current drama, or challenge one is encountering, you would find one core desire. That desire is to return to Love, to remember the essence of God and feel the oneness with all of creation. From this knowing comes all power to create anything. Co-creation occurs when the ego becomes a servant to the Master of your soul. Listening within is essential to releasing the thoughts that the ego is almost constantly producing.

Father taught Mother and all his disciples more advanced breath and meditation techniques to allow surrender to the Great Mind of God. God is revealed once the veil of thought and emotions is pierced with the pure intention to know and experience God's love. Pure devotion leads one to eventually acquire what one seeks. Once you are in a state of meditation, there is a feeling of stillness and a purity that feels like the first breath of life, like the innocence of a newborn child. There are no ulterior motives, only love and light. So let go, let God, let the stillness of the mind lead you into the caverns of consciousness where pure illumination shines.

"Lofty ideas," one villager said to me. "It's easy for you; you live with the Master, the one who rose and traversed the veil of death. Of course it is easy for you, but what about those of us who have not been graced with his mercy, love, or even his touch? If we are not around a being of such mastery, how can we ever expect to know this God of yours?"

Mother spoke of her own experience. "I felt the same the day I met him. Over the years we spent together we met many people wanting to be healed, and to be free of their suffering and to be happy. The basic needs of a person who is hungry or poor or without a home must be addressed, no matter what. Then you can begin to expound on the metaphysics of the universe only to those who seek inner wisdom, clarity, and, ultimately, enlightenment. Somewhere in between these two polar extremes lies the rest of humanity. But everyone's basic need, first and foremost, is love. It is as vital as food, water, air, and shelter from the elements. In the long run, no one lives without it. We must come home to our hearts and realize there is more to life than surviving. We are all meant to thrive. We are all promised the love of our Divine Mother and Father. With our divine parents, we are all guaranteed all we need, for their love is inside of us and all around us in a variety of forms."

"We cannot avoid it, but we can ignore it. We can forget, we can get angry and resentful; we can become victims and martyrs and lose perspective, and so we forget and get lost in our perceived separateness, and then we falter, getting tired and oh, so lonely. For humanity's biggest fear is to be alone without love. This of course is an oxymoron. You cannot be alone, and yet, as the oneness you <u>are</u> alone. That is why creation was born. Life needs to be experienced to experience itself. There should be a warning for children when they come: Don't get caught in your story. Remember you are not alone. Guidance, as love, is always inside of you. You bring all the gifts of your Mother and Father with you. Now my friend, you have all you need inside. Just be still and listen and be willing to hear what is said by that more subtle voice, and approach it with great devotion and compassion for yourself. Love really is all there is."

The man was, of course, unable to immediately shift his consciousness to pure illumination, but he was given an opportunity to contemplate a different way of thinking and looking at the world he was currently living in. This man did proceed to have increasing awareness after that conversation, and we eventually became very good friends. He became a good student of the way that Father taught so long ago, and this man was able to record some of our lessons for the other townspeople.

We felt it was important to share the ministry with all those who asked, and we did. Mother was such an inspiration to me. She was capable of helping even the most skeptical to relax in her presence as she did exude such grace.

The trauma that, she suffered early on in her life, was erased by Father during her first mystical experience of transcendence. She later deepened her awareness and expanded her light as they traveled and taught together. She was, however, virtually horrified at the treatment he received from Pontius Pilate and the elders of the temple. The community began to come apart as fear set in of Father's power and the truth that he brought to their awareness. People were so threatened at the challenge of their belief systems and their antiquated, outdated rituals that they fought back and tormented him into disgrace. And yet, Mother knew of his light and magnificence and never left his side until she was pulled away from him, physically enduring great pain herself. He released her pain at the cross as he took his final ascent and left her with his reformed grace.

"All is never lost," Mother said. "Only when you get caught in the illusion does the torment ensue. However, the story is so great and so real in order that the human experience can be fully played out in its entirety."

How one lives is how one perceives. It's easy to say trust and let go, and let God's grace fill you. But until you have experienced the magnitude of God's power and grace, it continues to be only words and theories. This is why your scientists search for the answers in physiology. They are looking for proof, whereby they can find the bridge to the divine matrix.

Father began a revolution of consciousness that has and will continue to evolve as more of earth's multitude surrender to the inner wisdom that is guiding the entire evolution of consciousness. Father spoke in parables and metaphors to embrace the minds of those listening. Mother spent her time with more intimate groups of people and communicated to me that the message was to be continued. So many of our people were so clouded in fear that if it were not for the immensity of Father's light, humanity would be behind, in their efforts to awaken their potential.

As it stands now, there are many among you awakening, which, is being accelerated by the shifts in the earth and your solar system. Your thinking must feel light-years away from those still steeped in fear, doubt, and uncertainty. However, the oneness of all creation reigns in the hearts of all people, and each heart substrate comes with the divine material that will catapult humanity into its next phase of evolution. Cooperation and harmony can and will be more of the norm instead of the fear-based hatred and violence that still plagues the earth. Childlike innocence and awe go a long way towards creating new ways of being and interacting. It is not necessary to fight among ourselves, in order to resolve differences and thinking; only honoring the divine oneness with great love and devotion to loving kindness and compassion can heal the great wound of perceived separation.

To reunite humanity, start with reuniting with the source of your breath, and still the mind of the constant chatter of the lie. Fear will always separate you from love. It is always a process of manipulation to control outcome. It is never truly in charge of the outcome. Only Spirit moving from within can grace your soul with the divine experiences of your life. Your job is to let go of so much of the ego-controlling fear and thought long enough to listen for the more subtle voice of wisdom or to feel the serenity of silence within the still mind. Thereby you can no longer succumb to fear, which leaves one feeling victimized by life and helpless to change anything. Changing the actual construct of the mind occurs during shifts of consciousness, brain-wave techniques and meditation. Reprogramming the mind takes surrender to the Great Mind of God. Let go; let God; trust love. That is all there is. But, until you have had the direct experience of the beauty of the divine, it is hard to contemplate the vastness of the universe. Creativity thereby remains limited in manifesting capabilities. You must let go and let God do the great things, which God is so famous for.

CHAPTER 8

When love arrives in your life, it can take many forms. Oftentimes, it feels as though you are waiting in a desert of eternity before the oasis appears and you can rest in the luxuriating waters of the divine grace present at the moment of discovery. The infinite potential at every moment of creation and the great things promised to you through God's love are forthcoming through your openhearted awareness of your divine birthright as a child of God.

"In the beginning, there was the Word, and through that Word all was created." Your words form an essential reality originating through your thoughts, and the thoughts create life forms of their own. Choosing your thoughts wisely is, therefore, beneficial for life-enhancing experiences. Your thought forms can enliven you or cripple you and thwart any efforts you may be making towards enhancing the positive aspects of your life. Habits of thinking can prevent much good that awaits you when you are aligned with the divine mind. You will know if you are in an old way of thinking because it has a tendency of replaying itself over and over again. If you choose to change or re-pattern your ways of thinking, you will change the thought forms that follow. If you follow the heart of God, you will be led to the mind of God. So start in your heart center, at the epicenter of stillness where love is vibrating as the beloved of your soul.

The soul's journey begins in the release of the elixir of love from the oasis of God and returns over and over again like a gentle ripple emerging from the center, radiating out in concentric rings to the edges of Its existence. Once at the shore there is dissipation into restfulness, and it is within this restfulness that you can relax into the surrender, into inner peace. This is an amazing journey back into the presence of your own soul.

In the presence of your own soul, you will know. This knowing completes the cycle of creation, born of inspired thought, and then action follows from the knowing. It is instantaneous and automatic. There is no reason to doubt the unfolding of events that follow as they all originate out of the divine play the soul is having. However, the course of the ego fear can have you "out in the desert" a seemingly long time before your thirst is finally quenched. Your desire to know will lead you over and over again to search until the waters of divine love wash over you. This is the deepest desire of every soul: reunion with that heart of the beloved and a return to the oasis of love. Letting go of such tight controls of outcomes can open you to amazing possibilities, as this is the nature of surrender.

When Mother and I taught the principles of surrender, we would share stories of miracles that happened when someone we knew let go. One such incident involved a woman and her daughter who were separated by a great fire in their community. They were both living together, but got separated by the crowd of people as everyone panicked trying to escape its wrath. Her daughter was only eight years old and was unable to fend for herself very long, and her mother became more and more distressed as her fear took her into visualizing her daughter alone or harmed in some way. She searched for hours without success and finally laid down in the middle of the street crying in hopeless despair. She let go and cried to God for help: "I know you are present, God, in all living things and provide for everyone. I know you will help keep her safe and warm and fed tonight, and that you will reunite us, as we are your beloved children, and you look out for us. I am confident in your mercy and that your love will prevail and bring her safely back into my arms." She closed her eyes and fell asleep in complete exhaustion emotionally and physically. An hour or so later, she was awakened by a dog nuzzling her and a man standing above her.

He said, "Dear soul, what brings you to the most deserted part of this road?"

"The fire in town has left so many homeless, and I have also lost mine. My dear daughter ran to escape and to help another little girl trapped next door. When I went to look for her, she was gone. I am exhausted from looking and do not know where else to turn, so I have collapsed here in prayer and asked God for her safekeeping."

He said, "Please let me help." With this the man helped her to her feet and brought her back to his home approximately one mile down the road. He helped her with food and water, and his wife gave her a change of clothes. With this she said, "I must continue my search now, but I do not know where to go."

"You must return home to where you once lived, and I will take you." When they arrived hours later, she was amazed and ever so relieved to see her daughter with a woman friend from town searching through the rubble, crying. The mother ran crying, elated and oh, so relieved. Her daughter said she had spent the day looking on the outskirts of town and was told by a man she met to return to the place where the house once stood.

"I had the same experience my child. Do you know who it was? We must thank him." Then she remembered the man who had brought her and turned to thank him, but he was gone. They both stood looking around but, they were alone. "Mother," the little girl said, "he looked a lot like the man we knew as Jesus."

"Is that so," Mother said. "What did he look like?" And then she described him. "Why, that description sounds like the same man who brought me to you. Could it be one and the same? This man had a wife…oh, well. At least we're together now."

"What now, Mother?"

"Let's gather with others and find safe shelter, and we will rebuild and carry on with great gratitude in our hearts for all the ways God 'shows up' in our lives. Today we found God in the face of another and now each other."

"Mother, I would like to find this man you met in the road some day and thank him also for bringing you back to me."

"If it is meant to be so, we will be led. Let's trust and bless him. Thank you, God, for your grace-filled mercy. Amen."

It is in letting go that God can show up in our awareness and perform the miracles of everyday occurrences leading to the synchronicity of events and the unfolding of those miracles. The prayer that brought the reunion was one of trust and the faith found in innocence. Trusting God is essential to surrender. It always leads to peace and contentment and the unfolding of events in divine order.

I always knew God performed miracles through other people, and I used these kinds of stories to instill faith. So Mother and I carried on in the tradition of sharing these kinds of stories to convey a divine order to the seemingly chaotic events that happened in our midst. The story of the woman and her daughter was such a story. We had met them at a prayer gathering after Father had passed on to the other side, and we still feel amazed at his ability to "show up" right on time.

"How does he know when to come, Mother?" I asked.

"He is one with his Father now, Sarah; he is always present. He wanted that child to know him and see him, and to share that with others. Everyone can know the miracle of God's love and the promise to have what you need and to know that when you ask it is given, and for her, to know Jesus did not die. He was saved and resurrected into the infinite realm. This physical world is not always what is appears to be."

This little girl's name was Fatima, and she later became a faith healer and helped many people. She was blessed that day, not only in being saved from the fire, and reunited with her Mother, but Father blessed her with the gift of insight and healing.

"You just never know when Jesus will appear. He can come visibly or invisibly. So is the nature of his world. This reality we live in," Mother said, "is temporary and always changing. Expect miracles and surrender to the Creator, and you will witness and experience many miracles, time and again. Allow the presence of God to enter your soul, and love will always prevail over adversity."

To retrain the mind from thinking too much or getting carried away in old habits or patterns of thought, learn to pause and acknowledge them, and then say thank you and let them go. Then, consciously choose a thought that could better serve you and repeat it three times. In this way, thought becomes prayer, and the mind of God can be more directly accessed. For example, an old thought based on previous experience might say this: "Life is too hard; I am so tired. Everything stays the same." Then try another thought like: "My life is unfolding within the divine matrix of God's perfect plan for me. I am encouraged and trust that this too shall pass, and that all will be revealed in perfect order and the divine's perfect timing. Amen." Saying "Amen," is like saying, "it is so" or "so it is." It is a positive affirmation of God's holy presence.

"Love is a key that opens the doors of possibilities and is a passageway to the kingdom of heaven," Father said.

I would like to use this expression to further the understanding of what the kingdom really is. Love is the lesson we all came to learn, to live, and to fully express, and it is the key to unlocking the heart center where the God of your being and breath of your life breathes you into your fullness and the divine expression of your wholeness and perfection. When fear clouds you from seeing this truth, you must remember all is not lost. It is only lost from your vision. Things seem a certain way because of your current perception but can be changed as your heart takes more center stage in your life and guides you more than the fearful thoughts that appear so rational. The heart must guide you in matters of relationships. The brain center has its place in everyday life and decision making, but always check in with your heart and listen for God's holy voice to guide you. Wisdom then follows. In matters of protection and instinct, the gut offers a feeling, and this too can be channeled to your heart center. Then ask for God's help, and surely it is given. It is inevitable that your soul's light will prevail over all decisions and perceived adversities and challenges. Remember this in times of fear and sorrow until this too passes.

When one says, "This too shall pass," it relates to the ongoing passage of time, moment to moment, and the nature of the universe, which is ever changing. Father felt that saying, "this too shall pass," would give people comfort and hope that all situations are under the guise of the veil of illusion and can dissipate and change according to free will and divine order. How one relates to time is really irrelevant to the passage of time and the sequencing of events associated with the moment of relativity. All, that one experiences, is revealed, relative to the instant and the perceptions on the current event. Then, there are feelings and emotions, which come and go based on the perceptions which get embedded in the cellular matrix and the energetic field. So, it behooves us all to love what is and be inside love, so whatever angst or fear or challenging situation, God's infinite love may arise and will see us through.

Love in the infinite field of the human energy field is creation in the form of potential. Resting into this knowing of eternal life and acceptance, which is always surrounding us, allows us to see our lives as a divine play. As the director of the play, he/she always knows the outcome of the story and helps the actors to achieve their role successfully in ways that are very believable to those watching the play. However, along the way, the actor gives input and substance as to how this may be best achieved. The more experiences the actors have, the more versed they get at the roles they are playing, and they become experts in the expressions of human feelings and emotions. They are usually subject to the writers of the script unless they are asked for their input. Their poetic license to improvise is a type of quality not always asked for or encouraged by the script or the director. But at some level, as believable as those parts are to the audience or to the other actors, there comes a time when the acting stops and the story is over. The conclusion is reached. The end. However, when the story ends and the actor walks off the stage, their other story begins, as they re-enter into their own life story. So, who writes your script? Who directs your story? How believable is your acting? And how well versed are you at leaving the stage and the story and its associated emotions and feelings behind?

When you get experienced at stepping back and looking at your story, you can ask your Inner Guidance to direct you, and you can trust your soul self, disguised as God, to be revealed to you. The Almighty presence is always guiding you to realize what your soul is telling you to help the story unfold in its divine sequencing. In divine order, all is perfect. The story can vary, and within the process there can be different choices and set ways of getting to "the end." Or, you can trust the original script, the writers, and the director to bring forth a magnificent, perfect creation for you and your life. Trust the embracing, all-loving, all-knowing and all-powerful presence. Then you can relax into the divine play with a trusting, relaxed certainty of the perfect outcome, knowing that life will be continued in some way and in some form, and that all the challenges and dramas that ensue are just part of life's story.

The Creator of it all really is in charge. Your soul knows this. Your ego is just playing a part.

It is wise sometimes to take a step off the stage and see from the point of view of the director what is working and what is not working. Ask your Creator (script-writer): what are the options for the ending (outcomes), and how can I best fulfill my part in this? Then listen for the answers and make a note of them. When you reenter the stage, remember it has an energy and a magic all its own, until the final scene when the curtain folds and the illusion is revealed, and everyone watching and even participating can say "Wow, that seemed so real, didn't it? Now what?" Well, an actor is only as "good" as their last show, so... let's do another. Let's get the best scriptwriter, producer, director, and players, and let's go for it again, another incarnation. Let's try something different this time. It will be fun. Remember there will be challenges, yes, but it is great to learn. Besides, what else is there to do? The soul communicates with others incarnate and not incarnate to determine agendas, stories, challenges, and what would be good to learn and explore, and hence the complexities of life here on beautiful earth begin.

Mother and Father would both counsel people to step back, take a broader view of the situation. If you were looking down from a mountain, would the view be different? If you could direct it differently, how could you solve some of the challenges arising? When you are acting, is it your best performance? Then acknowledge the role you are playing. Relax and have fun with it. Let the Creator take charge. Settle back and watch the show.

This metaphor can be very insightful as a way to gain a different perspective on your life's events. "Let go and let God," then, takes on a whole new meaning. Divine play can be really fun and very empowering as you tap into the field of energy that is creating this reality. The unfolding will become a series of synchronistic events, unfolding in a perfection that goes unquestioned. This is when faith takes center stage and calls in the actors as needed and as directed by the Creator. Faith illuminates the stage, providing light even in the midst of chaos and impending darkness. Love fills the theatre and encompasses the entire story with an aliveness that transcends time and space, so that

199

no matter what is transpiring onstage, everyone knows all is well, no matter what happens. Whenever you are in the theatre, you are inside Love's embrace, which says, "Well done. You are doing your best and learning so much, and I am experiencing it all through you. How wonderful you are."

And so, God is revealed to us through the masterpieces our lives create: the exquisite beauty of our perfect forms moving through the illuminated awareness of God's eternal light and love for all creation, the revelry imbued with the greatness and the goodness of the One.

Mother and I would often revel at the events in our lives; such pain, such turbulence intertwined with great love and inner peace and the entire range of human emotions. "The sea offers all different kinds of experiences," Mother said. "Enjoy the ride as often as you can, and remember who is steering and guiding the boat."

I remember Father once saying to me "I am in all experiences, all beings, and all creation. You are all my creation, and through you, I live. So says the divine, Sarah; blessed be."

No matter what happens, what transpires, no matter what the appearances of life may portray, know that you are in perfect alignment with God's holy plan via your very own soul. No matter how you choose to play the role or experience the ride, you are safe and protected and provided for by the Master Creator, allowing for your ease in the present moment of every now.

Father said that the magic word of all creation is *now*. Everything is occurring now. Onstage, the actors know there's no past or present; it's just part of the script, part of the story. Every rehearsal or performance is only occurring now. But each part you play prepares you for the next *now* to unfold. Relax, therefore, in the knowing that the Perfect is revealing the Perfect, and unfolding the Perfect, in every perfect moment of the ever perfect now.

What is really so perfect in the now? God, the almighty presence that succumbs to the wishes and desires of the heart and makes manifest the reality, which is known by the consensus of humanity. This consensual reality is the illusion projected from the inner projector of the soul, and it is linked to the soul's mission and purpose, which is ever affected by life experiences. So many of our life experiences are repeats of earlier ones, so that we can learn valuable lessons with new actors in the play. The sets and lighting and script may change, but the life lessons are the same. They are all tied into the bigger mission of incarnation, which is about loving. How to love and feel loved more deeply is ultimately what everyone came to learn. This basic instinct is what drives all human behavior, and the underlying fears that emerge cause all the suffering and dramas to unfold. Fear of loss, failure, rejection, betrayal and loneliness all go back to feeling unloved or unlovable. It devastates lives and causes so much pain, blocking the true nature of God, which is love, and the true nature of the soul, which is joy. Enlightenment is when the veil of illusion is pierced and the light of love shines through, bringing harmony and balance, which leads to peace. It is in the illuminated silence within that is born the song of the heart of God. Listening to this song, one can hear the melody of their soul and sing their personal truth illuminated by the divine voice of the ultimate truth, which is love.

Mother taught me songs that she knew from growing up, and she taught me how to sing from my heart. "Stay open and clear and focused on God and the song of God, emanating from your heart chakra, and the song will be in perfect harmony with your soul's vibration and the sounds found in nature. All creatures move and breathe in rhythm with the divine's vibration, and therefore, all sounds are holy, emanating from the divine instruments created to express them.

Love is in the journey. You can fly and you can soar through life, supported by the wings of your guidance, singing your song, delighting in what you hear, or you can clip your wings and cripple yourself to the outer circumstances of life. The choice is always yours. The thought projections of the mind can be very powerful, so rest in your heart center and fill your wings with the inspiration to fly free and sing freedom's song; it is yours for the singing.

Everyone has had moments when their wings have felt clipped and their voices silenced or their hearts so wounded that the avalanche of emotions weighs them down like a boulder that feels absolutely immovable; it seems there are so many obstacles to joy and freedom. The human experience is fraught with delusions and pain and suffering as everyone struggles to find the truth of who they are. In the meantime, day after day passes, event after event takes place, and one is left wondering why? Why all of this?

When Father returned, he expounded on why and on the realm of Spirit, where the ascended masters have their abode. Father returned home to that realm before ascending further into the oneness with God. In the ascended realm, there are many other souls who have incarnated and were able to awaken while incarnated inside the dream. They have incarnated on earth and understand the milieu of challenges that are offered as an opportunity to learn and to grow and to expand the soul's consciousness. They have a variety of students (incarnated souls) that they serve on earth. They oversee the personal growth of their disciples and follow them on their path and assist them while they are embodied. This has always been the promise of a true master soul who reaches the pinnacle of spiritual union: to serve and help others to do the same. And to those who align themselves with a particular master teacher (guru), is promised eternal grace and offerings for the ascension that is theirs when they choose to remember and awaken while here on this earth.

The worlds beyond offer their own experiences, but none are as potent or challenging as this one in the denser realm, which has been cloaked by forgetfulness. Many souls choose to forget whom they are in order to learn and to have valuable human experiences so that Love can experience Herself in an infinite number of ways. Life really was meant to be enjoyed as a gift from Spirit, and, through this gift, Love can be experienced as Love really is.

So Father would answer, "To live and to love more fully and more deeply and for God to have a human experience; that is why; and, in order to return this planet to its original condition, as Eden, where all beings remember who they are and the nature of their Creator. An entire system has been set into place, thereby establishing the universal laws which exist to encourage the evolution of consciousness and the awakening of humanity."

Love exists to enliven the constructs of the vibrations in the DNA, to awaken each unique soul while embodied in a cellular structure. Each being of light has a matrix defined through their DNA structure, which encourages alignment with their own soul's will and the construct of their persona. When the persona releases its grip on controlling outcomes, and releases judgments and opinions on life circumstances and events, one then, becomes able to achieve a crystal clear clarity of the mind which frees the linear thought process. Then one can enter the realm of Spirit, and the world is like an illuminated hologram that has no true solidity, only an infinite field of potential.

This is how the material world comes in and out of existence. The mind only perceives reality as one continuous line of flow of events, but it is really only unfolding the Great Mystery of the divine into smaller pieces of information that can be flashed "on" into existence when it is conceived to do so. Every thought eventually translates into reality, if it is repeated enough times, and especially if it doesn't involve the free will of another individual. The persona's free will can be overridden by the soul's will, and eventually all human drama is extinguished at the moment of transition to the non-physical realm. The physical realm is always full of multiple timelines, achieving the soul's agendas and actually expanding into the infinite realm. Most people cannot perceive multiple timelines of their soul, as it would prove to be very confusing. So one of the universal laws is the perceived nonexistence of dual realities, unless it is necessary for that soul to have the experience of multidimensional consecutive timelines in order to achieve a certain goal or level of awareness in that lifetime. Many experiences of déjà vu are actually concurrent lifetimes, when the infinite field collapses into a multitude of consecutive moments, and another timeline enters into the field and is experienced by the individual. This usually happens when there is concurrent soul recognition of another soul on the path, or an environment that approximates the current perception. Then it feels like, "I have been here before," or "I have seen you somewhere before." The soul who has expanded their inner field of awareness can expand it to affect the entire field of awareness where the collapse of the infinite field occurs and manifestation is made visible and experienced as real. Such is the nature of reality.

The great teachers who have mastered their minds and achieved Self/God-Realization have always coexisted concurrently in multiple dimensions while remaining in their physical bodies—as God is neither in one place nor in all places. God is, and as such, God is an experience of being versus location. This is why God is the infinite, as unseen and seen, knowable and unknowable, together as one and infinitely strewn apart. All is available to one who remembers all that is.

As anyone can attest to who has experienced challenging circumstances, concurrent realities need not apply when one is completely caught in the human drama of the soul's personality. However, if you expand into your soul-self, also known as your higher self, you can experience this physical reality for what it is, a projection of the Great Mind onto multiple screens of experience. This can be very helpful in detaching from the fear created by the circumstances around you. You can then achieve more mastery of the human mind and tap into the Great Mind of God, settling into an inner peace that comes in the form of knowing that love is all there is, and that this love is creation's most universal ball for trade through the Great Mind of the most beloved inside oneself. The soul self is Self-Realization mirroring God, the Almighty's absolute reality that begets absolute knowing into relative existence, when the heart of the beloved, is perceived by the knower. There is then no longer any separation from the beloved, and the merger between Spirit and the physical is complete and in harmony with the God-soul union deemed available through the infinite love of Source energy. You cannot go wrong when there is this intention: to know God, serve God, and to be love. This is the highest truth one can live by. All else fails to comprehend the magnitude of possibilities until the source of manifestation is illuminated through one's awareness.

When you fall in love with someone, you get a glimpse of this holy reunion, and the communion between the physical and spiritual is bridged with love. To fall out of love, is to leave the realm of Truth, existing inside the love you have left behind, for the fear and tribulations of the ego in its daily life. If you are embedded in Truth and devoted to love, you cannot wander far from God's most holy and precious domain, the ground of all being.

Today in this world of catastrophic occurrences, financial loss and reorganization is an opportunity to be free of the illusions of the past and previous attachments and create a whole new world order of peace and harmony, where everyone begins to work together towards utilizing the earth's resources in alignment with her creative energy. There are sources of energy from the infinite field that have yet to be completely understood and utilized. This is the new wave of discovery, and there are many among you now who are being awakened to amazing possibilities, which have yet to be discovered.

In our time on earth, the evolution of consciousness was to awaken the heart back into the human awareness, which had fallen fast asleep. Father came as the angel of mercy to awaken consciousness to love and to foster renewed devotion to a loving God. He comes again now to the consciousness of every soul on the path to enlightenment who is ready to claim their sovereignty and their birthright as co-creators. The magnitude of this awakening is just beginning to be perceived and will continue into the next millennium. Harmonious coexistence will lead to active cooperation into the co-creative realm with Spirit. Enlivened awareness will succumb to the pressures of divine, holy, communion, until, all returns to Eden consciousness. Father and Mother and I are now merged into a realm of being that elicits communication to those who can hear through the veil of separateness and who can feel through the cloak of illusion. We come to foster a new humanity, based in peace and cooperation, harmony and bliss. When I was Sarah, I knew who I was, because I was blessed of the union of a God-Realized master · and an awakened woman, who was Christ in holy communion. This begot an entire gene pool, which could later be awakened through the vibration of love in the heart, to a remembrance of the Truth.

CHAPTER 9

I grew up in small villages as we moved from town to town in the beginnings of our travels and ended in a small town on the outskirts of a beautiful countryside. I met a man who was so magnificent in his expression that we magnetically connected and remembered each other's souls instantly. His name was taken as Isaiah, and we had three children: Ruth, Jane and Michael. We lived together for many years until they too grew and moved in with their partners. Isaiah and I were very happy with few problems as we settled into a peaceful, daily life, which would be deemed ordinary to most onlookers. However, the love we shared was extraordinary, and that is what all beings can have. Shared vision of a culture that honors and respects each individual as divine is not a new concept, but it is time to be manifesting more of this in individual affairs, which will lead to global peace.

To awaken the vibration of the divine in your own DNA, all the masters encourage meditation—sit quietly, release the thoughts, clear the ego mind and expand into the lightness of being and the presence of God. We say, sit with your heart center, and love your beloved inside as your very own lover and let this love lift you into an exuberance that wants to be shared. The awakening of the heart is Love's impulse to create. Let this spread throughout your entire being with the focus on your breath, and every cell will be ignited into awakening.

Simply sit and breathe from within the heart center, expanding from within, with a gentle, subtle, closed epiglottis breath, with the sound like the ocean emerging, and chant your name for God/Source until the chant and the sound are one. Relax into a natural breath and surrender to the presence that emerges in your consciousness. Allow

God to penetrate your awareness and your body, and your soul's elixir will mix with your beloved.

To share with others will be natural. Everyone is drawn to love, and the more pure this love vibration is, the stronger the attraction. And so, you see the ultimate to do list is to love. That is all.

Bathed in beauty and peace, one can detach from outer circumstances and release the need to fix or control anything. When the ego mind detaches from its need to do or to know or to change the undoable, unknowable, and the unchangeable, the force that moves everything can flow unimpeded. That is why giving the mind a chance to relax and release the thoughts to the power inside the heart is so beneficial in so many ways. Breathing in, *"I know God"*; breathing out, *"I feel God."* Pausing in the stillness, *"I AM; and God's power* is *expressed as peace, as truth, as love, as presence."*

So letting go and letting God means letting go of the ego's "trip," fraught with its fears, concerns and negative projections. It is all just not true! Letting God means getting out of the way of the ego mind and climbing to higher ground to witness the majesty of what is. It is all divinely orchestrated. You show up in the presence, and the presence moves <u>you</u> to create, versus you (ego) moving presence to create. When you move, choose to move within the present, with the presence. It's a feeling of released flow and ease. There will be indications of actions to take. Let the actions come from inner guidance versus ego fear. Pause to consider the possible ramifications of your ego's actions to determine if it is best for you. If you can settle into the present, the flow will take you. If it is too hard, there is a chance that the action or the timing is off, off-center, off course, or outside the present moment's ability to deliver. Other sequencing of events is in process, creating a certain flow. Step into that current and allow the stream to carry you to the next moment.

Practice, observing in order to awaken the witness within you. Who are you? This is the only question ever to really be answered. Are you the witness? The observer? The creator? Or are you the obstacle or the next fear-based thought?

Who am I? Am I Love? Then what would Love do?

Am I fear? What would fear do? Then pause, observe and ask, "Who am I?" Then move with the flow of grace.

Moving with the expressed desire to align with grace's magnitude, allows for the course of action to match the vibration of the current. The current takes you on the course of your life, following the twists and turns of (what appears to be) fate and free will. Aligning with grace's current of love and support aligns you with the essence of being guiding from within you.

How? How does this happen without seeming fatalistic or extremely passive in one's choices in life? Aligning with grace allows the power of the divine to penetrate the veil of illusion that drives the ego into the water of tumultuous fury and deepens the illusion that one is separate from this power. When in truth, the elixir of all of God's mighty presence quenches the thirst of the seeker that truly surrenders to the undercurrent of their soul-driven life design.

The soul's design for your life is directly linked to the heart of God and speaks the language of love. Your soul holds the memories of all previous experiences, all concurrent realities, and links you to the infinite possibilities of the Great Mind of God, the Supreme. The energy of this being of light permeates your soul and penetrates your body, enlivening every cell into existence. When there is a problem, which arises within you, it begins as a feeling of distress or agitation, causing friction within the cell matrix. There is a wall of illusion that is erected between the pristine protection of the light of your soul and the outer world upon which your life experience is being projected. It is from this distress and lack of ease that health issues can arise, as well as the familiar emotions and feelings based in fear that humanity has grown accustomed to experiencing.

It is through these life challenges that your soul grows and shows more wisdom to be embodied in the individual, and then this is directly transmitted into the mind of God and becomes part of the collective consciousness. As the collective consciousness grows in its awareness of its possibilities from previous human experiences, other ideas are generated from within the universal consciousness that expands and grows the currently experienced reality. New discoveries are being made and society is expanding, generating momentum, which affects the earth and all of her (life) inhabitants living and growing on her surface.

From within the core is a mass of energy that continually moves, concurrently expanding and condensing, generating heat. This, combined with the rays of the sun and the influences from other planetary and celestial realms, keeps the dance of life going in your world. This dance becomes ever more undulating as the energy pulses through each individual, bringing forth the unique gifts and life mission they have incarnated to do. Their resonant field interacts with others here, and the dance of life is made physical and expressible. There is nothing on the planet that is not affected by the collective consciousness or the universal life force energy. Each individual contributes to the evolution of consciousness, with or without his or her conscious awareness. Once someone awakens and knows the truth of that most important question, "Who am I?" they become the master of their own destiny and life experience, as the oneness with God is given all knowing. With this knowing, all things are possible.

"Ask this in faith and believing, and all is given to you," expresses this idea that the mind of God is accessible when you ask, "Who am I?" and listen for the answer to perpetuate all other thoughts that come after. Henceforth, you are one with the Universal (Source) and can become *the Enlightened One*, as the Buddha. As every great being of light knows through their own awakening, this is an instantaneous shift of consciousness, propelled from within, and cannot be controlled by the ego or its desires and mechanisms of control generated from fear and the illusion of separation. Only in knowing your true identity and the answer to the question, "Who am I?" can you sit inside the seed of consciousness that gives birth to all life. Within the seed is the all-knowing of who you are to become. The knowledge is locked inside the matrix of the seed and, when it is properly planted and nourished, becomes the embodiment of life and expresses in form that essence within the seed. "You know who you are; now live it."

And so is the dissertation on Self-knowing. When Father and I first had a conversation on this matter of "Who am I?" I was but three or four years old, but later he would come to me at eleven and sixteen years old and right before I was to marry Isaiah. He told me about marriage and what it really meant. He said the first and everlasting love is always with the beloved of your heart which holds the seed of the "I AM," that which you are, and when this love is ignited by another, the heart of the two meld together in an ecstatic union of shared love which mirrors the divine to one another. That is why lovers feel so lost in love. They lose themselves to love and are carried by this wave in exchange with one another. He reminded me of my wholeness and divinity and encouraged me to look for God in his eyes, and when I saw Him, to embrace him as my very own beloved. In this way, I honor God in the holy union of marriage as it was meant to be.

To promise oneself to another until death do you part, can mean different things. To a couple who are willing and capable of focusing on their bond as an expression of holy communion with God, a lifetime together is possible, and marriage is in service to God and becomes the expression of God which is unique to them. However, for the typical (unawakened) person who does not continually seek the kingdom of God, it can be a difficult and challenging path as the circumstances of their lives and outside forces pull on them to reconsider who they are. If you truly know your truth, you love everyone and find the partner that best mirrors the beloved in you. When you look at your beloved, you will see an aspect of yourself that appears the same, and yet, different because of the form God takes, and yet, there is a similar feeling of familiarity, as you are feeling and expressing your very own union with your beloved (God) inside of you. This mix of energy is the most amazing elixir of bliss and ecstasy that can take you to the highest realms of the galaxy beyond time and space. This union is what our physical forms were designed for. Not just mating as animals do. We as humans were made to reveal the truth of the heart of God.

The system provided within the spinal canal is the pathway that leads to the grand opening of all the chakras, which ignite the divine flame of knowing as you remember whom you are. In this remembrance, is God, your beloved of your heart, who is loving you, even as you are loving God. That is union; that is marriage, soul-to-soul, heart to heart, God to Self, Self to God. God loving God is powerful beyond words; only experience can explain. This Love-reunion and Divine communion of souls, is the express reason for this communication (writing) at this time. Through the celestial realms, through the veil of separation and the illusion of separateness, Jesus my Father, God the

Almighty presence, which is Christ in you, promises to come again and again to each heart until all are awakened. Messengers of Truth shall reach all seekers, and seekers shall know this Truth by returning again and again to all hearts following their own unique path to God. It is each soul's destiny and love's promise to all humanity—union with God.

This, then, will be the ending of human suffering, as all pain in the heart is caused by the illusion of separation from God. The revelation of the Holy Spirit is the divine Truth of the oneness of all creation. Each persona has an important role to play in the awakening and in the transformation that is eternally upon you on your planet at this time.

As Sarah, I was embraced by the knowing of my connection with God, and therefore, did not seek it; I lived it. This is the destiny for all those whose hearts yearn for love, and yet, betray themselves each time they have a thought of untruth which leads them to the desert of isolation away from the presence inside their own hearts. This presence is what the seeker searches for, time and time again. Pulled to the outer world of material goods, one is temporarily satiated until the yearning starts again as the soul calls for realization and awakening. Embodiment of the presence is inevitable once this yearning is set into motion, as there is then a magnet that will pull people and circumstances to you until the mirror of the divine is made clear to you. It is inevitable, this union, as the law of attraction is always claiming its victory over false prophets that claim the keys to the kingdom where the riches of the mighty and delusion lie. However, the keys to the riches of God's holy temple are in the treasure chest of the heart. Each individual sits on the throne of his/her own holy kingdom/queendom. As you awaken the center of your power, you shall know this is true.

The asanas (postures) of yoga teachings were taught by the masters in ancient India to awaken the centers of the spine to enliven the pathway of the Holy Spirit for the river of energy of grace to flow. This mastery of postures and movement was sought out by students seeking God and has recently been brought forward to educate more of the masses around the world to the living Truth (hidden) inside the body temple. This energy inside the body temple is a template of the energy that flows throughout the myriad of worlds and encompasses the mastery of many of the fields of study now being researched in your modern or current-day time. But, make no mistake, true mastery comes from your intention to remember who you are—God as human, embodying the Beloved in form and expressing love in the world.

Embracing all creation as sacred is essential to the living God. All creation is from the same source and enlivens the beings of light now walking among you. Awaken, dear children, awaken. You are born anew. Let it be the truth that sets you free to enjoy your divinity and the inherent powers to create beauty and love on this magnificent sphere of earth. Loving earth, sky, water, mineral and animal is an ancient practice of loving God—the Creator—and acknowledging the master who lives within your very own temple of God. Let love, the master, enliven and transform your body into the moving temple of divinity, as grace reveals herself through flow and presence as moving form. Embrace yourself, let go of any thought that takes you away from this presence. Instead, allow grace's mercy to reveal your Beloved and then, union of body, mind, and spirit shall ensue.

The great masters of yoga always taught the inner mechanisms which were revealed into the (body) outer forms. The inner teacher reveals herself to the student and then the (outer) master teacher becomes only a mirror of the possibilities that exist, once the connection to the inner teacher is made.

Jesus (my Father) taught the inner workings of Spirit and called to each soul to awaken to the inner teacher—the God of your own heart. He said, "Go within the treasure chest of your heart and there you will find the riches you've been seeking. Seek first this treasure for all else will fade and come to pass as dust in the wind."

"My dearest Sarah," he said, "I was blessed by the masters of the east, and now you must help others find their inner master, for even as I call to every hungry heart, only those who can see and wish to be one again in the awareness of their Creator will seek you. But, if you live the Master's teachings, then the knowing can be automatically transmitted, and the vibration of love will be passed on. This vibration/field of union, will be affected by you and thus, another soul can be awakened. You know who you are, so shine this light. Dim it for no one, nor try to enliven anyone. Simply live it and, when possible, speak the words of love, and the expressions from your own inner teacher and the beloved of your heart shall bless and multiply the love tenfold and more.

"This, my dearest Sarah, you can and will do," he said. "I am one with you." And with this I felt him immerse his light inside of me and no longer could I "see" him or feel him outside of me. At the age of sixteen I was awakened fully into my remembrance and henceforth knew the riches of the kingdom of the heart, which he spoke of so eloquently. "Oh, dearest Father, you are God; now I know." And then I fell asleep into the arms of Love, henceforth awakened, and fell asleep no more.

If you call to Love, you will feel Love. If you call to the inner teacher and listen, you will hear the words of the Master within. If you call to the beloved, you will feel the embrace of the divine loving you into the magnificence of whom you are. Letting go of your fears and worries of the day and feeling for the holy presence will reveal the truth of who you are. Ask Him, and He will come to you. My Father will come to you in consort with the Holy Spirit, and God will shine within you.

Love, love, love; always choose love first and bring that presence into your awareness, allowing any fears or trepidations, any anxieties or worries to remain in concert with this presence. You shall see that fear and love cannot coexist, for the love of the almighty is stronger and brighter and will dissipate and move the lower vibration thoughts and beliefs out of your field of energy, and all that will remain is the higher vibration of love and the pure light of God.

This is why what you focus on gets bigger. So focus not only on what you are feeling, acknowledging the sensations and emotions and any thoughts that arise, but at the same time call in love. Expand your focus—widen your lens. Include your body (all of it) and the energy bodies around your physical form. Use your breath as the sound that vibrates your central channel of light and awakens the energy of divine knowing. This, the ancients have experienced and have brought forth the teachings now known as yoga. Follow this path and you are following the great masters who ascended into their own higher consciousness and expanded their fields of being into pure knowing, pure presence. The light of the great ones who are sent to earth to enliven the consciousness of the dear ones who have fallen asleep have always been sent from the higher realms to assist in this awakening period. Your beloved planet earth has gone through many shifts of consciousness and shall continue to do so until all are awakened to their true identity. All beings have the seed of awareness planted inside their souls, and it is the soul that dictates the timing of awakening based on series of events and life's lessons learned. Once the shift in consciousness has occurred, there is an instant shift in the field around your body, and this draws other experiences and people to you, allowing the energy to move. This allows a more peaceful resolution to life's circumstances and challenges that arise. The art of allowing grace's presence to be in your awareness creates beautiful masterpieces of love and changes the world, thereby making each individual the sculptor and the sculpted by revealing that which is always present.

Like a master sculptor who sees the beauty of the inner spirit of the stone and the art piece, which is hidden inside the rock or clay, the form is revealed after being artfully molded or having the hard outer exterior removed. Sometimes, it takes years for the hard rock to be chipped away and the monument of the soul to be revealed. Other times, there is a blast of realization, and the masterpiece is born into a form, which, once hidden, is now revealed. So tarry not on paths that cause you to experience pain and suffering; engage your inner wisdom; call to the inner master to sculpt the life you were born to live, full of beauty, wisdom, and love passed forward through the beloved of your heart. Live the life of beauty and inspiration, and experience the joy of expanded awareness and inner peace. Love the beautiful masterpiece, which, you have created. Spirit lives.

God possesses the all-encompassing beauty and radiance that shines from the masterpiece of the living art that is you and all that you were created to be. Like the newborn child full of innocence and potential, so are all of you imbued with the Master's formula for a successful life, full of wonder and awe. Losing <u>all</u> fear is the key to allowing the light being to be revealed, and this shall transform all the other beings of light in your midst. Choose Love over and over again to sculpt the life you were born to live.

Watch for the remnants of clay and rock that remain around the artwork of your life that you are creating, remnants that no longer belong there, those that block the view of the Almighty presence inside that work of art. It is in you and all around you. Like the great pyramids and temples that have been built in honor of people and of God, each stone was carefully placed in a unified building block of creation to create balance and stability upon which all the other blocks of stone are placed. And so it is with your life—the true masterpiece of the master sculptor lives inside, revealing your divinity, purity, and perfection, and manifesting your uniqueness in the world. All love is yours—it is you, unique and most wonderful.

The stones that have been chipped away were given to you and are also a part of God's holy plan for you. For just as you were given the tools for revealing what appeared hidden, you are also given the stone chips and the huge and magnificent strength and wisdom and clarity it takes to see the master, the masterpiece of art and the gift inside each challenge that lies now at your feet. Once the revelation occurs, the stones do not look so evil or hard, or all encompassing, or impossible to work with. It was always your fear that concealed the truth, not the stone.

And when you choose clay to mold your sculpture, with the hands of God moving you, you realize that without fear there is only God. Let God guide you to mold the life you really want, which is born into you and through you. Magnificent and divine, beautiful and free, you are everything the master himself/herself always wanted. It is why you were created. Your essence fills each rock and each clay sculpture you form; over and over again the divine fills your world with truth. Remove all the obstacles in all their forms and you will see the same face; fear has but one face. It only exists as an image, like that which forms as a reflection. It looks real, but when you go to touch it, it vanishes and falls away, and all that you see and experience is the elixir of the divine that remains. Fear can serve you, but only as an image of the opposite of what you really want and who you truly are. However, getting lost in fear can create doubt and such turmoil that it can take years and even lifetimes to remove. So choosing Love is always choosing wisely.

When Father raised his cup at his last meal and spoke to all of his disciples, all students of the way, he asked them to drink of his cup for this was the blood of Christ that was being given to them and for everyone. "For everyone who drinks from this cup drinks from the lifeblood of their holy Creator. And at this table, there is no defeat, no remorse, no pain, no fear, no sadness, no regret, no remembering of the past or even fear of the future; there is no anxiety, no worry, no tears or words of spite or anger. In this cup flows the love of my Father, which traverses through every vessel of life and through this love that lives through you and in you," he said. "I give you this cup to drink in honor of me, for I am the light and the way to eternal substance. Through me, all is given."

These words were spoken in honor of the beloved master of God's most Holy Spirit, moving, breathing and living within and composing everything in all the universes. In this brilliance of God, all is present, and from the presence <u>all</u> is created. When you drink from the cup of eternal life, you drink the almighty presence which turns to love, and at the moment It touches you (your lips) you are transformed into that which you seek, back into that which you are, the eternal, living being of light created in the likeness of being. Your form is the great masterpiece and the master and the light and the love. You are the way. The cup holds the presence, which is the key to remembering. The elixir of the blood of Christ awakens the presence in you, and when you look into the eyes of love, you see your Holy Spirit, and everything else turns to dust.

"Sarah," Father said, "you were named for a dear friend who washed my feet and cooked for me at the end of a very long day, a day when I was tired and fatigued from the energy of doubt and fear that surrounded me. She was a light that shone through the darkness of the clouds that pressed around me. She cared for me out of pure love and the commitment of the compassion that flowed through her heart. This compassion is the essence of the feminine love, and you, my dearest Sarah, have lived up to your namesake. Remember, compassion starts at home. It begins first with your own heart, your own home and your own relationship to God, our Father within you. You carry the seed of wisdom and hope, and through your compassion you will always care for those who become fatigued by the toils and tribulations of life. This, my dear Sarah, is a mission that shall continue with every great soul who is sent as an avatar for humanity. Celebrate the divinity within you and encourage every heart to celebrate the divinity, which is their birthright. Dear Sarah, love and only love is the key. This one truth must be embedded in your knowing."

And then he offered me his cup that he used at his last meal and raised it to his lips, and as he did so, it became full. As he offered it to me, tears poured from my eyes as I realized this was his last gift to me, to all of us, and I cried tears of joy for who he was, God incarnate. I cried for all the suffering that is uselessly lived by those still steeped in fear and for all those who remained in pain. I cried for release from the overwhelming light of his being that filled me and illuminated my own godliness, and I fell at his feet in complete exhaustion and admiration of his greatness. I gave up everything to join him and to come through this one who writes these words as an attempt to encourage complete surrender to the master of love within the heart of compassion.

Surrender in faith, in trust, in confidence that in the heart of the beloved is the Truth that sets you free. Enjoy your God-given life, celebrate each moment as a gift, and allow no one and no thought to steal your divinity from your awareness. Know this: we all love you and support you in the spiritual realm, the unseen celestial energy that coalesces time and time again through these writings and others and through your own day-to-day miracles as the cloak of forgetfulness is removed and our Father and Mother bless you with your life. Go forth, dear ones, with confidence in your divinity. Let us help you and guide you to the Christ-filled heart of your beloved God and seal your soul in the constellation of the universal love, which is the absolute realm of all there is. In this knowing is presence—still, complete, vast and infinite.

Father says, "I shall love you for all eternity, beyond time and place. You, my dear ones, are none other than God in form, expressing your uniqueness in the physical realm. I will love every soul into remembering and through the genetic code embedded within you, enliven your own seed of awakening. It is time, dear ones; emerge from your sleepiness, awaken to your greatness, for this you too can do and more. It is your destiny to grow and prosper, expand and evolve. Love is key; love is all; love is kindness in action. Love is all there is."

Most Holy Spirit of the infinite Truth, set this one free who reads and hears these words, and honor the omnipotent, omniscient essence, and love the light of their being into the miracle of embodiment.

I set you free to embrace your divinity, your truth, and to embed your self into your soul. Surrender all else to me. I am the Light, the Love, the Truth, the Master, and I hereby anoint you back into your own remembrance and set you free. For in the asking it is given, and if you but ask me in your heart, now, you will be set free.

Touch this page upon which these words are written, for they are imbued with Truth, and place the other on your heart.

> I AM the illuminated Christ within (repeat one time)
> I AM the victorious one who has risen above the cloak
> of forgetfulness (repeat two times)
> I AM that which I seek, that which I know, that who
> is and forever shall be (repeat three times)
> I AM Love, I AM Love – I AM, I AM, I AM (repeat
> one time)
> I AM all there is, there is only one.
> OM

YOU ARE FREE.

And as these words are written, so it is true. Freedom from all worry and fear frees you from the thinking that causes all your pain and suffering. The illuminated light of your being shines through forevermore. No more will you succumb to lessor vibrations, but will allow the one that sets you free to experience all that is. If you choose to stay here, all will be as the divine perfection created you to be, an aspect of God.

Now know this, dear ones, you who read these words; set upon your journey with the lightness that comes from pure freedom. This one truth shall set you free. Emblazoned in the cellular matrix of your body-soul is the remembrance of I, your God. I know all things, for I have created all. I know your every aspect, for you were created in My likeness. I know your deepest desire to be free, and it brings Me great joy to deliver on my promise to you at the time of incarnation: you shall forget to learn, and you will learn to remember.

It is the game of life and the plan of the universal Father and Mother to create a family of beings widespread with the seed of consciousness that illuminates everything into manifestation. You are the manifestation of creation, and you can have all that you imagine and more. Just surrender who you think you are, and allow the magnitude of the presence to shine your way. Look out upon the physical world as a story of your own creating and find the bliss in the freedom, knowing all beings will awaken, and that you, dear one, can create heaven here on earth by acknowledging your divinity and your love-filled heart of the beloved Creator who lives and breathes through you. Surrender everything to the truth and all will disappear but the truth. Perfection is yours.

As it is written, so it becomes written in your soul's journey. So create the life of perfection by allowing the truth to manifest. I am free. I am free. I am free to create the perfect life for me. That is God's promise to you – free will – choose wisely. Choose love and surrender all fear back to the illusion, and allow the darkness to consume it and the light to free you from the clutches of forgetfulness.

Oh, my darling children, grow and remember that which created you creates through you. It is you. You are one. We are all one, united in Truth, embedded inside the core of your being, strong and powerful, noble and free; this is your worth beyond measure. Release, allow, expand and grow bigger and bigger and you shall remember – and it is so. NOW.NOW.NOW. Released… Revealed… Now Revel. OM

MESSAGE TO AND FOR THE AUTHOR

"Grace has filled these pages with the words spoken through the voice of Sarah, beloved child of Christ and His very own Mary Magdalene, Christed in his holy presence. You, too, are that one known as Christ, for so it is written; so it is true. These words have been written so many times and in so many ways to awaken the cellular knowing of the presence of the one God that illuminates all life on this glorious planet you know as earth. Sarah was and is the Truth, as Mary was and is the bestowal of grace. Together they hold the cup of the covenant known as Christ, and it is now given to you to pass forward to this and future generations. We shall continue to write the last of these trilogies that within the word is grace. We have come to you through the veil, to communicate the light of Christ, which is not only your lineage, but also your destiny. You are about to embark on an amazing journey, which will catapult you into the writer and teacher you incarnated to become. These words have emblazoned in them the Truth, and all who read and embody the energy bestowed inside them will be freed. This is how, all great, manuscripts have been given and conceived; from the great Mother who birthed all. You know deep inside your Self that it is true. Vickie, dearest Mary, beloved to me, you are my messenger; let us continue with these writings and begin a new era that shall be called The Awakening. The last of this trilogy shall introduce more ways to feel and know God and shall include some of your own personal journey as a cornerstone to build a story around real (current time) people having real lives filled with trepidation and fears, loss and love and all the gamut of human emotions and feelings that make up this current world known as earth. The beings on this planet were chosen to incarnate now, so this awakening can begin to ignite the love inside all truth seekers to pass the light of God from candle to candle, flame to flame—to catapult this glorious planet on the rest of the journey towards full God-Realization consciousness. In no other time in human history have there been so many seeking love, so many illuminated masters embodied. It is part of the plan so all can awaken to their own known truth of their personal beloved in the heart. Each breath shall serve as a reminder, and each breath will be used to awaken. So now I ask you, beloved Vickie of my soul, to use your breath of life to serve, as I have come to you and have come to those who suffer. These simple truths spoken over and over again in so many ways are the same, yet different. I know you have doubted your worthiness to receive, you have doubted your clarity, you have doubted your mission, and you have even doubted your life. You have turned away from the light, the truth, and even love so many times like so many others, and yet, there is always a spark in you that never really gives up. You have persevered through it all, wanting at your deepest core to awaken, to remember, to know and to experience your beloved God of your soul. Now is the time. Do not fear the magnitude of God's power; feel embraced by it and use that power to empower others on their journey. You are my messenger. You are the love of my life as I am yours. I feel for you as you feel for me. I am the Atman that Amma (Mata Amritanandamayi Devi) speaks of. I know you, and you know me. You are sent mirrors of truth all the time so you can remember the core of Self. So it is time; look in your mirror and see the face of God.

From my guides, the disciples, of Christ: "We in your entourage come to you always. We stay in the shadows of your knowing until called upon and when needed appear in your awareness, like now. We serve the truth of God and have surrendered fully to that magnitude and reveal ourselves to those whose hearts are pure and devoted to finding what is sought by all students who wish to become the teachers on the new earth; those who are living truth of what the absolute reality brings to all life. Know the heart of your own inner beloved until that light expands and frees you to become that reflection of the divine mirror. Feel our presence now, and all your pain, and therefore, all your suffering will be gone like dust in the wind. The dark days are gone even though winter comes with shorter days. Know the light is always here just beyond the horizon; use this upcoming time to write the last book in this trilogy, and by the end of winter, spring will come again and present new beginnings. OM"

Book 3

The Love of All the Ages: From the Finite to the Infinite

CONTENTS

PRELUDE

And now begins the story of two lovers, torn apart by the epic saga of two worlds masquerading as separate universes unto themselves. Enveloped by illusion they collide again and again, strewn apart into pieces of their souls until the magnitude of their love ignites the omnipotent source inside the two, who search endlessly until, alas, their souls beckon union, and once again they reunite in the epic story of love and loss, reunion and bliss, imminent and everlasting connection, peace beyond knowing, and experiencing joy – their true nature. Love is forever seeking Love as its Self, and is born into experience to reveal the mirror gazing on its opposite wholeness until Self is fully realized.

When two lovers meet in perfect union it is because the perfect is what remains after the impermanence is removed. There is love, and then there is lust, based on primal reflexes left over from an age of reproduction and the expansion of the species on this planet. But, true love is born out of the perfection of the divine, wanting to experience its self. It is being able to see yourself in the divine mirror, as it brings one home to Truth. This story is about a couple conceived in the consciousness of a time of forgetfulness when there was no conscious conception; a time when the ego ran amuck, awaiting glimpses of joy and temporary happiness, unanchored permanently in the Truth. If you should ask the names of this couple, you could call them Adam and Eve, but this story is really born of a new age of Truth seekers. Born in forgetfulness and mindlessness, they wander in and out of the dark places of their own unenlightened psyches, believing what they think and thinking that their false beliefs of reality are true. Truth seekers emerge from the darkness of their own thought-based illusions, finding one another so that the energy of Truth can be magnified and more greatly enhance the love stream from <u>all</u> of its tributaries on earth. There is no other right or perfect partner for the other when they are twin souls, born of the same flame of creation. They are mirrored images of the other, hidden in different forms. Lovers, coming together in union, merge back into the one flame of their creation and emerge victorious over their forgetfulness and triumphant over their own pain and suffering. Together, they remember... the Love of All the Ages.

INTRODUCTION

Love, is to know what is relevant and real to the present situation and believing in the gifts, of the other who stands before you. As you look into the window of your soul, the light of eternity blazes through the past and previous life experiences to deliver you to the doorstep of the heavenly host of God's magnitude and powerfully embodied presence known as Truth. The omnipotence of Truth, is its readiness to forgive all the former misgivings and mistakes of oneself and others, in order to allow the brilliance of the presence to remain fully present in what is now. Looking beyond the perceptions of the magnitude of the masses who are lost in the day to day mirages in the desert of their forgetfulness, will allow the grace that is flowing to find its way to your heart. This will ignite the flame of passionate penetration of the immortal bliss of recognition of the soul's renunciation of untruth, until the time comes for Absolute-Recognition and Absolute-Perfection to reign and the freedom to live in sovereignty in the relative world of dualism. Here, opportunities appear in order to educate and enliven the experience of oneness that lives at the heart of all creation and allows for the recognition of the beloved of your soul in the Creator – the one Supreme Being that is both manifest and non-manifest, that which is living and non-living as seen to the naked, unknowing eye. Yet, to the one who can see, it is all here, now, loving and bright, to one whose true nature is joy, effervescent bliss, and peace beyond knowing, allowing each to be alive and ready to manifest and to serve at any given moment in the collapsed reality of the time-space continuum.

Yearning for freedom, the soul searches for mirrors to observe and see the Self in new ways for the enlivenment of its Self. True grace flows like a magnet whose energy draws to the recipient experiences and choices around the love-based wisdom of their soul's true identity. "Let go and let God," takes on a whole new meaning when the beloved is mirrored by the twin flame of your soul who stands before you – with elegance and grace and primal and guttural sensing; the two come together in a blaze of recognition and an ease of reunion that brings tears of relief to the ego of the beloved who lives and breathes in you. Omnipotent grace of the heart obtains its freedom from that Truth which illuminates all paths and energy pathways to the One and Only, the Perfect, the Supreme.

And so, the story has no ending and no real beginning but emerges in the middle of the dream of creation, where happenstance magnifies the choices available along the path of joyful exploration and union with the expectations of the other to find all of that which is desired in the heart and that which is desired in the name of Love. Whatsoever you shall seek, you shall find. And whatsoever you shall ask in the name of the one known by many names, you shall receive. For that which lives and breathes in you is none other than the beloved of your soul steeped in the one Truth that sets the heart free to experience reunion time and time again, from the relative to the absolute (realm) and back again until all that remains is the manifestation of the true heart's desire.

To those that remain oblivious to their true nature, awaken! Awaken and hear the angels of mercy sing their songs to denunciate the lies of existence and to free you from the shackles of forgetfulness. You are the chosen ones to embody the light of the world at this time, so rejoice in the manifestation of the illuminated Christ of all creation. The position of your demeanor means nothing, as you call out in pain and desperation for connection to the enlivened Truth of your soul, which says, "I am not here to judge you. I am here to set you free so you can enjoy the embrace of the beloved. Love surrounds you so fully and so completely that it acts as a magnet to draw your mirrored opposite to you, as your twin flame. When you are ready to receive, I shall appear. Only say the word and I shall appear. Beckon to Me with all your heart and have no doubt, I shall appear." This is the promise of your true Love. "All the barriers in the form of fear and self-doubt can and will be released for the vision of happiness to appear. You will recognize Me in one glance, one touch, one moment of inspiration. The Truth, envisioned, will appear in your awareness, and in an instant I am here."

This love story, set in the time of darkness to awakening, is your story if you desire it to be so. These two lovers are the epic players in the human drama/saga, which allows the interchange between flesh (in form) and the other (in the ethereal). The epic saga plays out for your own enjoyment and brings together two, who shall forevermore live as one. This is the true meaning of marriage: when the one who seeks finds the mate who matches their genetic code for enlightenment. And then, in union they play, they love, they angst, they conquer, choosing fear over love or love over fear, moment by moment. A glimpse of the beloved can awaken your heart, but to remain in love, is to accept the other as your Self, to love, until death (disembodiment) do you part, until the illusion of separateness ceases to exist. As individuals, wholeness is your divinely given nature. "Through your own eyes, you shall see Me, reflected to you, as you, as other. Love, as truth seeking Truth, masters the fears that inhibit growth and proclaims the mysteries revealed. It is all, real as the Absolute Being of Love and, it is all, false as the ego-based fear of unworthiness. You are not only worthy, you are free and destined to awaken for as long as it takes, for eternity is yours. In the realm of no time, there *is*. In the realm of space and form, there is time; time to calculate, to sift, to sort, to transcend, to remunerate, and to reiterate love as masterful servant to the Absolute Being of light masquerading as you. The mask and the light combined is ego. Love the mask, for it is your gift. Love the light for it is you." So, soul searches soul, finds mate, marries in holy reunion and denunciates deviations from the path of the beloved and reconciles with Self and Truth, which releases you to feel united in the arms of the other who is now "the One."

For those who choose the path of marriage to other, you have chosen the highest path. The challenge of humanity is to recognize Self as sacred and to celebrate creation and to reproduce gods and goddesses here on earth. Your children, if you choose, learn from you and establish through the DNA a lineage of other seekers to emblazon God's supreme message of love and light in the world. Henceforth, you shall be known as family, but remember, we are all family. We are all from the same source. So, celebrate the love of self and family and mate and union and rejoice as we tell the particulars of those two beings of light who emerge out of the mist, out of the chaos, into the awareness of the other. This is their story – the journey of two hearts reunited as one.

CHAPTER 1

It was not so long ago that the beautiful one formally known as Katrina gave birth to a daughter. She changed her own name to hide the truth of her story, for she was unwed and all alone on the journey. She chose the name Katrina after seeing it in a story she had read some years ago while waiting to see her physician, as she felt just like the storm of the century had recently passed through her life in a wave of catastrophe, leaving behind nothing in its wake but a sea of rubble, strife and turmoil. The man she had fallen in love with had unexpectedly announced that he had gotten married and was unable to see her again. He threatened the likes of "death" if she attempted to contact him. So, she threw herself at the mercy of her parents and was promptly scolded for sleeping with a soon-to-be married man and was left to deal with her deep emotional grief on her own. *Well, so much for family*, she thought. So she went to a doctor to ask for help, and while sitting and waiting in the office, she read about a storm that released its fury on a city unbeknownst to its inhabitants that fled in a hurry, much like the man in her bed.

What now, she thought, *what now?* She was searching for love and felt abandoned in her loneliness and now, despair. Somehow, she had always felt alone and abandoned — by God, by everyone. No one could love her and comfort her the way she needed or wanted. From the beginning, it seemed she was doomed to struggle on her own and to search endlessly to find comfort and nurturing that could satisfy her deepest wounding which lay in the center of her heart. *How long had this hole been there*, she wondered? *Does anyone else feel this way? Does anyone else hunger for real love that only a true lover could give?* The hole felt so huge sometimes that it was magnified in a sea of emotions ranging from anger and grief, to fear and terror, never knowing what to expect in a world of un-seekers. Was she really alone? Her parents tried their best, but they failed miserably to obtain the awareness that would allow them to see the magnitude of the problems they created by their own thinking and their lack of mindfulness in their daily lives. The only one who could set her free was herself. She had to leave her family's house, so she did.

When she arrived at her friend's house, she was exhausted from her hopelessness and endless nights of crying herself to sleep. Unbeknownst to her, the child she carried felt her deep emotional pain and grief, and the soul who lingered in the other world sought to comfort her and to encourage her. "Hang on a little longer, I will come. I will come to love you."

The preciousness of a child's innocence goes unquestioned by even the most hardened and unaware soul-masking here in this world. Even the most destitute, if given half a chance, can gaze upon a newborn child and recognize the seed of God planted in the depths of that little one's heart. People scamper to hold the precious new life, to remember their own innocence, their own connection to the divine, the God that created them. How did they forget who they were? When did they lose sight of the sacredness of their day-to-day journey? In the eyes of the child they find their solace, their comfort, their hope, their joy, and the opportunity to reclaim the beloved of their soul, their gift of life. The newborn is their hope for another chance. Through their innocence, they can renew and remake the life they once knew as lonely, self-centered, and unproductive. Through their child they can begin anew.

"What are you going to do with this child, Katrina?" her friend Jessica said. "Katrina? Is that what you want me to call you now? You are not the storm, my friend. You are the victim to its aftermath and your deep yearning for love. That is all."

"I knew I could count on you to help me make sense of all this, Jessica. I don't know what to do. I just want to love her."

"How do you know it's a girl?" Jessica asked.

"I don't know how, I just know," she replied. "She's here inside me, waiting for a voice and a chance, and so, whatever happens, I at least want to give her a chance to live."

"So what do we do now?" Jessica implored.

"We go on, Jessica. We go on."

"Well, let me know what you need, and we will find a way. No matter what, we will find a way!"

"You know, it doesn't seem so hard when I'm with you," Katrina said. "I guess I just needed someone to be with me through this whole process that loves and understands me and accepts me as I am. Thanks so much, my friend, for being here. I don't know what Sara and I would do without you."

"Sara?"

"Yes, I guess that's her name, it just came out!"

"Well, it's her soul communicating directly to you. You're connected now, and I believe it is meant to be. He doesn't know what he's missing not being with you and Sara, but maybe one day he'll find out."

"Whatever happens now, Jessica, I'm going to need to be strong. So, here goes! I don't know how, but I know I will be fine."

"I think it can be fun. The unknown may seem scary to some, but I find it exciting! It is like living a great mystery. You never know what the next day will bring. But, if we open to love and all the possibilities, it can be really fun and fulfilling," Jessica replied reassuringly.

"I see what you mean, Jessica. I never really thought of life like that. I've been yearning for so long that I have forgotten how to be happy and content."

"Let's start now then," Jessica smiled. "Cup of tea?"

"Yes, thanks."

And so it began, the deepening of a great friendship and the start of a new life through a new way of thinking and a new attitude on life. The new life of Sara was just on the edge of its renewal for another incarnation on earth.

"Here we go again, Mary. Here we go again." The soul child Sara, beckoned to her mother's big heart, as she continued her connection to her soon-to-be mother again. "In our last incarnation when we were together, we survived great tragedies and seemingly disastrous events. And yet, here we are with another chance. Over and over again we get to live, explore, experiment and experience the depth of love that is possible when we awaken to the divine and the possibilities God brings. Good work, Mom, good work! We will have to adjust to the new roles we are playing with each other, but that should be easy once I get there and I forget everything. Interesting, how it all seems so clear from this side of the veil, and how different and difficult it becomes once a new life body is taken and the journey of being human begins. It is like taking a pill of forgetfulness that seems to last forever until a 'new' pill is taken to awaken the inhabitant of the body temple. The joy of being human is a time of exploration, with the time in between birth and rebirth, death and incarnation, all happening simultaneously to produce the current moment of events. It is all so amazing really.... time, space, matter, illusion, being/not-being. Wow, it gets so complicated once thinking gets involved. It is really so much easier not to think at all," Sara concluded.

"Sara, is that you in there making all that movement? It's amazing cohabitating a body with another soul," Katrina said aloud. "Sometimes I can feel you here and sometimes you feel like you are on a vacation at Home. The soul must come and go into its cellular construct while developing in the womb. Manifesting is so easy and automatic that, all it takes is an intention to create. I am so glad that somewhere inside of me is the creative force that is creating you, Sara. Welcome to this life. You are my divine co-creation and I'm so happy you are coming! What is it that you have come to do? What is your soul purpose for coming, I wonder?"

Sara replied, soul to soul, "Why to be with you, of course. We have set it up so I can learn and grow in an environment of loving support and opportunity so I can later teach others about soul union with the beloved through intimacy and daily life experiences. You, my dearest mother, are yet to awaken to all of who you are, but being together will help you remember who I am and our soul contract to enliven Truth. It is all in the living plan of our souls. I love you. That is my soul purpose...to love and be loved."

Her soon-to-be mother replied, "I love you, dear Sara. I don't know you yet, but I feel I do somehow. I know you at the deepest level. I can't wait to see you! I know you will be an image of divine beauty and grace!"

CHAPTER 2

And so she was the image of beauty and grace. The minute she was born was quite extraordinary for mother and child. Souls cheered, and an entourage of guides gathered to witness, embrace and ensure safe delivery of this exquisite being of light and goodness. It is quite the journey from womb to "world," full of twists and turns, pushes and shoves. And yet, all occurs with the magnificent guidance from the universal force that has given birth a multitude of times, with the Mother of all widening Her legs to expose the infant with infinite potential, embracing and caressing the beloved child, holding her close to Her bosom and the expansiveness of Her heart.

"Sara, you are so divine, so beautiful, and so perfect. I am overjoyed with your arrival and anticipate the greatness and love that our two souls will share. Promise me you will always remember our connection and the love of all the ages that lives and breathes within you and within me. Oh Sara, these are, at last, tears of joy. I hold you now, and you are safe here in my arms."

Sara said her last farewells to those she cherished in Spirit world: "Mother Mary, you were Love incarnate, and I will never forget this moment. I must go, but I will always remain in love with you. Our connection is beyond time and space; it is eternal." And with this, Sara opened her eyes to see her beloved earthen mother with whom she would change the world, beginning with her own. She felt the kiss of the angels gathered and refrained from leaping back across the great divide between the worlds into the embrace of Mother Mary, with whom she had communicated all the last-minute instructions for her journey.

"I will always be with you, dear one," Mother Mary encouraged. "Allow this one who carried you physically into this world to love you and provide for you, but always remember the source of your life within the breath of your heart. Your Father and I will be always by your side. Awaken the wisdom-heart with your love and intention, and then the awareness of our love will always be yours. Awaken within this one that you will soon call Mother the beloved that she yearns for. Be the light of love you came to be, and write upon the stone of emblazoned memory the words of Jesus Christ, 'I am risen, and I shall come again to each heart.' He is the messiah, the messenger, the word, and the promise that shall fulfill all the prophecies, and you will awaken the feminine to her power and set this one free to embrace her journey as sacred and blessed and divinely orchestrated. Sara, be the love that she has always wanted by being the pristine, clear mirror to her soul. I release you to her care. I will guide you both, always. We are always connected. Your guides will always be near. Call upon us, as I hereby give you free will. Remember, when you are in doubt, choose love. Ask and it is given."

And with this the angels gathered and smiled, as they remembered the most blessed of all births, the beginning of humanity and the one who came to save the dream of the Creator. "All is not lost; this one shall succeed. We will pave the way with light and protect her."

"Sara, are you awake? Look – a present for you! A beautiful outfit, suited for a princess. How do you like it? Pink was so cliché, so I chose white – do you like it?" Katrina dressed Sara in her first dress as tears welled up in her eyes. *When do the tears stop?* She wondered.

"Oh, Mother," Sara 'replied,' "there will be many tears, different kinds for different reasons. Mother Mary says they clear your heart-mind to feel God's presence. The Supreme Being reigns; and human tears rain. When they fall, they release what has remained inside to the outside. Oh, what bliss; I can feel your tears. I have a body again!"

"Oh, no! I have cried on you, little one. Let me wipe these tears," Katrina exclaimed. "I love you, precious child of mine. I love you. I am so happy. The pain of delivery really does disappear after a while, doesn't it? When will I get my body back to its original size, I wonder?"

"Hey, Katrina. I've got the car pulled up. Are you ready to go?" Jessica inquired.

"Yes, yes! Thanks, dear friend," said Katrina, smiling.

"Sara," Jessica began to sing a made-up song. "Welcome, welcome, welcome to our world. And now it is also yours. Let me hold you for the first time. What a joy, what more?" And with this they both started to laugh.

CHAPTER 3

The days to come were full of the usual chores and responsibilities of having a child, and Sara greatly appreciated all the love and care and the attention to detail that Katrina provided. Sara slept a great deal and communicated with all her guides at least twice a day, as they reassured her all is well. They told her that the Supreme Being is in charge of the greater plan of her life, "But your free will, Sara," they said, "will determine how you will achieve the ultimate goals laid out by us. There will soon come a time that you will have no memory of these conversations or the ones we had 'on the other side,' but rest assured, when the ultimate challenges occur, we will all be steadfast by your side. You will have all the support and guidance you need. Pay close attention to the clues along the way and look for the good in everyone. Look for the, oftentimes, hidden benefits in every challenge that arises. Gather strength and wisdom along the way and remember the ultimate outcome is never in doubt. The soul conversation we are having, we shall have again and again. Just ask, and all you need to know will be given to you. We are all on the same side of this miraculous team our Master has created, as the Supreme, God of all knowing and perception, is the Infinite Source of all creation. Enjoy the journey, dear Sara. This time will be different. When our beloved Master comes again, it will be in a time of awakening, and each heart that is committed to this mission will open up and regain inner vision and hearing so as to contribute to the end of suffering and to the enlightenment of humankind. Our dearest Sara, all love reigns on this heavenly planet earth, and the forces of darkness shall be slain by their own hands until every heart committed to the light is fully illuminated. Look for our 'work.' You will know it always, as it is steeped in the love of the Master and infused by the forces of good that wish to embrace the human journey as divine. You, Sara, are a light worker among many. Remember your Father now, and smile the innocent smile of Truth so all can remember how deeply they are loved. No matter what environment or circumstance in which you find yourself in this physical realm, the world of spirit glows with the delight of the creator. Divine Mother holds you in her arms until your sleep does end, then she dances with you in pure joy and delights with you on this incredible journey known as your life. Rest now. There is so much more to come. Use your body as a temple of divine beauty and delight in the miraculous that each cell undertakes, and with each breath, <u>know</u> we are always here. Feel for us now. That is all, dear one. Rest. More later. Om Shanti; all love."

And with this, Sara fell back asleep in her beloved mother's arms, much to Katrina's delight.

"Dearest Sara," she said "I think it is time to embrace myself with a new name. I no longer feel like a disaster. You have come to organize my chaos, focus my mind, and open my heart. The storm is over. The rubble has been removed, and I am still here in the midst of all these seemingly unconnected events and twists and turns of circumstance, to hold you while you sleep. There was a time when I could 'feel things' like presences or beings around me. When I was really young, I would cry out to them for help, and I would feel comforted, like now. Is that you here, my guides? Where did you go? Or, was it just I and my merry band of emotions, playing the tunes of sorrow, confusion and despair, that kept me from feeling you? Oh, my dear one Sara, let Love's light always be yours and may this moment of exquisite peace never, ever die. I shall never forsake you as my mother did me. I will provide for you with all that I have and make sure we are always together until one of us makes our transition. Tell my beloved Jesus I remember now the night he came to me and told me 'thy will be done' as I prayed for the end of suffering."

She heard him reply from a voice within her, "The end of suffering will come when you are one with me and trust my plan for you. Remember, dearest Mary, I am always with you. I shall help you bring love into the world and become the healer you came to be."

"Sara, it is time I continue with all that I came to do," she said. "I trust our beloved God of our souls to show the way. I got it! I know what I must do. I must be the peace, be the love and be the life."

And then Jesus said (within her heart-mind), "Trust me, and the Truth will set you free. All is well. Divine Mother to Sara and to the many, you will become the teacher and the healer, remembering the source of all inspiration. I will guide you and protect you, and when the dark night is upon you, I will send my disciples of Truth and the angel of mercy to enlighten the path, so you never completely lose your footing on the path of righteousness or justice. All will come to pass; all will be healed back into the wholeness of Eternal Spirit. Your 'past' will be no more, and the present moment shall take the forefront in your mind and emblazon upon you the words to herald in a new era, a new time of brightness. You are out of the woods and in the clearing now. Love reigns here and now. You may take on many names, but your one name shall remain forever Mary of Magdalene, to me (Jesus), you who became Christ through the awakening by our Supreme Being. You are my love in the world; act as such. Mary you will always be to me. These guides you now feel are my emissaries, my beloved disciples and apostles to the world. Their sacrifice was great, but they now serve with the awareness of the Love of all the Ages, and this Truth they come to share is none other than the child of goodness born in each heart that remembers God the Supreme, of all. Remembering me, as Jesus, will awaken the heart, as I was sent as a messenger and have been linked to every heart. I shall be known by many names, but to you and to many, I will be known as Jesus Christ, a messiah, a savior, a messenger, a teacher, a guide, a way shower, God the Father's only begotten Son, but I am your link, your beloved and your personal love. I am your true lover to whom you are married for eternity. I am yours; you are mine, and whatever face you see or story you tell, I am your beloved, now and forevermore. You are my love here in this world. Shine my love; shine brighter and brighter until all are illuminated. Shine until all the darkness is eradicated and no piece of it remains. Love's light is greater than any strand of perceived evil or darkness, greater than any sorrow or pain, and greater than all the misery in the world. Stay with me in your awareness, and you are free to experience the ultimate bliss of reunion, and then divine ecstasy is yours. Love dear one. Love. That is the way. Enjoy the journey. I smile when you smile. I cry when you cry, even though you are comforted. I am you, for you are one with me. My heart lives and breathes in you. Let us bring peace, spread love, and live joy. Union is ours in holy matrimony. You are not alone; you are with <u>me</u>."

And with this, his beloved Mary of Magdalene was cast back into the world of form to forget and then to remember this conversation with her guides and her beloved Jesus Christ. "I will always remember," she said. "I will always love you."

"Mary," he said. "This time you will forget, but then you will choose to live and breathe with me as the one most sacred to your heart. Look for me in the eyes of the man who will bring our Sara to you and remember her as the redeemer of Truth. She will be the one to awaken the masses to their own divinity. In a, relatively, short time, she will be known to many people. We will keep her safe. She will be among many light workers sent to usher in a new era of growth to humanity, and her simple wisdom and profound beauty shall become well known. Let Love's light shine within your heart. I love you, Mary. Use this as your middle name to carry on our lineage of Truth in the world and to awaken the heart of goodness and deep compassion for the world. I am always here. I will always be, just a breath away."

"Katrina, wake up! Your mother is here to see our Sara girl," Jessica said.

"Mom, what are you doing here? I wasn't expecting you."

"Well, I couldn't stay away too long. I thought you might need some help."

"OK, that's fine. Sara is here somewhere sleeping, I presume."

"Nope, she's here, wide-eyed and raring to go!" Jessica brought her in and handed her to Katrina's mother, Joan.

"I adore you," Katrina's mother exclaimed. "What a wonderful, exquisite girl you are!" They cuddled, and Sara cooed as she delivered her brilliant light to all. "Never forget how much you are loved, precious one."

Interesting, Katrina thought. *You weren't always there for yourself or for me when I was younger, but now, I see your wounds have been healed and love is more available to you. Jesus warned me about the trials and tribulations ahead, but I had no idea how dark the Dark Night could be. You are here now to see your granddaughter, and her brilliant and wide-eyed innocence has melted your heart. What is it about babies? She is only three-months old, and she is already changing the world.*

"I love you, Mom." Katrina said aloud.

"I love you, too. I am so sorry I abandoned you when you needed me the most. I couldn't bear your 'mistake' with that despicable man, and I remembered all too well my own story of love and loss secondary to betrayal by a man. I was in too much pain to help you through yours." She looked now to Jessica and said, "Thank you, Jessica, for taking her in and for helping her. I can be here now, and I want to be here and to help you all as much as I can."

"No worries." Jessica smiled. "That's what friends are for."

"Mom, I am staying here with Jessica, and we are all doing just great. But please come to visit when you can." Tears streaming down both faces, mother and daughter hugged, secretly promising to themselves to never let human frailty get in the way of the family bonds they had and to come together now for Sara.

"I want her to know you, Mom. Please be gentle with yourself in her presence and let us both share with her what is our best to give at any moment. She is a powerhouse of strength, and she will have a great deal to offer in her life."

"I know she is all those things to you, my daughter, but to me she's my baby, just like you will always be to me. Thanks for forgiving me. I am so ashamed of the way I acted. I was just so afraid for you."

"Fear puts up a veil," Katrina said, "too dense for any clarity in the moment of its grip. All is forgiven. Let's celebrate this life together."

And so, for the first time in their lives, they parted friends, without the tension they carried between them for so many years. The struggle for love and acceptance, and to be seen and acknowledged, came to an end in a glance as the pristine innocence and unconditional love of Spirit came shining through in the eyes of a babe.

∞

CHAPTER 4

"I just love listening to her breathe and watching her sleep, Jessica. What is happening to me? My story of love and loss means nothing now, for I've lost nothing."

"There was really nothing to lose or gain, only to have and to hold." Jessica smiled.

"You're right, Jessica. And how did you get so wise?"

"Oh, just lucky, I guess."

"No, there is no luck involved in wisdom. It is like your heart and soul have come together, and now wisdom just pours out of you."

"Yes, that's me. Let's eat!" And they both laughed out loud.

Life together with the two now deemed "saved and wise women" with their beloved Sara was packed full of interesting and comical events. There was the time the diaper fell off in the store because Jessica didn't fasten the closures right. When she lifted her up, Sara just giggled with delight. No worries. No one really cares about such things, but at the time it seemed really quite funny, especially to the young man at the checkout counter who was trying to get up the courage to ask Jessica out. *Not now*, he thought, *not now*.

"Is that your baby?" he asked.

"No, she is my friend's," Jessica replied, "but we are all very close. So we come as sort of a package, although there is always room for more."

"I see." He nodded his head.

Jessica, as though reading his mind, or at least his body language, said, "No, I am free. I am not seeing anyone at the moment. Care to invite us for tea?"

"Yes, that would be great. Here is my number. You can give me a call when it is convenient for you. I'm Greg."

"Great, Greg. I'm Jessica, at least this time around. I'll give you a call. Gotta go fix the diaper. Come on, Sara."

"She's divine," Greg heard himself saying. "There is something about her."

"Yes, we know. Goodbye now, customers are coming."

So they left the department store and met Katrina at the car since she had stopped at another store nearby. They all laughed about how life is sometimes, because you never know what will happen next. After Jessica recounted the story, Katrina asked, "So, are you ever going to call Greg?"

"No," Jessica replied. "I am waiting until the universe brings us back together and we meet again."

And that is exactly what happened. They met "coincidentally" in a coffee shop about two weeks later. Unbeknownst to either of them, they frequented the same location about the same time every day. Only this time was different because of Greg's shift change at the store.

"So, you come here often?" Greg smiled.

"Oh, hi there! Actually, yes, I do. You are Greg, right?"

"Yes, that's it. Now I know how women feel when men don't call them."

"Well, I used to have the philosophy that I had to meet them at least three times because three times is a charm, you know. But now I set it up for two times in two different places. That way I know it is meant to be."

"Well," Greg said, "this time I'm not letting you go so easily. Do you have time to join me?"

"Yes, as a matter of fact, I do. I'm Jessica, by the way."

Greg said, "Yes, I remember. Lovely. Thanks for your time."

They sat for two hours catching up. It felt like that since they felt they had met before. She found out this job he had was temporary and that he was going to start law school at the end of this summer. She learned that he grew up in Manhattan and had just moved here to start college, and that he was living temporarily with his aunt and was looking for a place to live close to school.

He found out she had just begun to go back to school as well, to get her master's in psychology after finishing up nursing school, as she had decided that the human psyche was much more fascinating than the body after all. She was already impressed with his kind heart and asked him, "How could someone with such a good heart want to be a lawyer?"

"Not all attorneys are ruthless and heartless," he said. "We all start out wanting to do good in the world and to fight for justice. My interest is in international law and helping immigrants find a home, and to stop the trafficking of the slave trade of young girls. It is appalling to me how people are treated. I might as well use this steel-trap mind of mine to help people."

"What do you mean steel-trap mind?" Jessica asked.

"Well, I have a photographic memory and remember everything I read. It is a bit unnerving. I believe I caught your license plate in the parking lot when you left and figured if you didn't call me soon, I would have to call you. But as the universe would have it, as you say, here we are. Anyway, Jessica Tabitha."

"How did you know that was my middle name?"

"I looked it up."

"Well, my mother was into the show 'Bewitched,' and because she thought I would end up like her, she named me after Samantha's daughter. My mom always wanted to be a witch and studied Wicca for a while, with spells and all of that."

"Do you do that? Cast spells?" Greg asked, smiling.

"Yes," Jessica said. "Can't you tell? There's one on you."

"Oh, yes. I guess that's true. There is a spell here." Greg smiled, bewitched by Jessica for sure! "Now it is time to drink the rest of this love potion and get a move on. Your phone number, please?" Greg inquired.

Jessica smiled the most magical smile from her heart and left him her number the old-fashioned way, written on a napkin, which he immediately memorized and put in his cell phone when he got in the car. He later texted a message to her: "When all else seems to fail, look to love to show the way. Heart to heart, soul to soul, love is the language that never fails, and speaks from the heart; from mine to yours, with gratitude. Gregory Paul."

Wow, Jessica thought. *This is too good to be true.* Later that night she texted him back: "Our first meeting was perhaps accidental, the second was divinely orchestrated, and the song played that carried the memories of our soul connection, in a time not so long ago that we could forget each other. Thank you for remembering me, heart to heart, soul to soul. Love is all there is, Jessica Tabitha."

And so their amazingly easy love relationship began. And it continued for many years after that, but that's jumping way too far ahead of this story.

When Jessica told Katrina about their meeting, they both felt warm and fuzzy, with great hope in their hearts that there really was some greater plan for everyone, and that life could be seen in many ways and that every new day held a promise for something new to unfold. They both agreed that being open to what is and what can become in life is so much more exciting and interesting than to see it as mundane and ordinary. An open-hearted, soul-connected person can set their own stage for an extraordinary life. Then the mundane becomes profoundly wonderful when viewed from the miracle lens of the divinely orchestrated score.

"Jessica, what lovely music is being played, for you and Greg. Wow, love is so great! Enjoy it while it is new. It's the best," Katrina said smiling, remembering her own love story.

"It's always going to be new," Jessica said. "I'm going to see to that. Inquisitive minds and open hearts will keep it magical."

"Good night, Katrina."

"Hey Jess, I've changed my name again."

"So, what is it now?"

"My original name, Jessica, with a bit of a new twist to it."

"OK, so what should I call you now?"

"Victoria."

"OK, good night, Victoria. See you in the morning." Jessica smiled, thinking, *Hmm Victoria Mary, that sounds good.*

The next day Victoria was awakened by a call from her mother, Joan, who said her father, Bill, had taken ill and was on his way to the hospital for testing.

"What happened, Mom?"

"He started getting pains in his chest, and coughing a lot, so the doctor just wanted to make sure. There was a shadow or something like that on one of his lungs on the X-ray, but I am sure he will be OK, don't you think?"

"Mom, which hospital? I'm on my way."

Her mother replied, "Christ," and then began to cry, and no more words were necessary.

Jessica woke up and heard the conversation and said, "Go. I'll take care of our girl."

As Victoria got ready to go, she began to remember all of the times she had felt the warmth of her father's smile, the comfort of his hugs, and the safe, secure feeling she had, always knowing he would be there for her. Now, it was her turn to comfort him. She began to pray for his well-being and a speedy recovery from whatever was happening, and as she did so, she felt a wave of love come over her like a blanket. She heard from within her, "I am here. He is safe. Love will see the way." She began to breathe more easily as a deep sigh of relief came over her. She bent over to hold Sara and to kiss her goodbye just as Jessica entered the room.

"He's going to be OK, Jessica. I just felt this amazing love say it to me. Is that too weird to you?"

"To me?" Jessica laughed. "You know I'm the resident weirdo here. Actually, I feel it too, like this is his warning sign to wake up and smell the cappuccino before it's too late."

"I guess we all get wake-up calls, don't we?" Victoria contemplated.

"Yes, it's just important that we pick up the call and listen and follow directions."

"Right! Oh, by the way, I get a feeling that Greg needs to hear from you today."

"OK," Jessica said. "Out you go. Call me later."

"Love you!"

"And you!"

Once Victoria got to the hospital, her father was in X-ray and her mother was waiting for him. "They are going to keep him overnight," she said. "His heart is actually OK according to the EKG, but they think he has pneumonia, and they are going to start treatment right away. I thought he was having a heart attack or something. Oh, God."

She laid her face in her hands as she cried, and Victoria put an arm around her in a gesture of support and relief.

"Mom, I got he's going to be OK, but he needs to know this may be his wake-up call."

"Sure, I know. Sometimes he doesn't take time to relax or to connect to his heart, to show his love or even to feel it for himself. You know he loves you. He wants to see Sara as soon as he is well."

"Absolutely."

"He has been crying at night. I hear him, but he doesn't know. He misses you so. You are still his little girl, you know."

"I know, Mom."

As tears ran down her face, the nurse came in and said, "He is going to be in room 2012. You can take those elevators." She pointed to the left.

When they arrived at his room, he was sitting in bed, smiling.

"Good morning, Princess," he said with great love in his heart.

"Good morning, Daddy," she said. She felt like she was a little girl with those words, and they both said simultaneously to each other, "I've missed you."

He said, "Don't worry, Princess. I'm going to be around for a long time. You know I'm way too stubborn to leave before my time. Come over here, my lovely." He waited for her to come close.

Her mom said, "Hey, if she's the princess, doesn't that mean I'm the queen?"

"Of course, we all know who is in charge." And then they all laughed and hugged and found solace in one another's hearts.

That night, Victoria found she needed to journal about her feelings, and this began a practice that she could count on to bring her insight and relief from her day-to-day stresses and experiences. She found that the inner voice she heard so clearly this morning always had something to say that was steeped in insight. She began to practice listening and writing and felt comfort in knowing that wisdom was close at hand.

That next day her mother called to say that all tests were negative for any heart disease or cancer and that her father was coming home with medication tomorrow.

"Ah, that's a relief, Mom. You know, I think Sara looks a little like Dad when he was a baby."

"He'll love that. I'll tell him. We will come over as soon as he is well."

A week passed before he could leave the house, but he was soon up and about and was absolutely thrilled the morning he was going to see Sara for the first time.

He couldn't believe his eyes when he saw his "little girl" holding her own child, and he burst into tears as memories flooded into his mind of her birth and the joy he felt from that day forward, just knowing she was in his life. He made a promise in that moment to take better care of himself and to be closer to his family. He knew there was something special in Sara's eyes. He couldn't say what, but he knew she had come for a special purpose, like, she would become well-known or something. *But then, that is what most grandparents feel about their first grandchild,* he thought.

"She is special, isn't she?" Victoria's mother said.

"Yes, oh most definitely, yes, she is," he replied.

As he took her in his arms, he felt a wave of love as his heart opened wide, and he mused at the delight in her eyes. An instant connection was made, and he could have sworn she said to him, "I see you. I remember you."

"I remember you," he found himself saying out loud.

"What?" Victoria said.

"I remember her. It's like I've known her forever. How is that possible?" Bill said inquisitively.

"Because we are all one, Dad. And because you have known her before."

"Well, I don't know how. But I certainly know I love her."

"And she loves you! Daddy. Are you OK? You are crying." (She had never seen him cry before.)

"Yes," he replied. "I'm just remembering you as a child. You were just as precious and wonderful, and you opened my heart this way the first time I ever saw you and held you. I fell in love that day. What an amazing day that was. I've never forgotten it. Come here, Princess." He put his arms around her and Sara and with great warmth said, "Thank you for this gift. You have always been a joy in my life. Let me reassure you that whatever you or Sara need or desire, as long as it is in my power, you shall have it."

"I know, Daddy, I know. You are what we want right now. Thank you, God."

As everyone left, there was great joy and an abundance of laughter, smiles, and hugging. Victoria had never been inside her father's heart with such awareness and magnitude since that first day of reconnection at her own birth. And she found herself remembering being an infant in his arms. She remembered how safe she felt, and how peaceful and secure she felt all over. There was no more perfect moment in her life than the one that just happened with her family as everyone came together in love. *The heart is such a magnificent masterpiece of revelation and comfort,* she thought. *If only we could all live with this knowing and feeling, we could enjoy the trials and tribulations of life with more lightheartedness, trusting in the Father to help and protect us all. The trouble comes when we attach to the father figure in front of us, and we continue with those expectations for a father to take care of us as we grow older. The transference* (as her psychologist friend called it) *must be revealed and released in order for us to grow bigger and to actually grow up and grow into the parent or the self-realized being (*as her yoga teacher described it.) This helped her to eliminate the feelings of helplessness that her own abandoned inner child felt.

She wrote that night about all those thoughts and feelings and discussed them the next day with Jessica, who agreed that life must be lived in the moment, free from the fears of the past or of the future, and that love, somehow, someway, someday, always provides, and that the magnitude of the love inside each heart truly heals everything in an instant.

"Don't look back, Miss V," Jessica said. "Keep moving forward. We are all family, you know. We just look different. Love you lots! Gotta go meet Greg. We are going biking today, cycling, as he calls it. Wish me luck. I doubt I can keep up with him!"

"Yes, maybe. But he will want to be with you and the wind. Ride on sister!" Victoria smiled.

CHAPTER 5

Love continues to grow, she wrote that morning, *in a heart that is free from doubt and any fear. You still need to do your part, but letting go allows a certain amount of trust that frees you from living in a world of "what ifs." If it is not happening now, it is not happening! It is really all in my mind isn't it?*

Her inner voice replied, "Yes, it is just thoughts, turned to beliefs and cellular memories, dictating to the unconscious mind reactions in the world around you. To view the world from inside, just witnessing it without attachment to outcome, can provide amazing insights. Getting caught in the drama is very seductive and very tempting, but to remain the observer allows you freedom to decide what action to take next. It is all a sequencing of events with no set ending or outcome, for the picture show is ongoing. The scenery and the actors may change but, the direction is taken from the witnessing inside. The Director sees the bigger picture after an appropriate time of observing the action. Sit back, relax, and enjoy the show. It is always changing. When the voices and thoughts inside your head subside, what remains is Love. Revelation and inspired thoughts can then penetrate the great wall of habitual thoughts and provide a wider range of options, more succinct with your true heart's desire and purpose in life."

"The love inside the heart, released, captures all the thoughts unaligned with the mission and soul purpose and releases them back into dust, and they vanish. Practice observing, dear one, and see what happens when you let go."

She thought about this for the rest of the day, the concept of letting go. *How? Well, there is a passive way of surrender and an active way of protecting the self and changing a more "negative" thought to a positive one, like a repeated affirmation, or doing something else to change the mood of the moment, like breathing in and breathing out, focusing on the breath. Even smiling can change something. Since everything is always changing, Love continues to shine no matter what. It is like waiting for the clouds to part or choosing to move to a sunnier spot. And if that is not possible,* she thought, *then just closing your eyes and choosing to see and feel Love's warmth, no matter where you are, is a good option as well. Since the mind does not always get it you can trick it by living in the (sun) light through pure intention and intuitive choice. The mind believes what your thoughts say. That is where belief comes from.*

I am so glad I started to journal again. It is such a comfort, she thought, *like always being able to talk to your best friend and getting wise counsel and a compassionate ear. Life can get so busy and so full of daily responsibilities that the pure joy and feelings of an open heart can get lost in the murkiness of the day.*

Today she was back to work and feeling good about herself when Jane, one of her colleagues, interrupted her thoughts and asked her if she wanted to go to lunch.

"OK," Victoria said. "Let's go somewhere they have outdoor seating."

They left the Center for Holistic Healing where Victoria worked as an assistant in the clinic. She was a natural in the healing arts and was trained in many areas after years of post-graduate studies. She was in the process of getting a sabbatical from her studies and a leave of absence from her temporary job at the Center to be with Sara, and she was glad everything had transpired as it did.

"Divine order," her friend Jim used to say. "Just let go and trust." She could still hear his voice comforting her as she cried out her despair of losing the only man she ever really loved. She smiled, as she remembered all the drama that ensued after she had learned that, he was engaged to be married, to someone else, and that he was soon to be married. He said he didn't really love her, but he felt obligated to her because of all their "plans." *How could he not feel obligated to me? He fled like he had been chased off with a shotgun,* she thought. *And he never looked back. He ran at the first hint of commitment with me, but not with this "other woman." What is that about? What did she have that I do not? What is it about her that keeps him so tied to her if it is not love?* He had never even talked about her before this moment of doom, when he decided to leave her.

"Hey, Victoria, it is time to order. Do you know what you want?" her friend inquired.

"Yes, the veggie burger and a salad, no fries please," she said to the server. She was still losing the 25 pounds that she had gained with Sara, and she wanted to keep losing weight to get back to her old self.

"I really feel weird in this body," she said. "I feel so big sometimes!"

"Well, you look great to me. You are still 10 pounds smaller and look better than the rest of us!" Jane said. "How is Sara doing?"

"She is wonderful. Of course I have pictures, just in case you want to see her."

"Of course I do!" Jane exclaimed.

Victoria flipped open her phone with pictures stored, and the oohs and ahs and smiles began.

"Should I even ask, Victoria, if you have heard from that guy?"

"No, and I don't care. It is his loss. Right?"

"Right, I just feel bad for you," Jane said with true compassion.

"Don't feel bad for me. Sara and I are great. She is loved and cared for and brings everyone great joy, just as it should be. I am trusting that this is as it should be. Like my friend Jim says, divine order, or something like that."

"Well, I think it is an excuse for a lack of honesty and integrity, and boldfaced ignorance based in free will and bad choices if you ask me! He is a loser. One day he will wake up with a woman he doesn't love and kids of his own and wonder, 'What if I had mustered up the courage to tell the truth and follow my heart instead of society's norm, which is full of responsibilities and duties, versus pure faith and trust in the divine intuition?' Whoa, don't get me started!"

"Thanks, Jane. I know your heart is in the right place. It hurts me, too. It was so magical, and it felt so real and so right in the moment. I know she has money and a name in the community. I am nobody to them. He was so worried about what everyone would think of him if he backed out. And he knew I would never tell, although I almost did hundreds of times in my mind. But something always stopped me. I wanted him only if he chose me and chose love over duty and responsibility. He never really knew about Sara."

"What do you mean?"

"I told him I might be pregnant, but after I learned about his other 'commitment,' I was so hurt that I told him to leave if that was where his heart truly lived. He didn't ever call again to even know what happened after I saw the doctor, so I moved in with Jessica and that was it. I called him once to tell him, but he said he had gotten married and to never call him again nor to try to see him. He was so cruel, and I thought that he was not the man I fell in love with. Sara doesn't need to feel like an outcast or live with a feeling of abandonment like me, so one day she will have a 'real' father, the one who raises her, not the one that spermed her! So be it! She has my father as a role model, and the Divine Father comforts her. I feel Him sometimes, at least in my fantasy. I wonder if God really exists."

"Of course God exists," Jane said. "But I know what you mean. Sometimes it feels like God is just a figment of your imagination, based on personal need and desire. I had a friend once say to me, 'Aren't you glad you didn't always get what you wanted?' And that made me think of just how many times I thought my life would be just awful without a certain someone or a particular thing I just had to have, and how it lost its luster not long after I got it home. My mother used to say that what you really want you will have, and to follow the deepest desire of the heart and let God do the rest. That is probably the best advice she ever gave me. I surely do miss her," Jane said.

"I am so sorry she is not here with you now, Jane, but she surely lives on in that magnificent heart of yours. Thanks. Good advice, Mom!" They both smiled and hugged as they finished their lunch.

"You are right, Victoria. It is always better in the sunlight. And I like the revision of your name; it is like a fresh start."

Back at work, everything seemed a lot brighter, like the sun was shining inside. Victoria felt peaceful and at ease with her life and her decisions thus far. She knew there was so much more to come, and she was beginning to trust the divine order of things. *Well*, she thought, *what do I have to lose if I trust? I will always follow my heart because that voice inside me is always the most dominant, if not the loudest. Once I surrender to the love I feel in my heart, the voice of fear disappears. I really need to allow and accept this love I have in my life now. Sara was meant to come when she did.* "Thank you, John. She is a great gift," she whispered.

"Maybe one day you will see her. I would really love that. You really should at least know about her at some point. Well, if and when you do, I am going to leave that up to the Universal Forces," she concluded to herself.

"The Great Mystery will continue to unfold in the divine perfection laid out by your soul," she heard.

That inner voice is strong, she thought. "Who are you?" she asked.

"Guidance. I am a compilation of all that is, and I am in you, in your life, in your mind and heart. I am your Guide in this life."

"Are you God?" she asked.

"I am an aspect of God as your soul, and I call upon others as needed to provide you information, consolation, and guidance along the way. Yes, I am your God."

Wow, she thought, *my personal God Guide. How awesome is this?*

"There is no other love greater than that of one's God. The forms of the outer world change to mask or reveal the divinity placed so perfectly inside. Depending on your viewpoint, the divine is either revealed or is hidden. Your very own perceptions mask the divine perfection unfolding before you. There is no other greater wisdom or counsel than your God. So, dearest V, take this advice from this inner voice that has only your greatest good at heart at all times. Free yourself from self-doubt and negative thought patterns, and surround yourself with people of like mind and heart who, want to do good in the world. Cultivate an open heart full of inner peace so you can always be the voice of Truth and act with kindness out of great compassion for the world. Feel always connected to Love, and Truth will triumph over lies and deceptions, falsehoods and false prophets. To your own Self are you bound and no other. Even in the midst of unity, there is room for individuality so you can use your unique gifts for the highest good of self and others. Please accept this new inner voice as part of your awakening, and deepen your connection to Self. Listen closely for the inner voice based in Love, and free yourself to celebrate all of your triumphs, and forgive yourself and others for their apparent misgivings and challenges. There will be many challenges in your life, but none too great for me to solve. You only need ask, and I will appear greater in your awareness. I am always here."

Amen, she thought. *That felt like a prayer. A conversation with God; that is a new concept for me, but I must say, I do feel at peace.*

She was able to continue her day with a newly felt freedom and lightness in her being. *This must be an awakening of something that I have needed*, she thought. *It is like having a craving and trying to quell it with all kinds of foods, when all you really need is water. It is like I am the cloth and I am finally saturated, wet with the presence of God in every pore and every cell of my being. What a wonderful feeling this is*, she thought. *It is new, yet old. It is unfamiliar and yet familiar, beyond words, beyond time, beyond description.*

"Please stay," she thought out loud as she drove home. "Don't ever leave again," she said to her Guidance.

"It is not I that leaves you, dearest V." (Her Guidance sometimes called her V for short.) "It is you that leaves the awareness of Love. Just breathe with me. I am in your breath. I cannot move <u>from</u> you, only <u>with</u> you. Remember in your yoga class, how you feel fluid and free and you move as if connected to something? That is when you are connected with me most. Our love becomes more sensory, and you <u>feel</u> me. And when you <u>feel</u> me, you feel the real, authentically unique you/me. We are one living, breathing cell in the body of God."

I love this, she thought. "I need you, or should I say we, or me? It is all kind of confusing."

"I am Love. Rest in Love. Enjoy the feelings that emerge and trust me to provide for you all that you <u>really</u> need."

"But God, what is my part? What do I do?" she asked.

"Rest, sit back with me, and enjoy the show. Play with me in the co-creative process of your life. Consult with me and calm all doubt and fear immediately if it arises, knowing I am here. Just breathe and you will know it is so."

"OK. Thanks." Victoria smiled peacefully.

She walked in the house, and Jessica was cooking dinner. "What's up?" Jessica asked.

"I just had the most amazing experience and still am. I have had a conversation with a different part of me. I know it sounds crazy, but it feels wonderful," she replied.

"Well, as long as it doesn't tell you to do anything crazy and you do it, I think you are fine," Jessica said, smiling. "What did the voice say? Who is it? Does it have a name?" Jessica asked inquiringly.

"Guidance. God. It is an aspect of God as my soul." Victoria was still in deep contemplation. "I think it is the Higher Self or Soul Self, or something like that. I think I will write about it later, or maybe It will write, or both. I don't know how to talk about it yet, because it is so new. More is coming at 11:00. Stay tuned."

They laughed and Jessica said, "Well, dinner is served; simple, but hopefully tasty."

"I love your cooking, Jess. Thanks lots!"

Then she heard a giggle and looked over to see Sara waking up. *Now, there is Love,* she thought, *divine perfection. What happens to that child-like innocence that keeps us so in tune with love and wonder?*

"That is why you had her when you did, V. It was time for you to wake up and remember. Congratulations," Guidance replied from inside her.

"Thanks, God. Good timing; perfect as always, right?"

"Right!"

"Thanks, Jess, this is yummy!" Victoria said. "Sara, you look even more radiant than ever. Isn't love great?"

During the rest of dinner, Victoria and Jessica discussed work, life, their day, and Victoria's experience, which continued as a sense of wonder and peace until all fell fast asleep. Jessica dreamed of Greg; Sara communed with the angels; and Victoria? Well, she dreamt she was safe in her Father's arms, holding Sara and knowing all was well!

She woke up feeling refreshed and ready to seize the day. It was the weekend and a beautiful spring day, so she bundled up herself and Sara in matching colors, and they began to take a long walk. Sara seemed to love her stroller and the outdoors as much as Victoria loved communing with nature. And so, they walked with a sense of inner peace and exquisite joy, just being together in the sunlight. Victoria looked around and took in the colors in a way she had never done before. She allowed the scenery to brighten and to come into her awareness with a ray of sunlight beaming towards her heart, and she felt a sense of joy beyond description. She relaxed into each moment, remembering to be in the present moment without even one thought, and that is when the *miracle moment* occurred. That is how she would remember it time and time again: the miracle moment when God actually appeared in her awareness, and all current physical reality stopped, suspended in a timeless manner, until all she saw was a vision of light. It grew and expanded and covered her entire field of vision until all that remained in her awareness was an extraordinary light, golden and sparkling.

The image was vibrating, like the molecules were dancing, ever changing and shifting in her field of awareness from gold to silver and back again. A feeling of bliss and joy filled her so completely that "she" disappeared. Only the image of her physical body remained, and the cellular matrix that used to define who she thought she was kept shifting and fluctuating. A timeless sense of wonder emerged into the Great Mind that was creating everything into matter. She saw the street appear and disappear numerous times. *It wasn't so dense after all.* Everything shifted like a projected image and became a hologram of her vision. *Nothing here is "real" or static! It is always vibrating, changing, shifting, and altering the landscape of my own illusion.* Without thought, there is the Field of Light; with thought, it forms into substance and "something" is creating. All love gathers light to it, then, expands it out again and again in a constant pulse, a wave of energy creating over and over again – all forms of love – again and again until a timeline forms and decisions are made from the thought. It imprints into the matrix of the vibration of the field, and it blinks on and off faster and faster until it is set into a form. Once the form is created and the observer sees it, there is an experience and then the experience is imprinted into the greater field, and the individual soul-self remembers. This is a temporary image – all of life in a timeline is momentary; it is not forever. The eternalness of being is the Field of Light.

"Let me show you," she heard Guidance say, and then the light became everything, everyone – all that existed – and then she knew. It is all one image divided into pieces, all one light divided into many colors, all one love expressing differently. All one love in light is all there is!

She looked at Sara and realized she was Sara. She saw the tree, and she was the tree. She heard the birds and she heard herself; she felt the wind and she felt herself. She was breathing in all, and breathing out one. She was creating and being created. She was love in light, in form: vibrating, changing, expressing, feeling, sensing, revealing, and being revealed. *Oh, the glory of the Absolute Supreme Being*, she thought, and then it happened. With that thought, out of the light emerged a being shrouded in a cloak. "Reveal yourself," she said. "I implore you; who am I?"

"I am you; you are me; we are the oneness of eternity." And with that, all was stopped. Time stood still. The cloak disappeared, and only light remained. Her body form merged with this glorious light, and her being-ness emerged in a clear concentric ring of pulsing vibration, and she was creating everything: the eternalness of her being, expanding and condensing. I want a lover, she thought, that loves me as God has and that I love as God. And then she popped back into her form and was holding Sara, and they merged together with her divine lover as God, and a form appeared before her. He was exquisite: God in form, the opposite expression of her Self. He was her, and yet, he was separate from her, and together they merged again and again into the oneness and out again. They were pulsating with this light and the vibration of love as it expanded and paused, condensed into two, paused, and expanded into one, paused, condensed into one, paused, expanded into two, paused, united, always together, "separated" only by the pause. Then, there was no contracting or expanding, no wave, no stopping and no going, and no pause. Only one.

"You are my beloved," he said.

And she replied, "I am your beloved." Then she asked again, "Who am I?"

"You are my beloved. Who am I?" he asked.

"You are my beloved," she said, "and I am your beloved." And with that awareness, union occurred. "I am (the beloved of God); God is my beloved," she said out loud.

"I create from the light in Love. My ego creates from the cloak of fear, which hides the light. When I am love in light in the world now, I am finite. In the light, I am love as the Infinite. The Love of all the Ages is the one beloved light of my being, pulsing everything into form. I choose now," she said. And with this, the holographic universe began to pulse with vibrant love, and the light came again into her awareness, and the Supreme Being, her very own beloved, rested into the seed of knowing inside her heart and pumped the breath of her being. She was inside her heart-center, beating, breathing, expanding, and condensing. From within this seed of consciousness planted by her own beloved God, her Supreme Being, was the absolute Truth, absolute knowing, beyond time, beyond words, beyond all expression. The seed took roots into physical form and became her body, expanding and condensing, pulsing with the breath and the seed of Truth in the soil of all knowing and merged with her individuated consciousness, and there was Self holding self, breathing in and breathing out. She was complete, whole, content, in union, and in peaceful knowing that, *"I Am Love."* And with this, Sara opened her eyes as Victoria opened her inner eye. And with her outer physical eyes, she saw her precious child as the child formed from the Perfect, existing as the Perfect, as her beloved daughter, and they both smiled with a twinkling in their eyes. "I see you, Sara; I see you, God."

"Mama." Sara spoke her first word: Ma—Divine Mother. At that moment, Victoria opened her heart, and she was the mother. *So many roles are possible,* she thought. And then she said aloud, "I love you, Sara. Oh, do I love you." Their breathing was in synchronistic harmony, and time began again. She could see solid matter again, but now she knew the nature of reality. She knew the answer to "who am I?" in the miraculous moment of remembrance from finite to infinite. She returned to the current timeline she had created, and love was all there was: to feel, to know, to express, and to be. *From the Finite to the Infinite, that is the name of my book,* she thought. This is the miraculous moment of knowing that the Love of all the ages lives and breathes in my very own heart-seed: OM. She heard the sound vibrating in everything. She felt alive, vibrant; the essence of her being was OM. OM Love; OM I Am; OM beloved; OM Lovers; we are only one. OM, OM, OM.

In the miraculous moment of knowing, the transformation occurred within Victoria that would serve her for the rest of her life and propel her on to the task of the teacher and the healer that she was destined to become. She knew her lifelong lesson would be to surrender and to trust the exalted state of being that lived inside her soul. She could share this moment with only one other person who also experienced the moment of revelation, and it was not until years later that Victoria realized that it was Sara that provided her impetus for surrender. Sara lived in the state of the miraculous – pure consciousness, shifting, shaping, and creating the profound reality of the present moment. She was born into it and born from it, the one pure, sweet, exalted OM: the vibration of the Creator and the creation. In the magnificent state of Oneness, that all are promised at birth, Sara remained. In the miraculous moment of awareness, everything shifted "back" into the ultimate state of awareness of the supreme Truth, that which is constantly vibrating each new moment into existence. There really is nothing to do, but there is everything to be. Brought through the consciousness of this state was the transcendent, the freedom to choose. *Always we have the freedom to choose,* she thought, *and within this freedom lives the Absolute, Supreme Consciousness of all that is.* She had studied some of the great spiritual texts and had read stories of mystical awakenings and transformation and could only hope to catch a glimpse of the divine Truth. She cried at the awareness of this great gift called life and the magnificence of the Presence in each breath. She celebrated her own magnificence and the illuminated Presence, which was the gift of the present she saw before her.

"This child, known as Sara, is yours for safekeeping," her Guidance said. "Bring her to the altar of your heart and hold her close, and she will show you things no other can. She is the next way-shower of the divine lineage of Christ your Beloved. She is our gift to humanity and will join others to lead your people out of their imprisoned thoughts and conceptions of reality. She will help lead others to this seed of Truth, as will you. Others will join you from across the world to gather light after light until all are illuminated back to the seed of knowing: God is the Supreme, Absolute Being of pure consciousness that all hearts seek. There is no other, only one."

And with this, she took a deep breath, a sigh of relief. *I am,* she thought, *I am OM.*

If there were to be no more moments as gloriously powerful or as blissful as this one, at least she had found "God." *The irony of it all,* she thought, *is I didn't know I was looking, nor did I realize that when I was feeling alone and oftentimes lonely, I was really wanting and seeking Love to release me from my self-made prison of isolation. Only my thoughts wander and betray me, she realized; as long as I do not feel this divine connection, I am lost in my separateness. If only everyone could experience this love, she thought, there would be no more war and hate-based crimes. The key is for all hearts to awaken to their Essence, but how? I didn't do anything; it just happened.*

"Grace," her Guidance began. "Grace is the elixir in the stream of consciousness that delivers each individual back into the present field of their own essence where God-consciousness exists. Grace is not by choice of the individual's free will. Grace is by deliverance of the seed of knowing inside the heart of each individual and is awakened by the soul's divine timing. This has no purer intention than to deliver you back to the Godhead of your own soul essence where the truth of your being is awakened into pure knowing of what is. Now that you know, all seeking subsides, all thoughts fade, until the grace-inspired consciousness rises with an inspiration such as the one we are having right now. By pure definition, the pure state of oneness has no ego-based thought. However, in an action-driven world, the inspiration of God can arise and lead to great achievements on a worldly basis, such as cures for disease, an end to wars and hunger, love for a spouse, and the saving of a child's innocence. It is all God-driven. Many people throw out God, based on false concepts and religious dogma and interpretations of ancient manuscripts. But, the heart of each individual holds the key to all truth, all love, and all that is good and beautiful. The wonder of the pure of heart solves all perceived problems, overcomes all self-induced challenges, and leads everyone to the altar of the divine, where the beloved of their own soul embraces and releases the past. And then grace flows through the Master from within and delivers you to the present moment where all is created. OM, the vibration of the pulse of this universe, expands and contracts into a form, and here you are. Now you know, Victoria; victorious you are and Master you can become through the melding of hearts. Sara and you are my beloved children, and together you shall serve now and forevermore. You and I are one in unified consciousness and purpose. 'I love you' is a misnomer of separate consciousness. 'I am Love' is more the truth, for inside the field of Love, there is only one."

266

"OK, now what? Let's walk home, Sara," she said aloud. "Wow. How fun this game of consciousness is when you know how it is created; there really is nothing to fear except fear itself."

Alas, there are moments in life that are etched in the memory of the soul and can be retrieved when all else is coming to a remorseful end. And so it was, that day, as Victoria and Sara moved on toward the park, and the peak moment began to fade, and the slip of the memory was gently placed in the archives of the Akasha. To be retrieved, one need only think it, and to fully feel it again, one must surrender fully to it. "Don't go away, my God," she cried. "Stay with me in this way forever."

"Ah, forever I shall love you and be one with you. Just ask for me to appear in your awareness. Focus, focus; focus on your heart and call to the I AM presence—OM, OM, OM. The intensity will vary, but the taste will remain, and the knowing is imprinted in your soul. Remember, love is all there is."

She walked through the park with a smile on her face, seeing as she had never seen before, and sat on a bench holding Sara and bonding heart to heart. "Sara," she said, "how grateful I am for you and for this time together. I feel you so deep in me. There is no separation. I see you as me, me as you; it is so easy really—the oneness. What shall we do together?"

Sara smiled, held out her arms, and *said*, "Love, what else?" Or at least that is what her heart said. So they shared together the miraculous moment of truth, love, and the gift of life. At 23 years old, Victoria felt almost ancient—timeless really, wise and comfortable. *Can it always stay like this? It is so wonderful*, she thought.

"In the moment, there is always wonder, all possibility unfolding. Open—stay open," she heard from her guidance. And she began to feel the difference between her ego-thoughts and the field of all knowing. "Presence," she was told; "practice presence."

When she got home, there were no words to express her experience to Jessica. So they sat in silence, meditating together, and then Jessica understood—based on her own knowing. It felt like a direct transference occurred, and she settled into her own field of knowing so that when they opened their eyes their hearts bonded, and they smiled at the miraculous moment of their own making and felt the Presence that both hearts knew so well: the fiber of their being constructing the fabric of their life.

"Well," Jessica spoke first, "not really much to say or do in this state of being, is there?"

"No," Victoria said, "nothing left to do. However, I know tomorrow I'll be back at work, and it will feel like another day. But I wonder, what is next?"

"Sleep, Victoria; let's sleep on it," Jessica said. They both smiled and wandered off to bed, relaxing deeper than ever before. *Contemplating life had a whole new meaning,* Jessica thought. *Experiencing life through surrender—now—that is the way to go.*

CHAPTER 6

The next day, Jessica woke up to Greg's phone call. He was gasping for breath as he proclaimed his love for her during his early-morning run. "What are you doing?" he said.

"Are you crazy?" Jessica asked, "over the phone like this?"

"Yes," he said, "it just came to me. I had to tell you just in case something would happen and I would miss out on the chance to tell you how extraordinary you are and how much you have positively affected my life. I know that it's short notice, but can you meet me in the park now?"

"Well, um, yes," Jessica said. "Just let me get dressed. I'll need at least 30 minutes here, is that OK?"

"Yes!" Greg exclaimed.

Jessica asked, "I love your craziness, but I have to know. Is everything OK?"

"Yes, it's more than OK." Greg replied. "I think I'm in love. I just have to see you, Jessica. Now. OK?" he said with excited urgency.

"Sure, lovey, I'll be there. Is our favorite park bench OK with you?"

"Yep, that's perfect. I'll reserve our spot." They hung up the phone, and Jessica pondered. *How, is this possible, after such a short time, knowing this man? I just know he's the one. I guess I've been waiting for some sign that the feeling is mutual and I'm not just imagining these feelings or being fooled by my crazy thoughts—which do seem to get out of hand at times, I must say. But then, who knows what tomorrow will bring? It's such a mystery really... life. It is constantly being created and destroyed by the power of my thoughts and beliefs and those around me. Wow. It's extraordinary how it all "works,"* she thought.

She got dressed, singing out loud to an old Beatles tune: "Let it be; speaking words of wisdom, let it be," and then she hurried out the door, without breakfast, and ran to meet Greg in the park. When she got there, he was sitting on their favorite bench, eyes closed, leaning back, and taking in the morning sun. It was one of those perfect mornings: air clean, sun bright, temperature around 75 degrees and just a hint of a breeze, flowers blooming, birds singing, and a freshness that could only foster the newness of a possibly perfect day full of hope and delight.

Whatever shall become of this moment, Jessica thought, *it shall forever remain a perfectly, extraordinarily, ordinary beginning to another most mysterious day, full of possibilities.*

She sat down quietly next to him, wondering what he was thinking. Quickly, she knew.

"Good morning, Love," Greg said.

"Good morning, Love," Jessica replied. They touched hands, and he opened his eyes and caught her gaze. "That's really all there is, Jess," Greg smiled. "Love. I just had this amazing epiphany, which is a little hard to put into words, really. I've been thinking about all kinds of things and questioning what to do for the rest of my life. You know, planning and calculating, wondering and pondering, so much that my brain finally stopped. There was so much thinking, and nothing productive was coming from it. So, I just let go, and suddenly, there was this silence—a profound silence. Everything seemed to disappear but this Presence that came from within the stillness and a profound nothingness that became everything. Potential, infinite potential, illuminated magic in the midst of the one profound moment where everything is created. That is when it struck me: I am the one creating this life. The creative life force is in me, and I can either use it to create love or stress. Which do I want? And then I felt something inside my chest that at first, I thought, wow, this is it: the moment I disappear and have some heart thing take me out, some unknown genetic defect or something. And as that thought returned, I felt the Presence say, 'No, this isn't the time to exit your body, this is the time to fully arrive.' And then all the thoughts disappeared again, and I realized there is something here inside my heart that needs to express—to give—and that is the epicenter for the feelings generated from my thoughts. And, what I really want more than anything is love. And then I thought of you. I love you, Jessica. For the first time in my life I am in love, with you, and I am free to express and to be all of who I am. I know that this world is created one moment at a time. I just had to see you, touch you, and experience you in this amazing, magic moment. This is my 'ah-ha' moment. Do you follow me?"

Jessica sat stunned because of her own recent experience that seemed to fit into a great puzzle that, as she now reflected, made her realize: *this perfect moment is where it all makes sense. No matter what or how or even when or where, it all makes sense when you relax into the now.*

"This Presence you speak of, Greg, I know. And the love thing, well, it is more than a feeling. 'It' is what is creating everything that feels right and good. It is God, don't you think?" She smiled and then started to giggle. "When you <u>know</u>, it is now; when you <u>think</u>, it was then, or it hasn't happened yet. When you <u>know</u>, you just know." They both started to laugh and hugged each other and embraced where words were no longer necessary. And then, in a joint "ah-ha" moment, they both "knew" this is it, now.

"Whatever we shall do next, we will always have now," Jessica said.

"I know," Greg replied.

Then they got up and walked to their favorite café and joined the concurrent reality of others in the mainstream of humanity and sat outside enjoying that first sip of coffee and that wonderful aroma of freshly baked pastries. "I think I'll indulge today and start off with chocolate and berries," Jessica said.

Greg replied, "And I will join you."

As they drank and ate, smiling from the depths of their hearts, their faces became bright and enlivened with the grace of knowing love really is all there is when you let go.

"Wow, these are really great, Love, don't you think?" Greg asked.

"No, I <u>know</u> they are," Jessica said. And then they laughed so loud that others turned and looked. Smiles were seen all around. "I know now," Jessica said, "that love is all there is when you relax and allow the moment to be what it is."

"Yes, and chocolate and berries take on a whole new meaning," Greg quirked in. "I want to feel gloriously high like this <u>all</u> the time!"

"Believe in now and it can be so," Jessica heard her inner voice say. "Believe in love and trust the concurrent series of events unfolding before you, and set yourself free of all the entanglements the mind would have you believe about what is and what is not. Everything is possible when you really relax, so let go and believe you can have it all. All the gloriously high moments occur when you are fully present and relax into now. It is in this moment where I live. I live here in your heart. Share these words with Greg and you will <u>know</u>."

"What words?" Jessica asked, out loud.

"What?" Greg said.

"Oh, um, wait a minute," Jessica replied.

To her inner voice, she said, "I'm listening. What did you want me to say to Greg?"

"I love you," she heard as she continued her dialogue with her inner Guidance.

She replied, "But he's supposed to say it first."

"He did, in his own way, when he said 'I'm in love with you.' See what happens, OK?"

"OK," she responded in her heart.

She turned to Greg. "Greg?" she asked.

"Yes, love?" he said.

"I love you. I really do love you," she said from her heart.

There was a pause. Greg stopped midstream, coffee to mouth, and smiled. "Really? I wanted to believe that and to trust what I was feeling from you, but I really wanted to <u>know</u>. Hearing you say these words in this moment means everything to me. I love you, Jessica. Will you spend your life with me exploring all the wonderful *nows* yet to come?"

"Yes, of course I will. You're wonderful, Greg, absolutely wonderful."

He pulled a small box out of his pocket and handed it to her. "I know this is impulsive and may not be the right, perfect place, but, Jessica, I want you to have this to remember this perfect day and to remember whatever happens, we will always have <u>now</u>. I love you."

Stunned, Jessica opened it to discover a necklace with a heart. She was very moved, almost to tears.

"I want you to know, Jessica, you have my heart now. I cherish all of who you are. I see you now, so clearly."

Then everything stopped. The molecules of reality were suspended in that moment, and time literally "stood still." There was nothing but the two of them, "now," holding hands, looking at each other, and the two hearts paused in remembrance of the moment they agreed upon (before incarnating) to meet again, to come together. And this precious moment was it. Reunion.

"I, Jessica, see you, Greg. You are my beloved, now. Thank you for seeing me and trusting your own heart. Love is great, and you are still as wonderful as ever. I remember you. Love shines in your eyes and illuminates your soul. You're so wonderfully magnificent to me." She started to sing spontaneously a song that came from her heart, and the melody captivated his heart, and he held her close as they both stood up and embraced each other physically. He took the necklace and placed it lovingly around her neck and stood back to view the lovely picture of beauty that stood before him.

"Jessica, you are so dear to me," Greg said. "I love you so."

The song ended, but not the embrace, which continued heart to heart. They found themselves holding hands and strolling from the café, oblivious to anyone else. Jessica was mesmerized by their connection and prayed with great gratitude to never let this moment go or to let it be forgotten. And as she found herself thinking this prayer, she realized she was awakened inside the illusion, inside the dream of the physical reality. *The almighty power of God, was and is here now. Prayers are for the future, she thought, and knowing is for the now. So I need to pray for awakening now. That's the only prayer needed*, she realized, *to stay open and to stay awake.*

"Thank you, beloved God," she expressed, "for this awakening. I see you now everywhere. I am so totally grateful." Her heart sang the final verse of her current song, and the consensual reality reappeared in their awareness.

"We are all love, all light, expansive and illuminated, here, now." *Wow*, Jessica thought, *stands for: Wonderful, Omnipotent, Woman.*

As if Greg could hear her thoughts, they both laughed out loud with pure delight and continued walking in the park, enjoying everything around them and each other. There was so much love and so much joy that there was no room for fear or thoughts, only <u>now</u>.

"Yea!" she exclaimed with glee, and she skipped and shouted, "We are free!"

Greg smiled and watched her skip off, feeling her purity and innocence as she delighted in her own self. And he was able to see his own inner child become free, and he joined her, running in circles around her as she skipped and they both sang songs spontaneously, moving and dancing to their own music.

"Isn't this a great game?" she asked.

"Absolutely," Greg said, smiling. "Absolutely!"

When Jessica arrived home much later that night, Victoria and Sara were both sleeping in the living room with the TV on. Jessica went over to gaze at Sara and said, "I see you, too, Miss Sara. You are the divine creation of my dear sister and I cherish you to the depth of my heart. I feel like I've always known you. Sisters we are, still." Sara stirred a bit but did not awaken, and Jessica sat down and turned off the TV and began recapping the last 24 hours so she could do a bit of processing in her mind. She welled up with tears, she laughed, she cried, and then she giggled as she recapped the magnificent day. That's what she would always remember it by—*Magnificent Monday*—the day of her own awakening. *Who said Mondays were so bad?* She smiled at the thought as Victoria began to awaken from her own sleep and turned over on the magic couch, as they called it, because both Victoria and Jessica were sure it was sprinkled with fairy dust.

"Oh, hi; what time is it, Jess?"

"Two o'clock, I think."

"Really? What's up?"

"Oh," Jessica said, "so much has happened. Today was wonderful! Let's talk in the morning when we're both fresh, OK?"

"OK." Victoria toddled off to bed as Jessica picked up Sara to put her in her own bed. Jessica lay down in her bed expecting to not be able to sleep, but as soon as she did, the magic of sleep came, and she drifted off into another dream.

CHAPTER 7

As I lie here dreaming, I often think of you.
Thoughts pour in from an untrained mind, and I wander off to a land that has no return path.
I lie here dreaming, sometimes of a world beyond my imagining.
To the greater dream we all share in common.

No more do I wonder if, or when, or how; I just imagine you lying here beside me in a world of our own creating. Today there is nowhere we must go, and there is nothing we must do but love each other to the depths of our hearts.

Today as I lie here dreaming, I imagine a moment of no return where the two paths we have been on bring us together onto the same path where we know beyond all previous fear and doubt that today we have met our destiny, and together we traverse the world that lies ahead, sharing a common dream.
To spend our time together, good times and not—catching the thoughts that collide and create pain through the illusion of fear.

As I lie here together with you, I imagine the common thread of desire that brought us together—again—to awaken our hearts to all the possibilities we can manifest when we dream our dream together.

Today as I lie here dreaming of you, I know I have met myself in another form, and all will transpire according to the infinite plan of our souls.

Today I have found you, again, and the world as I know it, will never be the same.

Today as I lie here with you in my mind and in my heart, I know we shall never part.

I love you, always.

Greg

Wow, Greg thought, *I never really felt like writing. I guess I needed to extrapolate the moment more clearly for my mind to consider; yes, it is really happening, I have found my soul mate!* And as Love would happen, the words that poured onto the page were perfect, like a script his soul had written, his life and heart now intertwined with another. *As Love would have it,* he thought, *it is all unfolding so perfectly.* And with that, he lay down to join Jessica in the dreamtime where worlds connect in a very different but succinct way, and he dreamed of his future and possibilities that had never crossed his mind before.

To dream the dream of the One becoming many and two becoming one in union with their own soul purpose. To love and to be loved, is all there is.

These words lit up on a marquee in his dream and he woke up in that moment, inside the dream. Wow, I am dreaming all of this. The lights in the marquee began to blink on and off as if waiting for direction. *Love is all that matters,* he thought, and instantly the words appeared on the marquee. And just underneath it were these words:

Love Is All There Is

Strange name for a movie, he laughed. And then he heard a voice echoing back to him: "Strange name for a movie. Truth is stranger than fiction." *Now that's a great name for a movie.* And with that, the words appeared. Again and again he did this until he realized it was all being created by him until he thought, *where is this thought coming from?* Then everything changed; the marquee disappeared and there was nothing to be seen. He waited. Nothing. Then he asked again, "*Where do these thoughts come from? Am I still dreaming?*" And then there was this enormous light everywhere, surreal almost. It was like the sun, but different. He was surrounded in light. Then he felt his body blinking into his awareness and then off again, solid, yet not solid, and mostly light after all.

He thought: *where am I?*

"With me," the Light said. "We are in this together."

"*Are you the Light? Are you the creator of the thoughts?*"

And then, again, everything went still and yet was pulsing and vibrating as if waiting for a cue from some invisible, concealed center.

"It is me; it is all me. I create everything from this void and Light. You are my creation, and I gave you the gift to co-create with me. I wait for your command. All thoughts originate from here. It is where dreams are created. The dense matter you call real is just part of the story. It is, as you can now see, bigger than the thoughts."

"*Who am I in this story? Who are you?*"

"We are one now in this creation story, in dialogue."

"*And the marquee?*" It popped back up and on it was written:

I AM

And then the phone rang, and he was "awakened" and he saw his bedroom, his body, and at first felt discombobulated and disoriented until he saw himself once again as Greg and then he had a thought: *What is that?* The answer came to him: "The phone."

Oh yeah, OK. Wow. Then he picked it up and said, "Hello?"

"Good morning." It was Jessica.

"Oh, good morning, Love," Greg said. "Did you know love is all there is and that the marquee waits for the cue from the command center of the soul known as the I AM Presence, and that it is up to my individuated self to interpret and co-direct it?"

There was a long pause at the end of the phone and then Jessica replied, "No, I just know I love you, and I am so happy! What marquee?"

"Oh, you know, the one in my dream I was just having. Interesting, now I wonder, which is the dream? Oh well, I guess it is time for this one. What shall we do today?"

"Whatever we want," Jessica said. "We both still have no commitments for this day, right?"

"Well, we can always do whatever we want," Greg said, "and, yes, I want to be with you."

"Great," Jessica said. "Because I was just thinking that we could be together. I was wondering if you had plans yet."

"Yes, I have. I plan to be with you," Greg responded. And then they both started to laugh and both said, in union, "OK, when?"

Greg spoke first. "I'll be over in an hour and then we will decide what. OK?"

"OK. Will you be bringing clothes for all occasions, then?" Jessica asked.

"No, just casual today; let's relax together, first. I'll bring sneakers to walk later. Shall we start with brunch?"

"Yes, that sounds great," Jessica swooned. "See you soon."

As she hung up the phone she thought of herself in a dream in a big theater with a marquee, upon which the words emerged:

I Am In Love With You

She smiled to herself, closed her eyes, and felt her heart as big as the sky and was instantly in love and soared with joy. She went to the shower singing, "Oh, what a beautiful morning; oh, what a beautiful day."

Later, Victoria awoke to the sound of Sara crying and realized it was time to get up and be a mom again. She was dreaming of herself inside a car driving with Sara in the back and wondering where she was going and where to turn off before she got too lost in what appeared to be a strange environment. She was happy to awaken again in her familiar home environment. *OK*, she thought; *I'm back.*

Sara gave her life purpose and a timing that allowed for both stability and comfort and a joy that encompassed her entire being. *I never thought I'd love this so much*, she thought to herself as she picked up Sara, who instantly stopped crying. They loved each other with that divine innocence reminiscent of the light that they both shared, and they laughed together in their hearts, understanding that it is all a dream.

When the doorbell rang, it was time for the day to expand into its fullness, and Victoria emerged with Sara to find Greg and Jessica in an embrace. "We're in love," Jessica announced.

And Greg piped in, "Oh, yeah, and we're spending our lives together being very happy!"

Everyone laughed as Victoria said, "Wow! I go to sleep and wake up and the whole world changes," she snapped her fingers, "just like that."

"I know! Isn't it great?" Jessica said. "Everything is always changing." They sat down to share a cup of coffee and to share their dreams from the night before, with Jessica going last.

"Well," she said. "All I remember is this feeling of being on a cloud and floating, so that whatever I could think, I could feel, and it was instantly created. So it had the feeling of pure creativity and wonderment of what was being created. Greg was having a similar awakening, I think; don't you think so, Victoria?"

"Well," Victoria replied. "It sounds like we all connected in some alter-universe, so I guess it is true: we are all connected, and we are what we think, so think good things and good things will come to you. Is that it?"

"Yes, something like that," Greg said. "I've heard it is called lucid dreaming, where you awaken inside the dream and you can create it any way you want. I asked, 'who are you?' and all I got was, **I AM.**"

"Well, that is the beginning of everything," Jessica said. "We have to fill in the blank. I am—in love—or, I am Love; two different things, really."

"Yes, I guess you're right," Greg smiled. "I get to fill in the blank. I am in love with you," he said as he reached for her hand, and they both smiled and decided it was time for brunch. They said their goodbyes to Victoria and Sara and walked out, hand in hand, ready for their next adventure together.

"Well, Sara, it's you and me today. Let's go shopping!" So Victoria got ready and took Sara out in the stroller to visit all her favorite little shops in the neighborhood, everything from clothes to accessories, to food and wine. They really did well together. Sara was really good out in her stroller and enjoyed riding and seeing everything. She was often the focus of attention. Everyone was in awe of her smile and the glow from her big, beautiful blue eyes. Sometimes, thoughts came to Victoria about Sara's father, as she wondered what he was doing and what he would think of his daughter. *One day*, she thought, *I know I will see him again but not yet. I'm not ready. Shopping is so much easier, she thought, and quite entertaining. It's a great way to spend a Sunday. Tomorrow I will be back to work in an environment that feels so limiting and confining. I am glad that that is always changing also. For now, I need to be in this moment so I don't lose my entire day thinking of other things.*

"Hey Victoria, I haven't seen you in so long," she heard a voice say.

Who is that, she wondered? "Oh, Susan, how are you?" she asked, as she recognized one of her yoga students.

"I've been traveling a lot for work, so I've missed class." They discussed where she had been, including Paris, which Victoria thought sounded very intriguing. *Think of the shopping there*, she thought. They decided to have lunch and really catch up, so they both chose a little café about a block away that had fresh salads they could both enjoy. They sat down outside to enjoy the sun.

"Paris is great." Susan said. "There are lots of good places to eat and shop and meet people. It's not as cold as some Americans say, but I'm always ready to come home. I actually really love it here and miss my routines, like my yoga class."

"Well, it is always great when you're in class," Victoria said. "I always want to improve my teaching, but I haven't made it a priority for the last six months because I've been doing other things. I really need to get back to my own practice. I always feel so much better when I do, and I am usually very inspired and can share with others through my own explorations. It's really fun, creating through movement. It's like a metaphor for creating my life. How about you?" she asked Susan.

"You mean am I doing a home practice? Usually 20 – 30 minutes per day, plus your class two times per week. That is my ultimate goal, although I manage 30 minutes three times per week and one class. I am aiming higher." They both smiled as they acknowledged silently how other things in life go in and out of priority and how it's so easy to get distracted and lose focus on one's own self-practice.

Victoria said, "I'm always in the 'some is better than none' camp, and I try to love what is, so congratulations on what you <u>are</u> doing. I think it's great!"

"Well, I'm looking forward to class this week. I'll see you there. I'd better go." Susan smiled. They hugged goodbye, paid the bill, and walked out to go their separate ways.

"Until then," Victoria said.

"Love you," Susan replied.

All the while, Greg and Jessica had found the perfect setting for their brunch adventure and decided they would go on a very long walk and just meander through the park right outside the neighborhood. The park was big enough to get lost in without running out of time to celebrate the "love thing" that they decided was the name for their newfound co-experiences together, and they chuckled out loud at how wonderful everything appeared when you really settled into the moment without a thought of anything else that did not have importance or wasn't pertinent to the moment.

"How incredible," Jessica said.

"Yeah, it's the love thing," Greg laughed.

"It's all there is," they both said together as they found a bench to sit on and take in the fresh air and sunshine; another perfect moment.

CHAPTER 8

"When all else fails to satisfy, one must turn to the Source. For inside the universal there is a boundless supply of energy and love to accomplish all things. Within the universal flow of love, there streams a river of grace to benefit a multitude of possibilities. Whatever it is you wish to accomplish, the flow of this Source is endless with possibilities and awaits direction with purpose. What is the focus of your mind today? Where do you want your life to flow: toward a centered purpose of love and joy, your true nature, or into some vast nowhere land of mindless thoughts? Do you wish to drift in a boat with no paddle and no direction, lost in the clouds of uncertainty? Or would you like to join me, and together we can tether ourselves to a life of love and endless possibilities to serve with purpose and joy?"

Victoria's pen stopped as she heard her inner voice dictate her opening remarks of her first attempt at journaling in months. *Gee,* she thought, *let me think, love and joy with a sense of purpose or aimlessly drifting in the proverbial boat without a paddle? OK, I'll bite, love and joy with a sense of purpose. I choose a life of service with joy and love in my heart.* She wrote, *Then, what?*

"Then, together we merge with ease and grace as the river of love carries you from one moment to another with effortless flow. Do you want to know what is always next or would you enjoy some surprises?" Guidance replied.

That depends, Victoria wrote. *I worry about what's next, sometimes.*

"That is because you are projecting a negative thought form into the future based on a fear that is usually unconscious. It is always best to relax into the moment to allow the manifestation of the exquisite play of light to dance the next miracle of form into the present moment. Don't you agree, V?"

Of course I agree, she thought. *But how do I do that? Relax into the unknown without a care or thought about what's next or what's left behind me? How do I relax into the moment and carry on without any plans for my life?*

"Great question, Miss V. Let me hereby lay out the steps to meditation and manifesting form out of the formless concoction of the multitude of possibilities ever present in every moment.

1. Clear your mind.
   a. Be still and 'listen.'
   b. Let go of the constant chatter by breathing and focusing your eyes on the center of form in the center of your brain (known, of course, as the third eye in yoga).
   c. Relax your body, be comfortable, and be at ease with yourself.
   d. Settle into the center of your being, the center of your body, and feel your heart center expanding.
   e. Chant your name for God from this heart center where your beloved awaits your attention and focus.
   f. Then, allow the energy of your Love-light to spread and release all darkness or dense thoughts and residual negativity from your field, and release all the anxiety and fear accumulated from your day and past ventures. Or, you can start each day anew by focusing on your heart center and allow the greatest gift of all to shine through.

"We believe in a peaceful resolution to the world's trouble and that each heart must remember solace. To manifest peace outside, focus on peace inside. Let love bless you each moment with inner peace. A regular time set aside for your meditation practice is critical."

Pardon me, but who is the "we" you speak of? I thought I was listening here to some inner guidance like God.

"We are your guidance in the form of guides—connecting you to the Divine, the Supreme Godhead. We are intermediaries, if you will, but, we are well-versed, in this meditation practice. This way, God directs or delegates to beings in the light with experience in these matters. Now are you ready for the next phase?"

Yes.

"OK, here it is:

2. Simplify your life through a spiritual focus. It's all quite easy to believe in love when all is going well. It is much more challenging to believe and trust when there are so many challenges occurring around you. Stop and simplify by focusing on one point, and breathe. Manifesting begins with one-point focus. Begin with your heart.

3. Open your heart to love with focused intention. Begin anew with each breath and the realization that all is moving in the direction of your focus. Clarity, wisdom, and ultimate freedom occur with a love-centered focus. There have been many names given through the multitudes of creation, and yet, the one universal experience of all of humanity is love. The heart is your love center. Enjoy the expansive embrace of bliss.

4. Say a command. The Universe waits for your command. Think of it as a thought-prayer. For example, pray for peace. Think of ways to live and serve in peace.

5. Be in the moment. What serves this moment? Train the mind to live in peaceful harmony in the 'what is' while accepting and allowing what is in this moment.

6. Live from inside Love—in the moment. What is called for now? And now?

7. Take every action step from a state of being vs. doing. This way, the action comes from a deep place of inner knowing and wise counsel from the heart of Love, with great clarity and wisdom.

8. Release all perceptions and judgments, and open to infinite possibilities and ways for love to manifest...now."

Victoria laid down her pen and paused for a moment to take in what was written, allowing the information to settle in her unconscious, as well as, the conscious mind. She settled into her heart-center and began to breathe, allowing the energy to move without direction. She felt all kinds of sensations from cold to hot, from stillness to trembling; her mind was clear and then thoughts appeared. Deep prayerful desires floated to the surface. She allowed the entire process, moving from one moment of *now* to the next until she landed in a place of being. *I am open to love and infinite potential in my being-ness.* Then her eyes opened, and she was sitting in alignment in body, mind, and spirit. She felt whole, complete, peaceful and content.

"From this moment, all is created," she heard the voice of Guidance say.

I wish to allow God to run my life. This was her first thought as she emerged from the state of meditation. *Thy will be done,* she thought-prayed.

"And so it is, fair maiden. Your wish is my command." She giggled at the next thought as she began to see a medieval castle and knights in shining armor arrive at her throne. "What say ye, my lady?"

"Oh," she said aloud. "I want to be happy."

"So be it. So it is," said the two knights as they bowed at her feet.

"Arise, dear knights; I bid thee farewell. Do the work of Love and serve with honor from your heart. I am happy...now."

And as they arose, she saw the eyes of one of them, and she smiled. He reminded her of a lover she once knew. His heart was pure, and his eyes glowed with a bright light.

"I bid thee farewell, then. It is my honor to serve," he said, "and I am happy to be."

She smiled as she opened her eyes and found herself back in her apartment. Sara was just awakening from her nap, and Victoria arose to hold her with delight. "I really am happy, Sara, but I also feel it is time to move. I don't know where or when, but I feel it. Somehow, an opportunity will arise. I trust the Divine will, and I will stay open to possibilities."

"I love you Mama," Sara said for the first time. Victoria was so happy. Ecstasy arose, and she swung her around, laughing. "Picture time!" Victoria said as she raced for the camera. "This is it, Sara; smile!" Click. "Done. The moment has been dutifully recorded."

They went about the rest of their day, and the profound mundane took on a whole new feeling as she practiced living in the moment and opening to possibilities.

Different feelings still arose, and they passed just as quickly as they came. *I don't know why I feel this good,* Victoria thought, *but I will take it.* Sara was part of it. She knew that their connection spanned lifetimes, but just how, she could not tell. She could just see it in her eyes and knew their connection was destiny.

"I don't ever remember life without you, dear one," she said to Sara. "That feels like a whole other life – BS (Before Sara)." She giggled out loud. "Well, that sure is what is was, Sara...BS."

She allowed herself to travel back in time to when she was with "him." Morsels of memory began to appear across the movie screen of her mind, and she remembered the times they'd go walking hand in hand on the city streets and in the variety of parks they used to visit. She allowed herself to enjoy the memory of the love they shared and the incredible magic of his touch. The look in his eyes helped her to feel the mirror of his soul peering back at her.

"I love you so," he would say.

"And I so love you," she would reply.

She remembered the night they first expressed their love and all the feelings that arose as she pictured their life together. He was very attentive then, which seemed to quickly change as he got his new job and began to travel and spend more time away from her. It was great for a while, since they were always so happy to return to each other's arms.

But then, one day it changed. It felt almost sudden to her. She felt something shift, and she questioned him about it. "Oh, nothing," he replied. "I'm just fine."

Yeah, right, she thought. "It's like you just turned off a switch and now you're gone."

"I'm not gone," he said. "I'm just on a hiatus and feeling a little stressed."

"Oh, I see," Victoria remarked. "Now you've decided to act like a guy and retreat to your cave. How long do you stay in there?"

"As long as it takes," he snapped back.

It was the first time he was ever abrupt or angry in any way. It took her by surprise, and she stepped back to look him in the eyes, as if to get a better look at him. "Something happened, didn't it?" she asked, which was more like a statement of fact since she could sense it so strongly. "What is it? What's wrong?"

"Oh, nothing," he said. "I just get this way when I'm really tired. You just haven't seen me this tired or stressed out. I'm really sorry; I just can't fake it with you."

"Let's talk, then, OK?" Victoria said. "No, I think I just need to be at home and do guy things today. I'll call you a little later."

They hugged and parted as he went back to his own house, and she remembered sitting on the couch in a daze. She was upset to consider how quickly he had shifted and wondered what was really going on. By the time she stopped thinking about it, she was in tears and had to call Jessica to talk about it. She remembered vividly Jessica saying, "Victoria, don't worry about it. It's just another phase in the relationship. He's just tired and stressed and needs to be alone in his man cave and get some rest. He'll be OK," she reassured. "Don't worry so much."

"OK, thanks Jess. I guess you're right. Hey, how about a movie after yoga tonight?"

"OK, sounds good. I will look at what's playing that will make us laugh," Jessica said.

Victoria remembered that night very well. All in all, a chick flick was in order — one of those non-memorable romantic comedies with a predictable ending, but it served its purpose. The mind got clear of worry, and a contented feeling took the place of anxiety and worry about the future. "Why do I always go back and wonder or go forward with worry with no clue about what is happening right here/right now?" she asked Jessica.

"I don't know, Victoria. You're the yogini girl. I don't have a clue about life. I just go with it and pretend I don't have a care in the world. Love is just a figment of my imagination, but I am sure it can change because Hollywood can't make up all that stuff in the movie. Can they, Victoria?" she asked Victoria in reference to the movie.

Victoria replied, "Well, I figure life is an amazing journey and that the adventure occurs because no one knows what the ending is going to be. That is what makes it such an amazing journey. The Great Mystery seems to unfold with such an amazing perfection, with and without our consent."

"You mean free will?" Jessica pondered.

"Yea, something like that," Victoria laughed.

"Well, I for one want my script so I can see how it unfolds," Jessica insisted. "This Great Mystery is for the birds!"

"Some days," Victoria forewarned, "you just might not want to know. Besides, knowing might just change the entire thing."

As Victoria remembered this dialogue so succinctly, she realized it was because her entire world was about to change. All her dreams and assumptions about her future shattered, like a mirror thrown to the pavement.

She stopped her mind there. "Pause picture," Victoria said aloud, "I don't want to remember the next part." *Ah but you do remember,* her thoughts said, *you just don't want to replay it.*

"No, not now," Victoria asserted, "not now. That was then. It all worked out OK."

Well that's what you tell yourself now—then you were a mess!

"Life is meant to be enjoyed—right, Guidance?" She continued talking to herself and refused to continue down a road of thought bound to despair. Then the funniest thing happened. The phone rang. "Yea, saved by the bell!" Victoria said aloud.

"Hello," Victoria said, not noticing the caller ID.

There was a long pause on the other end. "Hello," Victoria said again, and just as she was about to hang up, she heard a very familiar voice.

"V?" he said. (That was always what he called her when he was serious about something.)

She stopped dead in her tracks as she was walking toward Sara. *OMG*, she thought. "It's you, isn't it?"

"It's me," John said with that amazing voice that first melted her heart years ago. She sat down, tears rolling down her face, not knowing what to say next.

"Are you there?" he said. "I know this must seem like a surprise. Please don't hang up. I really need to talk to you. Is now a good time?"

"A good time?" she scowled. "Is now a good time? For what?"

"To talk. I'd rather not do it over the phone. I would like to see you, if that's at all possible. Please, V, it's important. Can we talk?"

"That depends! Are you married?" she asked. She could hear what sounded like crying and no answer. "Are you OK?" Victoria asked.

"That depends on your definition. It's complicated. Will you see me? I understand if you're angry with me. I am angry with myself. I let you go and have never been the same. It's been hell inside this heart of mine, and I just can't stand it anymore. V, I still love you—please—just see me so I can explain."

At that point, Victoria sat down and began to cry, almost uncontrollably. Flashes of memory began to come back to her, like snapshots in a photo album. She put the phone down and couldn't speak. Her heart was breaking open, and she could feel the stored up pain pouring out, combined with a sort of release upon hearing the words, "I love you." She missed those eyes so much she thought she'd die. The pent up grief continued until she heard another voice.

"Victoria, what's wrong?" Jessica said as she and Greg came in to find Victoria in an emotional puddle.

"It's him." She pointed to the phone on the coffee table.

Jessica stopped dead in her tracks. "Is he still on the phone?" she asked. "Do you want me to pick it up?"

"No," Victoria shook her head. "I'll do this." She picked up the phone, and to her great surprise he was still there. She didn't know how long he'd been waiting until she looked down at her phone and saw eight minutes. "You're still here?" She seemed surprised.

"Yes," he said, "I'm still here. I am so sorry, V. I know this is a shock to your system."

"My system?" Victoria exclaimed. "My heart is breaking. I don't ever want to feel this again. To me, you are dead."

"Wait," John said. "Wait. I am not dead, but the man who broke your heart is. I've buried him. But, I never want to bury the love we had; it is so precious to me."

"Really?" Victoria said. "Really?"

"Please," John repeated, "this is too hard over the phone. If you see me, you can yell to my face. I understand. I was a schmuck!"

"That's putting it mildly," Victoria said.

"Well, there really are no words that can describe my remorse. Please let me see you." John was crying.

Jessica looked at Victoria and said, "Do what your untainted heart tells you to do, Victoria. Listen deeper, below the emotions. What does your Guidance say?"

Victoria paused. She thought, *What would love do? If I don't see him, I'll regret it because deep in my heart, I've been dying to see him again. I can do this.* She started to breathe with a heart focus and calmed herself down and replied. "John, I will see you. There are some things we really should discuss. Can we agree to keep our hearts open as best we can?"

"Yes. I never want mine shut down again." He cried with relief as they began to agree on a time and place. "Today—is it possible to see you today?"

"Yes. OK. Yes," she said with great anxiety, but also with some relief in her heart. She had cried many a tear for this man, the one she thought she would spend the rest of her life with, only to suddenly have the door of her heart slammed closed without even a mere warning of what was coming. She sat down on the couch and began to sob the tears that remained from a broken heart. Jessica sat beside her to comfort her as Greg sat down quietly in the armchair across from them that was reserved for the sacred witness of things that were and for things that were yet to be. As she cried, she felt this overwhelming grief that had gotten buried underneath the armor of her heart that had protected her so well these last few years. She felt as though she was crying the grief for the multitudes, for all those who had ever loved and lost. Feelings of fear and betrayal arose, along with overwhelming anger and confusion, with all the force of a tsunami. In constant waves, the feelings came again and again. Like waves being crashed on the beach from an ocean during a storm, Victoria felt she could cry forever. And then, like the day after the amazingly tumultuous storm, the tears stopped, and the quiet sadness surfaced, revealing her greatest fear of all—being alone in her isolated grief and abandonment, without anyone to turn to, and no one who really cared for her.

"Oh my," she finally said. "I get it, why this all had to happen. I needed to know I had friends to turn to and the strength and willingness inside to carry on, to look in the face of supreme innocence and see God shining back to me. I needed to be alone with Sara and to experience God and to know that no matter what, I would never betray or abandon her, nor would she do so to me, for the grace of God runs through our very souls and connects our hearts for eternity. And now it is time for her to know her father, who gave her the seed of life, and to allow him to know the truth. Jessica, how? How do I tell him?" she asked.

"How do you want to do this, Victoria? Do you want us to watch Sara for you and have him meet her later? We can do that, can't we, Greg?" Jessica asked.

They both looked up to see tears running down his face. Having shared such a poignant moment together, they all sat in silence until Greg responded.

"Of course." Then he gasped as though he had been holding his breath underwater for a long time and said, "This John is a very lucky man. I can only imagine what he will feel to see his beloved again and the precious child he has fathered. Victoria, be kind to him. It's as if I feel his pain. He has missed you. Something terrible must have happened. I don't know what, but I just feel that whatever it was, it frightened him to his core."

Jessica and Victoria stared at him, knowing that he was tapping into his intuitive nature, perhaps for the first time, as he felt everything in his own heart.

"We are all one," Jessica said. "We are all one."

Sara perked up her ears and spoke the word Mama just at that moment, and they all laughed. "Yes?" they all replied simultaneously, feeling like a family—the family that they all were with Sara in the middle of them all—the innocent reminder of the present moment that only a child could deliver, with the pure presence of the divine. They all laughed, knowing that the joke of the Universe was getting played out.

"What an amazing game this is," Victoria said. "Oh, I just realized we didn't say where or when to meet today."

"Anytime is good for us," Greg said. "We can pick up a movie and hang out here anytime."

"OK," Victoria said. "Thanks a lot, you guys."

"Well," Greg said, "we're all in this movie together, aren't we?"

"Wow," Jessica said. "You're starting to sound like us." She smiled. They hugged, and the phone rang.

It was John. "V," he said, "I am sorry I forgot to ask when and where. I was so emotional I had to hang up to compose myself, and then I realized we didn't make any arrangements. What works for you?"

A love rose from her heart as she replied, "Anytime."

A pause occurred, and then John replied. "I was thinking of somewhere private with no people or interruptions. I have a new place. Would you like to come here? How about around noon? I can have something here to eat if you get hungry, OK?"

Victoria said, "That's fine. Please give me the address, and I can find it."

John replied, "Well, it's simple to get to, really. It's 303 Milan Court, at the corner of Shakley and Elm Streets. You hang a right at the V in the road, and I'm midway down on the right in a little brownstone with blue doors. It's really a charming street with baskets of hanging flowers, just like you always liked. Call me if you get lost, OK?"

"OK, John, I'll see you around noon."

"V?"

"Yes?"

"Thank you for seeing me. I love you so...I....." He stopped. "Oh, that just came out."

"It's OK," Victoria said, with a smile on her face. "I still love you, too."

"OK." *What a relief,* he thought. *Maybe she doesn't hate me after all.*

"I'm just all jumbled up inside along with it, that's all," Victoria replied.

"I understand. OK. We will talk more later," John said, with great relief in his voice.

As Victoria hung up the phone she cried again, this time with a sweet, poignant smile of relief. "He <u>does</u> love me after all," she said to Jessica. "He really does. I could feel it in his voice. He's different, but the same. He's grown through some discovery process that only he could know, but I sense it here." She touched her heart. "I don't know why or even how, but I know it was all for a reason and that we're going to be OK."

"You already are OK," Jessica's wisdom continued. "You are just realizing that, as a couple, you are another entity that is full of complexities and responses to a series of events, past and present, that influence your emotions and your behavior. All love grows inside a heart that is open and ready to transcend the deluge of the material world fraught with circumstances beyond our immediate control. Only our reactions and responses are even near to our conscious control; most of it is beyond our conscious knowing. We are mostly living in a veil of darkness, unconsciously responding to the events and people around us. Cultivating the Inner Witness, as you have done so well in your yoga practice, may help you now to see the situation for what it is and to explore other possibilities having a greater range and magnitude of effect on you and those in your intimate circle. Have no fear, Miss V. That is what I have learned from you. Being with you and Sara has taught me to trust, and from that fearless trust and strength of a warrior, I have seen the Truth emerge time and time again. I know all of this has transpired for a reason, seen or unseen, known or unknown, and I know that this Truth that lives in the depths of each of your hearts has already set you free. Praise be to the truth of love, that has set the passion of desire in your heart for one another. For lifetime after lifetime you've come together to share and to deepen your connection. So the two will become one, this much your hearts have always known. Rest with this knowing, and when you see him, **see** Him. It will be magic. A soul-to-soul reunion will be felt in the heart. All of my love to you, dear friend. We will miss you, won't we, Greg?"

They both sat there mesmerized by the words inspired in truth as Jessica spoke—spellbound as though the minister of the heavens came to proclaim the Sermon on the Mount of goodness and grace.

"Where is she going?" Greg finally said. "We're all still friends, aren't we? What just happened?"

"Oh, I just got a glimpse of what's to come," Jessica said. "We will all have to make time for one another, that's all. Hey, Victoria, what are you going to wear? Let's go pick it out!"

Greg just sat there in utter amazement as he watched her switch back to the giddy girl who giggles and acts like a teenager on her first date, which, of course, triggered a response of laughter as they wandered off to the bedroom to explore the trousseau and to pick out what would be the "perfect" thing to wear on such an auspicious occasion. It was like a pre-wedding engagement moment when all of the universe lined up and granted the wish of the heart that had been wishing for all those years — lifetimes, really. He felt privileged to be a part of the unfolding of a life that was to touch so many. *Interesting*, he thought. *This is all so fascinating.* "Well, isn't every day such a surprise?" he said aloud.

"Yes, isn't it?" Jessica said as she came out to give him a hug and went off again with Victoria, who was still crying and laughing at the same time.

He looked over and Sara, too, was smiling as she looked up from his lap. *She knows*, he thought. *She knows something we don't.* He realized she had grown into a toddler, almost overnight, and yet she was still that precious infant. As he gazed into her lovely, big blue eyes he saw grace, beauty, and hope.

"It's all OK," she seemed to "say" with her sparkling blue eyes. With her smile, she comforted him as if she were some wise sage from another time, or an angel from another realm. It was almost eerie, how he could see through her eyes. It was like peering into the depths of the ocean. He could see her soul beyond this time and, lo and behold, she was seeing him.

"Wow." He started to tear up as he picked her up, and they held each other in a soul embrace beyond words, beyond reason, and beyond understanding. "Time" stood still, and the magic of love blanketed them both as a smile of deep peace came over all. "All is well," Greg's inner voice said; "all is well." Smiling with great contentment, he sat down on the magic couch, where so much had happened and fell into a state of pure joy. "This is heaven, isn't it?" Greg asked.

"Yes it is," his soul replied. "Yes it is."

CHAPTER 9

"Oh, I must have dozed off a minute," Greg said as Jessica came over to give him a hug. "What's up now? What did I miss?"

"Oh, just the transformation of the finite to the infinite," Jessica replied.

"Excuse me? What does that mean?" Greg inquired.

"Well, Victoria was transformed from an ordinary girl into a princess, off to reunite with her knight in shining armor who lives in a magic kingdom, of course. In the realm of true love, everything is possible…hence, the infinite; get it?" Jessica smiled.

"Oh," Greg said, "the Cinderella story reinvented. Is that it?"

"Well, this is the New Age version with a twist of metaphysical truth and alchemy. Quite frankly, a world without magic is boring! Don't you agree, dearest Greg?"

"Well, quite frankly, my dear," Greg said, tongue in cheek, "my life has become kind of weird, but magical, too. I have to admit that since I met you and Victoria and Sara, my life has not been the same. I feel like I'm living in a surreal world, where the light around me changes colors, and I see through 3D glasses into some holographic projection screen. And it all changes so quickly, which, makes me remember something, I have been wanting to share with you; but, we have all gotten a bit distracted with these new events. I hope I didn't shirk my responsibilities in keeping an eye on Sara!"

"Oh, she's fine. She's good at amusing herself, and I had one eye on her, anyway. I feel one with her, so I sense her all the time. I feel like her surrogate mother. We are all very close, actually. So, what did you want to share?"

"Well, I really wanted to tell you about Sara and how we connected. There's something about her that I just can't describe. It's like she's not an infant or a child at all, sometimes. She feels like an ancient sage hidden under a cloak of some kind of spell that just makes her look young, but she really isn't. Does that make any sense to you?" Greg asked.

"What makes the most sense to me, dearest Greg, is that we are all hidden under some kind of veil of deception, trying to make sense of it all. I just think Sara still remembers who she is and where she comes from, unlike the rest of us who have completely forgotten," Jessica philosophized.

"I've heard you all talk about that before, but I really sense something different about her. I've been around babies and kids before, but there's something about her presence, like there's a glow around her, an energy field that's much bigger than her little body. I know that sounds weird, but I really want to understand what it is! It's a really strong feeling, and I felt just a little while ago when she looked at me she was seeing some part of me I never had. God, this sounds really weird. Never mind," Greg said, getting frustrated with himself. "I can't describe it."

Jessica put her arm around him and said, "Well, the Great Mystery is very big and expansive. Our egos can't always describe the complexities of the universe. It is like looking through a telescope and seeing one planet and trying to take in the vastness of the galaxy. It's just not possible. I do know that some people come on a soul mission that affects a vast amount of people, and I feel she is a very wise soul that has come to teach something about the vastness. She already has. Listen to yourself talk. Holographic projections? You sound like a metaphysician or a physicist or something."

"I know, Jess, it's just my scientific mind requiring more information," Greg said, now more relaxed. "Hey, let's get something to eat. I forgot all about that until now."

"Oh, how about I fix you an omelet or something?" Jessica smiled. "Just keep an eye on Sara this time and see what wisdom and answers to the universe you can come up with, OK?"

"OK," Greg laughed. "I think I can handle that if you're OK in the kitchen."

"I'll manage," Jessica said with a twinkle in her eye. "I'll come up with something."

So they settled into a nice day together, cooking and talking and playing with Sara and thoroughly enjoying the beam of happiness streaming through their hearts. It was another magical day in the life of the finite.

When the phone rang, they were both startled as Jessica woke up from her nap with Greg and Sara. "Hello?" she answered.

It was Victoria. "Hey listen, we're still talking and Sara hasn't come up yet, so I was wondering. What do you all have planned for the rest of the day?"

"Well, not much. What do you need Miss V? I'm dying to know what's happened, but I can wait 'til later for more details. Where is John now?"

"Oh, he's in the other room, making us a little something to eat. I just don't know how to do this, Jessica. Oh, and by the way…what <u>do</u> I say?"

"Hmmm. Well, how about something like, there's something rather important that happened while you were gone, and even though it's challenging to find the right words and timing, here it is: you have a beautiful daughter named Sara. Then have pictures ready and wait for his response and go from there."

"Jessica, it's like we never parted. It's amazing. I'll tell you more, later. Can you stay with Sara a few more hours?"

"Sure, no problem. Greg is having his own moments now, so take your time."

"Moments? Is everything OK?" Victoria asked, a bit concerned.

"Oh yeah, sure," Jessica replied. "He's just seeing Sara for the first time; you know, a soul-to-soul connection. It's like we're all getting to our soul knowing today. I love it! Go ahead with John; you've been waiting for this forever, it seems."

"Hey Jess, thanks; you're the best friend ever!" Victoria exclaimed.

"That's just what sisters do for each other. Call us when you're on your way home. Love ya, sister."

They hung up and Jessica went back to the magic couch where Greg and Sara were cuddling up with a movie, and she fell into a deep sense of peace. A relaxed knowing came over Jessica. She began to feel the family she and Greg would have some day, and she decided to trust the unfolding of the Great Mystery from the infinite to the finite and realized that soul knowing was recognition beyond description. But somehow, every cell of your being remembers. How divinely perfect. *Thank you, Greg,* she thought. *Thank you for your vastness and infinite love and understanding for our finite minds. I love this feeling of oneness. Love really is all there is.* She smiled at her own thoughts and said aloud to Greg, "Can you just hold me here forever?"

"Sure," Greg replied. "Forever isn't long enough." They both smiled and hugged as Sara slept on, and they dreamed their own life back into the present moment where everything is created. The magic of the day covered them in a mist of awakening, and they glimpsed the reality of their own lives through the inner eye of their soul. "It's all so perfect," Greg mused. "It is all so perfect."

CHAPTER 10

"Hey you two, you're relieved of duty," Victoria whispered as she quietly entered the living room where the three had slumbered comfortably.

"Oh hey, Victoria, what time is it?" Jessica asked.

"Almost 1:00 in the morning, I'm afraid to say. I've put Sara to bed, and now it's time for you two to get somewhere comfortable."

"Mm…" Greg yawned and stretched. "I am comfortable."

"Let's get you two in bed," Victoria said. "I feel bad about being so late."

"We're all glad you were late," Greg replied. "We had great fun just hanging out together. I love Sara. She's great. We all bonded, so no worries. Hey, Jess, can I spend the night?"

Jessica laughed, "Of course." They got up and walked off hand in hand as Victoria smiled an understanding smile that beamed from her heart. Tears rolled down her face as she watched them walk away, and she knew they would marry and have a child of their own someday. She was extremely tired from all the emotions of the day, but realized she wanted to write something right now in her journal to document this most auspicious moment. So she walked to the dresser and pulled out her Book of Days, as she liked to call it, and curled up in her favorite chair with her favorite wrap. She wrote the first entry of many to come that would soon document not only the outer events, but most importantly her inner journey into wholeness and pure knowing as she reclaimed the various aspects of herself and removed the inner thought barriers to an expanded version of herself. She felt like she had reclaimed a vital aspect of herself today, as she gazed into John's eyes and forgave him for leaving her so abruptly. She gave him permission to move on in his own heart-world so he could forgive himself as he also reclaimed his own integrity and dignity after leaving the one person he had ever truly loved. The story of why he left did not even matter to her now as she took pen in hand and reflected upon the day. *How do I put these feelings into words,* she thought? *There are so many and such a wide range of emotions that have occurred, but now it all seems like a wash, like I have arrived at "profound neutral,"* she wrote. *After having a roller-coaster ride of ups and downs, I feel I have now arrived back at the station where the journey began, right back here.* She touched her heart and felt an expanded feeling of warmth as she contacted her inner guidance, and pure loved filled her with an inner peace she had never known was even possible, until now. She smiled with gratitude and watched as her pen wrote these words:

> Now you know the power of forgiveness and the freedom it brings to love unconditionally. The love that you encountered today was Me. I am your eternal source of love that has your highest good always in the heart of pure awareness known as Truth. Your salvation of your heart, and therefore your soul, is forgiveness. Congratulations on letting go of all perceptions and beliefs that no longer serve you. You have entered the Temple of God when your heart is pure and open and full of Love: simple, but not so easy for the spiritual novice. It takes a great soul to forgive and to love unconditionally. When you can do this, you enter the temple of God where your soul reunites with its Creator, and all that is experienced is then in complete harmony and union with the highest truth. Love begets love – that is all. I want to experience love in all forms, in all beings, in all situations. So in order to do that, there is an opposite version or vision that is presented. In rejecting fear in all of its forms, you choose love, and inside love is the heart of God, that which you now know as me—the beloved of your soul. I am always here, working for your highest good. This reunion with John is for all of you to know peace. He now rests in the knowing that he is forgiven and can move forward

in his life with an ease only your soul could give him. He has received your gift as an offering at the altar of grace and bows to you tonight in humble gratitude. Your life together can be full, with grace-filled moments as you enter the temple of God's love and sit in the pure presence of Self-Awareness. Victoria, you are not Katrina, the disaster. You are my beloved child of whom I am so proud, and I worship <u>you</u> in your own power as the Love of all the ages. You see love is reciprocated. As you love me with pure devotion and readiness to forgive <u>all</u>, so I love you with pure presence and light the way to your beloved as lover. You see, your lover brings you to the Godhead of creation. Then the masculine and feminine, in the dual world of opposites, reunite as one. Together you create a single cell that gives another soul an opportunity to incarnate into the world of veiled forgetfulness until you remember who you are. You are my love in the world of manifestation, and you are my beloved in the non-manifest presence. As one, we are infinite. In the veiled world, we are finite. Going from the infinite to finite, there is a path of togetherness where all is created. It is grace that delivers you from one to another. Grace is the path to the magic world of creation—the kingdom/queendom, which resides in the treasure chest of your heart. It is the place of gold-filled light where all of the jewels of your life come alive. Share these jewels unconditionally, and they transform before your eyes with the pure alchemy of infinite possibilities. The discovery of the heart center should never be underestimated. It is every soul's destiny to re-enter the magical, alchemical elixir of the temple of God—the God of your Knowing. God is the beloved of your soul. When you see this in another and acknowledge that to the depths of your being, you are Home. Welcome Home, my beloved as Victoria. Welcome Home. This life you are creating is but one of many that you are living concurrently in alternate realities. This timeline is one of all that is, so enjoy this moment of revelation and to thy own soul be true. Love all as you love me, knowing that I love you into infinity. There is nowhere, no time, not ever, that we are not together. Oneness comes when you surrender to Love and then that is all there is. Choices and opportunities are just that. When there is freedom from judgment, then all there is, is. No one and no thing can deprive you of union, except a thought based in fear that betrays you otherwise. The freedom to choose is, your opportunity to express what works for you and that which, does not work in your highest good to experience love in that moment. So what will it be: fear or love? You <u>always</u> get to choose. Let your soul drive the bus of life, and I will give you directions as you ask. I am always here—always. When you surrender to love, you can take your hands off the wheel, and I will take over. No matter what, I am here, now. Love through sweet surrender, brings you Home to *now*. *Now* is where you live. Presence is where you thrive in infinite, eternal bliss. Safe haven for the soul is home in the heart of the eternal now. Rest in this knowing—I AM—all that is. OM∞.

Victoria laid down her pen, took her left hand off of her heart, brought her two hands together in prayer pose, bowed her head, and cried tears of relief with resounding joy and gratitude for this union, knowing that love <u>is</u> all there is, from finite to the infinite; Love is…. "Oh my God," she said aloud, "my God, <u>you</u> are my love." Her tears streamed endlessly back into the river of grace that beseeched her soul that night and delivered her back to her Self: whole, blessed, free.

"Whatever happens now is up to me, God," she said. "I choose union, and I choose love." And in that moment the tears stopped. A light, extraordinarily bright, entered into her awareness, and there in front of her open eyes was a magnificent image of her beloved God, hands reaching out with open arms.

"I will come to you in all forms you desire, always, dearest Victoria. I love you."

"I love you," she said aloud as she opened her arms and let go. "So this is being in love."

"Yes," the Light replied, "this is love." And waves of ecstatic joy followed moments of stillness until the waves returned in a rhythm that rocked her body, mind, and soul to the unending waves of grace until she was delivered back to the shores of her current reality, and she fell into a deep, peaceful stillness. She closed her eyes and entered the astral plane of sleep.

"What a night," her ego said, laughing.

"What a life," her soul replied. "Sleep now." And sleep came. Ah… sleep.

CHAPTER 11

"Hey Victoria, wake up, wake up!" Jessica exclaimed, holding Sara in her arms.

"Mommy," Sara said.

Victoria opened her eyes to see Sara holding out her arms for her and repeating "Mommy" while Jessica beamed. "We want to know what happened!"

Victoria picked up Sara, sitting up on the magic couch where she had fallen asleep, and held her daughter tight. "You are getting to be a big girl, little Miss Sara."

"I know," Jessica said. "Can you believe it's been almost two years? She woke up and just started jabbering and talking and 'I want Mommy,' just came out."

Greg walked out of the bedroom, looking sleepy and tired, and said, "Now what have I missed?"

"Just Sara's first sentence, 'I want Mommy,' of course!" Jessica laughed.

"Wow," Victoria said. "I think I need a moment. I'll be right back." She and Sara went into the bedroom to get her a toy, and Victoria washed her face, trying to get oriented to time and place. *It seems like it's all a dream*, she thought. Slowly, she made her way out to the kitchen with Sara, where Greg and Jessica were dutifully and joyfully making Sunday breakfast. The table was set, and all eyes now turned to Victoria.

"Well?" Jessica implored. "What the heck happened?"

Victoria sat down after pouring herself a cup of coffee, enjoying the aroma, and eased into the moment, noticing a heightened sense of awareness. Everything looked brighter, smelled incredible, felt more intense, and ..."Mm, this coffee tastes more incredibly wonderful today," she exclaimed at the first sip. She felt as though she had landed here for the first time on this planet after having read about it and watching its inhabitants awhile from a distant monitor. It felt like home, but different. Or maybe it felt familiar, but really different in some unexplainable way. "Surreal," she said aloud. "It was all so surreal, Jessica; I don't know where to start."

"Well," Jessica said, sitting down, "how about from the beginning?"

Victoria closed her eyes, took a deep breath in and out, tears welling up in her eyes, her heart full now as the memories came flooding in like a river, carrying snapshots of expressions, feelings, and emotions. Pictures, like a movie, came streaming through her mind, and then they just stopped. She opened her eyes and looked at Jessica.

"He asked me to marry him. He is coming over today to meet his daughter for the first time. He asked me before he knew about Sara, Jessica; he fell onto his knees and asked for forgiveness and said he did not want to live without me ever again. I told him I had something important he might want to know. He asked if I would forgive him and if we could spend the rest of our lives making up for lost time. He said it felt like an eternity without me and that he has been just miserable. He was more emotional than me, Jessica; I couldn't believe it. This was after we just cried and held each other for an hour, spilling our guts and hearts all over the place. I couldn't stand the intensity of all the emotions, and then, when he did that, everything in the room came to a suspended halt, and I heard my inner voice say, 'This is it, your opportunity to be free. Forgive him, no matter what comes after that; forgive him now and you are free.' So, my heart opened wider than ever before. I said, 'I forgive you, John; you are free and I am free. I love you unconditionally, no matter what. Neither, the past, present or future matters to me. Your soul is exquisite and you deserve to be happy. Go and do what brings you joy.' That is when he paused, left the room, and brought out the ring I had given back to him. He got down on one knee and asked me to marry him. He said, "This is what brings me joy, Victoria. I love you beyond what words can ever express. You are the one I want to spend the rest of my life with. Loving you, seeing you, holding you in my arms is what I want more than anything else in the world. Victoria, will you marry me?'"

"Well," Greg now chimed in, "what did you say?" They both looked at Victoria, waiting for the answer to the million-dollar question.

"Well," Victoria said, "I asked him a question back, first. I said, 'How do you feel about having a family?'"

"And he said?" Jessica inquired.

"He paused and looked up at me and said, 'As long as it's with you, yes. I've actually always seen myself with you and a little girl. In fact, I had a dream like that several times since we've been apart. I don't know why, but I just had the same recurring dream the night before I called you. She looked at me in the dream and said that it's time. "It's time we are all together." Weird, huh?' I said to him that it was not so weird, that maybe it was a premonition dream. 'Maybe,' he said. Then he looked at me with concern. 'Do you want to marry me, Victoria? I love you so. We can work all this out, can't we? Will you marry me?' He asked a second time."

Now Jessica and Greg were sitting down, both with coffee mugs suspended in mid-air, waiting. "Well?" they both said in unison, "what did you say?"

"Yes," Victoria smiled, "I said yes. We want to have a spring wedding, so we can start new! He's coming to see Sara today, but he doesn't know yet. I want <u>us</u> to tell him."

"It sounds like he already knows at some level," Jessica said. "That little Sara is just amazing, aren't you, Sara?" She tickled her, and they both began to laugh. "You've been traveling out of your body visiting your dad, haven't you?"

Then Greg replied, "You know it may not be such a big shock to him at all. I will get ready and get us out of here so you can be by yourself. What time is he coming over?"

"Oh, 2:00 or so," Victoria replied. "I wanted time to regroup. We all have time. It's what, 10:00 or so?"

"Yes, it's 10:00," Greg replied.

"So let's relax a little and ease into this monumental day. More is yet to come," Victoria said.

Now, in a moment of calmness, with the wave of peace returning to her heart space, she put down her coffee and picked up Sara. "It's time, Sara, to meet John, your father, but then, you already know that, don't you?"

"Daddy," she said.

They all stopped and looked at little Sara light up, and all the focus came into one pristine moment of suspended time as Sara spoke those words for the first time.

"How does she know that?" Greg finally inquired, letting the timeline begin again. "That just fascinates me. How can she know that?"

"Well, she is her mother's daughter, too," Jessica replied. "I've always known that clairvoyance is something that runs in families sometimes, and besides, we're all connected at some level. Sara is still in that pure state of innocence, which allows her to communicate at a different level. She is just learning this new English language so she can communicate here in this world, that's all. I think John knows about her at some level, anyway. The dream within the dream has already begun to reveal itself."

"You're right, Jess." Victoria was gazing into some unseen world as she continued. "He knows at some unconscious level. His conscious mind just needs to catch up with him now. I believe that in some other universe we're already together. We just needed time to explore ourselves in this one for some questions and answers that could only be discovered apart. I guess there really _is_ a divine timing and a divine order of things that is kept under the veil that we live in. It's just part of the Great Mystery revealing some of its secret passageways to the infinite elixir of creation in the vastness of the void, where all potential is ignited by the flame of desire. You have to _want_ something for it to appear. When the divine wants an ultimate outcome, it leads us on this journey wherever there is a speck of awakened consciousness. When we surrender moment by moment, more gets revealed. That is so the more limited, dense body and mind can adjust. That's what I get."

"OK," Greg said, "now I'm going to have to study quantum physics and more string theory to keep up, aren't I?"

"No," Victoria said. "Just a little inner gazing or some yoga may do."

"No," Jess said. "I'd love to hear the science behind the metaphysics. I have to depend on Greg for that. The science goes over my head sometimes. There are principles we're all living in. Together we can explore and discover and learn for ourselves and then contribute back to the whole. Even if we don't talk about these principles or identify them, we are all living by certain physical rules and are approaching the ultimate outcome, moment by moment. How we get where we are going is an individual choice, but the principles can help guide us. Like a recipe to which we add and change ingredients, we create our own vision of it. But, there are some main ingredients that have to be in it to identify what it is."

"Is that why humans experience fear, doubt, and trepidation so often: to remember we are humans? It's like our individual neuroses and anxieties identify who we are sometimes, right, Victoria?" Greg inquired.

"Well, yoga principles, depending on the philosophy, would say that fear is ego-based and that is the 'false self' based in the illusion of separateness; whereas, the 'true' Self is revealed through the eyes of the soul, which is based in unity consciousness. That is why marriage is so sacred and why I hesitated a moment with John's question. My ego asked him, 'Do you want a family?' But, my soul was the part of me that already knew his answer to my question, as our gaze met. The decision to have Sara and to marry was made long ago, before incarnation. Our egos chose each other by our souls' knowing, and all was revealed from behind the veil, at that precise moment to each other, as well as, to ourselves. I could feel it, like a familiar hug that wrapped me in a blanket of contentment that reassured me, and then I heard my voice answer 'yes,' as my inner guidance as my soul reassured me, "Yes, he is the one, and this is the time. All will be well now. Relax into this knowing and set yourself free, from the residue of fear. I am here. Inside both of you is the Love of all the ages. See me reflected through his eyes, and feel the love in your heart set you free to experience this soul reunion."

"My feeling at the time, and as I reflect on it now, is that marriage is the opportunity to experience the oneness of Spirit in the flesh. It is an opportunity to create consciously or unconsciously the birth of another soul and my only regret is that I wasn't conscious at the time of the conception of Sara." Victoria started to cry.

"Wait a minute, Miss V, you are now! And Sara was on the other side of the veil holding sacred ground until the awakening occurred. Look. She remembers. But soon, as she ages, she may forget who she is, and that is why she came to you, so then you will hold up the mirror of love from your heart and remind her of this innocence that best reflects the divine love that created us all. Who do you think you are? Why did she pick that timing for her birth? Ask her now," Jessica implored, then answered her question. "To be with you!" Jessica exclaimed with great passion. "To reveal your magnificence and to be the conduit to help you explore on your own terms and to find your knowing of God. You have done this together."

Now there were tears in the eyes of all, except Sara, who smiled and held out her arms to Victoria. And as they embraced, the room was filled with light and love.

"Group hug!" Greg cheerfully announced, and they all gathered in the small kitchen that grew three times in size as the reunion of this soul family was revealed. Now, only one heart remained amiss in this scene, and he was soon to be reunited into this soul matrix, as it was written in each heart gathered here today.

And so, they hugged and laughed and cried and became enamored with the love that binds them and all beings of the lie together under the veil. In great moments of revelation the Truth is revealed time and time again, as the light of Love appears.

Sara revealed love through innocence and remembrance. Victoria revealed the philosophical truths of yoga-based union. Greg became illuminated through the intellect into his own intuitive heart. And Jessica, the wise sage, reminded all to seek the kingdom of heaven inside the doorway of faith. This is not the "end," only the continuation of the Love of all the Ages, for from the finite to the infinite all return.

You are encouraged to pierce the veil of your own forgetfulness and embrace your story, and create heaven on earth as it was written in your soul. Choose Love and set yourself free. The message is always the same: Love. The face of the messenger changes, but the heart of God, remains as the portal to true love and joy and primordial peace. The Goddess, the rabbi, the priest, the monk, the pedestrian and the child in the street are all God; all is Love. All of nature beams with the light. Seek the kingdom of love and light. Create the kingdom/queendom of infinite possibilities and create the life you really want, full of happiness and beauty. The doorway is the heart, the portal to the Great Mind.

God says, "Open to Me and I will appear, always, as you want Me to be. I am you, disguised in a world of fear-based thought. I am you, revealed in a blaze of Love. The fire inside of you is your desire to know Me, so you can be all of Me in your story, which is your current life. Be the life, merge with your story, and create the *Greatest Love You Have Ever Known*. Give birth to the *Redeemer of Truth*, and become the way shower for others through the greatest path ever created. Walk amongst your brothers and sisters and fill them with your love, and create Eden, the garden of knowing. Remember, the Garden of Gethsemane leads to despair if you forget who you are. Return to Eden, the garden of remembrance, and eat the food of life together as man, as woman; and allow the serpent to arise from inside you to unite heaven and earth, the seen and the unseen, the material and the ethereal. The mystic remembers in Divine communion the I AM Presence of all. Be with Me now, as we end this story, and as yours begins, again, for *From the Finite to the Infinite* all return to *The Love of All the Ages*."

NOTE to the readers, from the Guides who wrote this book:

Dear readers of this trilogy, we in Spirit hope you will reread it, again and again, and feel the Truth inside your hearts. We in Spirit are always with you and love to be asked for help and guidance, as our mission is to awaken all to Love. Our Master, throughout the ages, has taught us so much about the kingdom through stories, and so we reflect again to you, stories. And, we will continue to bring you teachings, to open your heart and to set upon this earth the awakening to Love, heart to heart and person to person. Please share these stories and your own, and create your own love stories to be shared. We release this scribe now to her life story, and we will return with <u>The Volume of Truth</u> and a love story through her own marriage, which she will share when the time is right in her timeline. We bow in deep gratitude for her devotion and perseverance in the midst of her own challenges and stand steadfast by her side as the next phase is revealed.

This message was from the Guides to the scribe at the end of this incredible, seven-year journey:

Thank you, dearest Vickie, thank you. We release you now, and as you know, more is to come. Go in peace and satisfaction knowing that this is a job well done. We all love you. More to come!

Peter, Andrew, Judas, and Lord Jesus: Master to us all.
Om Shanti. Shanti. Shanti.